The Ma Place

A Collection Of Recipes
Published By
The Augusta Junior Woman's Club, Inc.
1986

AUGUSTA JUNIOR WOMAN'S CLUB, INC.
AUGUSTA, GEORGIA

The Augusta Junior Woman's Club, Inc., is a non-profit, charitable organization dedicated to improving the quality of life in our community. Through volunteer service, members strive to accomplish something—not merely to exist. Proceeds from the sale of this book will be returned to the community through projects sponsored by the Augusta Junior Woman's Club, Inc.

Copies of *The Market Place* may be obtained using the order blanks in the back of the book or by writing to:

The Market Place
Augusta Junior Woman's Club, Inc.
P.O. Box 3133
Augusta, Georgia 30904

Copyright© 1986 by Augusta Junior Woman's Club, Inc. All rights reserved. No part of this publication may be reproduced, stored in retrieval system or transmitted in any form or by any means, electronic, mechanical, photocopying, recording, or otherwise, without the prior written permission of Augusta Junior Woman's Club, Inc.

First Printing   1986   10,000 copies
Second Printing   1987   5,000 copies
International Standard Book Number 0-9615980-0-X

Printed by
WIMMER BROTHERS
Memphis   Dallas

All recipes herein have been tested and represent favorite recipes of the Augusta Junior Woman's Club members, their relatives and friends.

INTRODUCTION

The Mart of the Whole Country

In 1783, the year the American Revolution ended, Chief Justice George Walton predicted that Augusta "will soon become the mart of the whole country above it." He was right. Augusta served the thousands who flocked into the Georgia backcountry as a place to exchange the produce of farm and plantation for supplies and manufactured goods. Broad Street had over a hundred stores by 1800 which a wide-eyed visitor described as "filled with all the necessary manufactures of the Northern States, of Europe, the East and West Indies." Augusta was where the frontier met the world.

Although the whole city was a virtual market and buying and selling the order of the day, the heart of the city was the building simply designated as The Market. It stood from the earliest days in the center of Broad Street at Fifth or Centre Streets. This was just as Oglethorpe intended and one reason Broad Street was wider than the other streets. The Market was the place to which farmers brought their fruit, vegetables and livestock for sale to the city dwellers. The practice of marketing was as ancient as farming itself and the basic reason for the existence of towns.

In Augusta there was a succession of market buildings. The longest lasting was called The Lower Market to distinguish it from the Upper Market at 12th and Broad. Erected in 1826 it was blasted by a cyclone in 1878. The proud tower which crowned a facade of four columns and the building with its stalls along the sides collapsed like a house of cards. The only part of the structure left standing was the end column nearer the south side of the street. It was carefully moved to the corner as a gesture of respect for the venerable building and its importance to Augustans. In fact, the citizens thought they could not do without a market and built a new one in the same location. However, times were changing. Grocery stores and neighborhood markets served an expanding city. The new market was pulled down after only twelve years and sold for scrap.

Although supermarkets have replaced most of the neighborhood groceries, there are still some which remind us of the old days. The Farmers Market next to the Fairgrounds best represents the continuity of the tradition. And there are still the roadside vendors who sell their produce from moveable stands, as if displaced by the disappearance of the old central market.

It is ironic that the guidebooks single out the "haunted pillar" as Augusta's tourist attraction. The idea of anything being haunted, hexed or cursed seems to intrigue people. But apart from the legends which have become attached to the pillar, it is important as a visible relic of the venerated Lower Market. It is a reminder of the reason for Augusta's existence.

Edward J. Cashin
Chairman, Department of History, Political Science and Philosophy
Augusta College

About the artist: Randy R. Lambeth is an Augusta born scientist-turned-artist. A 1967 graduate of Butler High School, Lambeth majored in biology at Augusta College. Following a two year career in research protein immunology at the Medical College of Georgia, Randy discovered his artistic talent. With the encouragement of an artist friend, Lambeth began his own career with studies of Augusta's neighborhoods and their residents both of which remain a favorite subject of Mr. Lambeth's watercolors and oils.

About the artwork: Augusta's neighborhoods boast such colorful names as: Frog Holler, Harrisburg, Pinch Gut, Hawks Gully, Nellyville, Lick Skillet, the Terry, West End, Sand Hill and Summerville. Each neighborhood had its own family owned corner grocery stores. The cover design and divider pages record scenes from this vanishing part of Augusta's heritage. The cover painting is in oil. The Eve Street Market is located on the corner of Eve and Jenkins Streets.

CONTENTS

Introduction 5

Appetizers 7

Beverages 25

Soups and Sauces 33

Salads and Salad Dressings 51

Breads 73

Cheese and Eggs 89

Poultry and Game 99

Fish and Seafood 119

Meats 135

Vegetables and Side Dishes 159

Sweet Tooth 185

    Desserts 186

    Cakes 197

    Pies 211

    Cookies and Candy 221

Something Special 235

Substitutions and Equivalents 247

Index 249

APPETIZERS

CHEESE AND DATE DIP

1 (8-ounce) package cream cheese, softened
1 (8-ounce) can crushed pineapple
½ cup whole pitted dates, snipped

Drain pineapple, reserving 2 tablespoons of juice. In small bowl, combine cream cheese, drained pineapple and reserved juice. Beat at low speed until blended. Add dates. Mix well. Cover and chill. Serve with assorted fruits. Yield: 1 cup.

CHEESE SPREAD

1 (8-ounce) package cream cheese, softened
8 ounces sharp Cheddar cheese spread, softened
3 teaspoons horseradish mustard
½ cup mayonnaise
½ teaspoon Worcestershire sauce

Mix all ingredients together with electric mixer and whip at high speed until mixture has doubled in size. Serve with crackers, melba toast rounds or pumpernickel sticks. Yield: 2 cups.

CHEESE IN A BREAD BOWL

1 (3-pound) round loaf rye bread
1½ pounds sharp Cheddar cheese, shredded
¼ pound crumbled bleu cheese
1 teaspoon dry mustard
2 tablespoons butter, softened
1 teaspoon Worcestershire sauce
2 teaspoons grated onion
1 (12-ounce) can beer
parsley and paprika for garnish

Slice top off bread and hollow out loaf to form a bowl. Tear center section into bite-size pieces and set aside. Place all ingredients except beer into a bowl. Mix well. Slowly add beer, beating with mixer until fluffy. Fill bread bowl with mixture. Garnish. Serve with torn bread pieces. Yield: 2 to 3 cups.

SPINACH FETA TRIANGLES

Filling:
1 (10-ounce) package frozen chopped spinach
½ cup chopped onion
3 tablespoons olive or vegetable oil
ground pepper to taste
⅓ cup ricotta cheese
¼ cup crumbled feta cheese

Pastry:
1 (1-pound) box or 24 sheets phyllo pastry
melted butter for brushing on pastry

FILLING: Defrost spinach; drain and squeeze out all moisture. Sauté onion in oil until tender, about 10 minutes. Add spinach and cook over low heat for 10 to 15 minutes or until mixture is dry. Season with pepper. Cool to room temperature. Stir in ricotta and feta which has been crumbled into small pieces.

TO ASSEMBLE: When working with phyllo pastry, keep unused portions covered with a damp towel. Remove 1 sheet of pastry and brush with melted butter. Stack a second sheet on top of first and brush with butter again. Cut pastry into fifths (cut from short side of pastry to short side). Place 1 teaspoon filling in center of 1 strip about 1 inch from top. Fold one corner over filling and continue to fold up the strip (as if folding a flag). Tuck under any excess pastry at end of strip. Repeat process until all pastry is used. Place triangles on buttered cookie sheet and brush with butter. Filled, unbaked triangles may be refrigerated (up to 24 hours) or frozen. Bake at 350° about 25 minutes or until browned. Serve immediately. Yield: 60 servings. *Do not defrost frozen triangles before baking.*

PECAN CURRY SPREAD

2 (8-ounce) packages cream cheese, softened
½ cup bottled chutney
2 teaspoons curry powder
½ teaspoon dry mustard
½ cup chopped pecans

Mix all ingredients. Using hands, shape into a round ball. Refrigerate. Remove from refrigerator 15 minutes before serving. Serve with crackers. Yield: 2 cups. *Keeps refrigerated for one month.*

APPETIZERS

EASY CHEESE STRAWS

½ cup butter or margarine, softened
½ cup vegetable shortening
4 cups (about 1 pound) grated extra sharp Cheddar cheese

2½ cups all-purpose flour
1 teaspoon salt
¼ teaspoon cayenne pepper

With electric mixer or food processor, cream butter and shortening. Add cheese gradually, and blend well. Sift flour, salt and pepper together. Add to cheese mixture gradually and mix thoroughly. Load dough into cookie press or gun and press onto ungreased cookie sheet. Slice to desired length. Bake 10 to 12 minutes at 350° or until edges begin to brown. Carefully remove from cookie sheet to cool on paper towel. Yield: 8 dozen.

HAM CHEESE SPREAD

2 (8-ounce) packages cream cheese, softened
10 ounces extra sharp Cheddar cheese, shredded
1 (4½-ounce) can deviled ham

2 teaspoons grated onion
1 cup chopped nuts
pimento strips for garnish
assorted crackers

Combine cream cheese and Cheddar cheese, mixing on medium speed with electric mixer, until well blended. Add ham and onion; mix well. Chill. Form into ball, roll in chopped nuts and decorate with pimento strips. *(Shape into football for your Super Bowl party!)* Serve with assorted crackers. Yield: 2½ cups.

VARIATION: Omit nuts and pimento. Add 2 tablespoons milk to cream cheese and Cheddar cheese in saucepan; stir over low heat until smooth. Stir in ham and onion. Serve warm.

PARTY SANDWICH BITES

⅔ cup grated carrot
¼ cup minced green pepper
¼ cup minced onion
¼ cup chopped cucumber
¼ cup chopped celery
1 (8-ounce) package cream cheese, softened
¼ teaspoon salt
2 tablespoons lemon juice
1½ tablespoons mayonnaise
1 loaf sliced bread

Combine vegetables, mixing well. Combine cream cheese, salt, lemon juice and mayonnaise. Beat until fluffy. Fold in vegetables. Chill to allow flavors to blend. Cut bread with cookie cutters in party shapes. Spread filling on bread. Sandwiches may be open-faced or topped. Yield: 20 servings.

PINEAPPLE CHEESE BALL

2 (8-ounce) packages cream cheese, softened
1 (8-ounce) can crushed pineapple, drained
1 teaspoon seasoned salt
¼ cup chopped green pepper
2 tablespoons chopped onion
½ cup chopped pecans

Mix all ingredients except pecans. Form into a ball and roll in nuts. For variety, cut a pineapple vertically through leaves. Hollow out pineapple and fill with cheese mixture. Yield: 3 cups.

CHEESE-OLIVE BALLS

2 cups shredded sharp Cheddar cheese
½ cup butter, softened
½ teaspoon salt
1 teaspoon paprika
dash red pepper
1½ cups sifted all-purpose flour
25 to 30 medium pimento stuffed green olives, drained

Combine all ingredients except olives. Mixture will be coarse. Roll into small balls and press flat. Wrap dough around olive. Bake in 400° oven until golden brown. May be served hot or cold. Yield: 2½ dozen. *Dough may be prepared ahead and kept in refrigerator.*

12 APPETIZERS

SOUR CREAM DIP

2 cups sour cream
4 teaspoons prepared horseradish
1 tablespoon paprika
1 tablespoon minced chives
1 teaspoon salt
1 teaspoon minced tarragon or dill
¼ teaspoon monosodium glutamate
⅛ teaspoon ground pepper
1 clove crushed garlic

Mix first 6 ingredients. Add rest of ingredients and chill 1 hour to blend flavors.

Smoak's Bakery
Augusta, Georgia

PIMENTO CHEESE SPREAD

1 pound sharp Cheddar cheese, shredded
2 tablespoons green onions, chopped
1 (2-ounce) jar diced pimento
¾ cup mayonnaise
¼ cup chopped nuts
dash of salt and red pepper

Bring cheese to room temperature. Add remaining ingredients. Blend until smooth. Serve with party bread, crackers or celery sticks. Yield: 3 cups.

CHILI CHEESE CUBES

8 eggs
½ cup all-purpose flour
1 teaspoon baking powder
¾ teaspoon salt
3 cups shredded Monterey Jack cheese
1½ cups cottage cheese
2 (4-ounce) cans mild green chilies, drained, seeded and chopped

In a large bowl, beat eggs until light. Stir together flour, baking powder and salt. Add flour mixture to eggs and mix well. Fold in cheeses and chilies. Turn into greased 9x9x2-inch baking dish. Bake at 350° for 40 minutes. Cool for 10 minutes and cut in 1-inch squares. Serve hot. Yield: 3 to 4 dozen.

BACON TATER BITES AND MUSTARD SAUCE

25 bacon strips, cut in half
1 box (50 pieces) frozen bite-size potatoes

17 American cheese slices, cut into thirds

Sauce:
½ cup prepared mustard
¼ cup brown sugar

½ teaspoon ginger

Cook strips of bacon until brown but still limp. Prepare potatoes according to package directions. Wrap each potato with a piece of cheese. Wrap limp bacon around cheese and secure with a toothpick. Broil, turning once, until bacon is crisp.

SAUCE: Blend together all ingredients in a small saucepan. Heat until ingredients are blended. Serve as a dip with Bacon Tater Bites. Yield: 50 appetizers.

BACON-RYE BALLS

1 pound bacon
¼ cup evaporated milk
1 (8-ounce) package cream cheese, softened
1 cup fine rye breadcrumbs

2 teaspoons finely chopped onion
1 teaspoon Worcestershire sauce
¾ to 1 cup chopped parsley

Cook, drain and crumble bacon. Combine bacon and remaining ingredients, except parsley. Chill 2 hours. Shape into 1-inch balls. Roll in parsley. Yield: 2 dozen.

APPETIZERS

BACON WRAPPED OLIVES

3 slices bacon
12 pimento-stuffed olives, or pitted black olives

Cut bacon into quarters. Wrap one piece around each olive. Secure each with a toothpick. Place on a dish or cooking grill. Cover with a paper towel. Cook in microwave, covered, on full power for 2 to 2½ minutes, or until bacon is crisp and thoroughly cooked. Serve hot. Yield: 12 servings.

COCKTAIL MEATBALLS

1 pound lean ground beef
½ cup dry breadcrumbs
⅓ cup minced onion
½ cup milk
1 egg
1 tablespoon parsley flakes
1 teaspoon salt
⅛ teaspoon black pepper
½ teaspoon Worcestershire sauce
½ cup shortening
1 (12-ounce) bottle chili sauce
1 (10-ounce) jar grape jelly

Mix ground beef, breadcrumbs, onion, milk, egg, parsley flakes, salt, pepper and Worcestershire sauce together. Shape into 1-inch balls. Melt shortening in large skillet and brown meatballs. Remove meatballs from skillet and pour off fat. Heat chili sauce and jelly in skillet, stirring constantly until jelly is melted. Add meatballs and stir until thoroughly coated. Simmer uncovered 30 minutes. Serve hot in chafing dish. Yield: 5 dozen.

HOT RYE ROUNDS

1 pound hot sausage
1 pound processed American cheese
1 loaf party rye bread

Fry sausage and drain. Add slices of cheese and warm until cheese melts. Spread mixture on rye bread. Place on cookie sheet and freeze until set (about 1 hour). Store in airtight container in freezer. When unexpected guests arrive, place on cookie sheet and broil until bubbly, about 2 to 3 minutes. Yield: 20 to 30 servings.

CURRIED CHICKEN BITES

1 (8-ounce) package cream cheese, softened
3 tablespoons mayonnaise
2 cups finely chopped cooked chicken
1½ cups finely chopped almonds, toasted
3 tablespoons chutney, chopped
2 teaspoons curry powder
1 teaspoon salt
2 cups flaked coconut

Beat cream cheese and mayonnaise until light and fluffy. Stir in chicken, almonds, chutney, curry powder and salt. Mix well. Shape mixture into 1-inch balls; then roll in coconut. Chill several hours. Yield: 4½ dozen.

CHICKEN NACHOS

2 cups cooked chicken, cubed
1 cup sour cream
½ teaspoon salt
½ teaspoon chili powder
½ teaspoon powdered cumin
¼ teaspoon garlic powder
1 bag of nacho corn chips
1 cup Monterey Jack cheese, shredded
½ cup green olives, sliced

Place chicken, sour cream, and spices in food processor with chopping blade. Process just long enough to combine. Dot chips with mixture. Sprinkle with cheese and sliced olives. Microwave on medium until cheese melts. Yield: 20 to 30 servings.

CURRIED HAM ROLL

½ pound cooked ground ham
⅓ cup raisins
1 tablespoon grated onion
⅓ teaspoon curry powder
⅓ cup mayonnaise
1 (3-ounce) package cream cheese, softened
1 teaspoon milk
fresh or dried parsley

Mix ground ham, raisins, onion, curry powder and mayonnaise. Shape into long roll. Wrap in waxed paper and refrigerate until thoroughly chilled (at least 1 hour but no longer than 48 hours). Before serving, blend cream cheese with milk and spread over ham roll. Sprinkle with parsley. Serve with crackers. Yield: 8 to 10 servings.

RED DEVIL BALLS

1 (8-ounce) package cream cheese, softened
1 (4½-ounce) can deviled ham
1 cup chopped walnuts

Cut cream cheese into small pieces. Place in blender with ham. Blend until smooth. Remove and chill until firm. Shape into small balls and roll in chopped walnuts. Return to refrigerator until ready to serve. Yield: 30 balls.

PIZZA BREAD

3 eggs
3 teaspoons dried oregano
3 tablespoons grated Parmesan cheese
2 loaves frozen pizza dough, thawed
⅔ pound pepperoni
1 round of provolone, cut in half and shredded

Beat together eggs, oregano and Parmesan. Set aside. Roll bread dough into two 8x14-inch rectangles. Spread with egg mixture, reserving 3 tablespoons. Layer pepperoni and cheese on top of egg mixture. Roll up jellyroll style. Place seam side down on baking sheet; seal ends of roll. Baste with reserved egg mixture. Bake at 350° for 20 to 30 minutes. Yield: 2 loaves. *Bake on pan that has sides!*

SAUCY FRANKS

½ cup ketchup
¼ cup maple flavored syrup
3 tablespoons prepared mustard
¼ teaspoon ground ginger
¼ cup water
2 (16-ounce) packages frankfurters
1½ cups frozen small whole onions

Mix ketchup, syrup, mustard, ginger and water. Slice franks diagonally into 1-inch lengths. Stir franks and onions into mixture. Cover. Chill 3 to 24 hours. Before serving heat mixture to boiling. Reduce heat; simmer 5 minutes. Serve warm with toothpicks. Yield: 60 servings.

CAVIAR PIE

4 hard-boiled eggs, finely chopped
1 small onion, finely chopped
2 (3½-ounce) jars black caviar
1½ cups sour cream
chopped parsley

Combine eggs and onion; press firmly into a 9-inch pie plate. Spoon caviar evenly over the egg mixture. Carefully spread sour cream over caviar. Sprinkle parsley around edge of pie. Serve with crackers or party rye bread. Yield: one 9-inch pie.

HOT CRAB APPETIZER

1 (8-ounce) package cream cheese, softened
1 tablespoon whole milk
6½ ounces crabmeat, flaked
2 tablespoons finely minced onion
½ teaspoon prepared horseradish
½ teaspoon salt
dash of pepper
⅓ cup slivered almonds

Blend ingredients well, except almonds. Spoon into ovenproof dish. Sprinkle with almonds. Bake at 370° for 15 minutes. Serve with crackers or fresh vegetables. Yield: 2 cups.

CRAB MEAT DIP

1 (12-ounce) bottle ketchup
1 (12-ounce) bottle chili sauce
¼ cup horseradish sauce
juice of 1 lemon
dash of hot pepper sauce
dash of Worcestershire sauce
2 (6½-ounce) cans crab meat

Mix together all ingredients. Serve with ruffled potato chips. Yield: 4 cups.

18 APPETIZERS

SALMON PARTY BALL

1 (15½-ounce) can salmon, drained and flaked
1 (8-ounce) package cream cheese, softened
1 tablespoon lemon juice
2 teaspoons minced onion or ¼ cup chopped onion

1 teaspoon prepared horseradish
¼ teaspoon salt
¼ teaspoon liquid smoke
½ cup chopped pecans
3 tablespoons parsley flakes

Blend salmon and cream cheese. Combine with all other ingredients except nuts and parsley. Chill. Shape into a ball and roll in mixture of nuts and parsley. Serve with crackers or quartered bagels. Yield: 20 servings.

SEAFOOD SPREAD

2 envelopes unflavored gelatin
½ cup water
2 tablespoons lemon juice
1 pint sour cream

1 (12-ounce) bottle chili sauce
2 tablespoons horseradish
1½ cups finely choppped cooked lobster, shrimp or crab

In medium saucepan, sprinkle unflavored gelatin over water and lemon juice. Let stand 1 minute. Cook about 5 minutes. With wire whisk or rotary beater, blend in sour cream, chili sauce and horseradish. Fold in seafood. Turn into 3½ cup mold; chill until firm. Serve with crackers. Yield: 20 to 30 appetizers. (Cook over *Low* heat!)

LOBSTER DIP

2 tablespoons butter
2 cups sharp processed American cheese, shredded
2 drops hot pepper sauce

⅓ cup dry white wine
1 (5-ounce) can lobster, drained and broken into small pieces

Melt butter in small saucepan over low heat. Gradually stir in cheese until cheese is melted. Mixture may appear separated at this point. Add hot pepper sauce and slowly add wine. Stir until mixture is smooth. Add lobster. Stir until heated through. Pour into chafing dish. Serve with assorted crackers. Yield: 1½ cups.

SHRIMP BEIGNETS

1 (7-ounce) package frozen cooked and cleaned shrimp
1 cup water
2 tablespoons butter
¾ teaspoon salt
⅛ teaspoon celery salt
⅛ teaspoon white pepper
1 cup all-purpose flour
4 eggs
1 small onion
vegetable oil for frying

Defrost and drain shrimp. Grind shrimp in food processor or blender. Bring water to a boil; add butter, salt, celery salt and pepper. When butter melts, add flour all at once. Stir well. Remove from heat and stir until flour is absorbed (batter will be very stiff). With electric beater, add unbeaten eggs, one at a time, to flour mixture mixing well after each addition. Grate onion into batter. Add ground shrimp and mix well. Cover batter and refrigerate at least 2 hours. Heat oil to 370°. Drop batter by heaping teaspoons into oil. Turn once to brown on both sides. Drain on absorbent paper. Serve with hot mustard. Yield: 4 dozen.

SHRIMP CELERY

1 (8-ounce) package cream cheese, softened
½ pound shrimp, cooked, peeled and chopped
½ teaspoon Worcestershire sauce
1 tablespoon chopped onion
2 teaspoons mayonnaise
1 bunch celery
paprika for garnish

Mix first 5 ingredients with a fork. Cut celery into 4-inch lengths and stuff with mixture. Garnish with paprika. Yield: 15 to 20 servings.

CREAMY TUNA DIP

1 cup sour cream
1 cup mayonnaise
1 envelope buttermilk salad dressing mix
1 (7-ounce) can tuna, drained and flaked

Combine all ingredients and mix well. Chill until serving time. Serve with raw vegetables. Yield: 3 cups.

ASPARAGUS DIP

1 (16-ounce) can chopped asparagus
1 (8-ounce) package cream cheese
1 teaspoon dehydrated onion flakes
1 (4-ounce) package chopped almonds
1 tablespoon mayonnaise

Drain asparagus well and mash. Add cheese, onion and almonds. Add 1 tablespoon mayonnaise, more if needed. Refrigerate overnight. Serve with corn chips or small wheat crackers. Yield: 6 to 8 servings.

ARTICHOKE SQUARES

2 (6-ounce) jars marinated artichoke hearts
1 small onion, finely chopped
1 clove garlic, minced
4 eggs
¼ cup dry breadcrumbs
¼ teaspoon salt
⅛ teaspoon pepper
⅛ teaspoon oregano
⅛ teaspoon hot pepper sauce
2 cups Cheddar cheese, shredded
2 tablespoons minced parsley

Drain both jars of artichokes, pouring juice from one jar into a 7x11-inch baking dish. Chop artichokes and set aside. Microwave baking dish with juice for 1 minute on high. Add onion and garlic; cover with waxed paper. Microwave on high for 3 minutes. In a small bowl, beat eggs slightly and add all other ingredients. Add to mixture in baking dish, mix well and cover with waxed paper. Cook 8 to 10 minutes on high, turning dish after 5 minutes. Let stand, covered, 10 minutes. Cut into 2-inch squares. Yield: 15 to 20 servings.

BROCCOLI DIP

1 (10-ounce) package frozen chopped broccoli
1 package dry vegetable soup mix
1 cup mayonnaise
1 cup sour cream
4 green onions, chopped
1 (14-ounce) can sliced water chestnuts

Thaw and drain broccoli. Mix all ingredients. Chill overnight. Serve with crackers. Yield: 3 cups.

FRESH VEGETABLE DIP

¼ cup shredded cabbage
⅓ cup shredded carrot
2 tablespoons finely chopped green pepper
1 tablespoon finely chopped onion
1 (8-ounce) package sour cream
3 tablespoons mayonnaise
1½ teaspoons tarragon vinegar
½ teaspoon garlic salt
fresh vegetables for dipping

Combine cabbage, carrot, green pepper, and onion; mix well. Stir in next 4 ingredients. Cover and chill. Serve with fresh vegetables. Yield: 10 to 15 servings.

CON QUESO DIP

2 cans (6-ounce) Jalapeño bean dip
1 cup sour cream
½ cup mayonnaise
1 package taco seasoning mix
3 ripe avocados
2 tablespoons lemon juice
½ teaspoon salt
¼ teaspoon pepper
1 cup chopped green onions
2 chopped tomatoes
1 can (6 ounce) pitted chopped black olives
2 cups shredded Cheddar cheese

Spread the bean dip on the bottom of a 13x9x2-inch glass baking dish. Mash avocados and combine with lemon juice, salt and pepper. Spread this mixture over bean dip leaving ½ inch around the edges. Mix sour cream, mayonnaise and seasoning mix together and spread over avocados. Next, layer in order: Green onions, tomatoes, olives and cheese. Serve with tortilla corn chips. Yield: 12 servings.

HOT BROCCOLI AND CHEESE DIP

1 (10-ounce) package frozen chopped broccoli
3 ribs celery, chopped
¾ cup chopped onion
1 (3-ounce) jar sliced mushrooms, drained
2 tablespoons butter
1 (10¾-ounce) can cream of mushroom soup
1 (8-ounce) jar processed cheese spread

Cook broccoli and drain. Sauté celery, onion and mushrooms in butter until tender. Add broccoli, soup and cheese. Mix well and warm over low heat. Serve in chafing dish with patty shells, party bread slices or crackers. Freezes well. Yield: 4 cups.

MUSHROOM APPETIZER

½ pound fresh large mushrooms, cleaned and stemmed
½ cup Cheddar cheese, shredded
¼ cup bacon bits
¼ cup mayonnaise
½ teaspoon prepared mustard

Finely chop enough stems to make ¼ cup. Combine stems, cheese, bacon, mayonnaise, and mustard. Fill caps with mixture. Place, filled side up, on broiler pan. Broil with tops about 1½ inches from heat until cheese is golden brown and bubbly, about 4 minutes. Yield: 12 servings.

VEGETABLE MARINADE

1 bunch broccoli
1 (8-ounce) bottle wine vinegar and oil dressing
1 teaspoon garlic salt
¼ cup pink chablis
2 (2.5-ounce) jars whole mushrooms

Remove broccoli stalks and discard. Wash tips and drain. Combine with all other ingredients and marinate in refrigerator at least 3 hours. Drain and serve on lettuce with toothpicks. May substitute cauliflower or sliced squash for broccoli. Yield: 20 to 30 servings.

ZUCCHINI BITES

4 small zucchini, unpeeled and grated (about 3 cups)
1 cup biscuit mix
½ cup onion, finely chopped
¼ cup Parmesan cheese
1 tablespoon dry parsley flakes
½ teaspoon seasoned salt
½ teaspoon oregano
¼ cup vegetable oil
4 eggs, slightly beaten
1 cup sour cream

Combine all ingredients. Pour into greased 13x9x2-inch pan. Bake at 350° for 30 minutes or until golden brown. Cut in 1-inch squares. Yield: 4 dozen.

CHEESE CRACKERS

1 cup margarine, softened
2 cups all-purpose flour
½ pound sharp cheese, shredded
1 teaspoon salt
¼ teaspoon cayenne pepper
3 cups puffed rice cereal

In a large bowl, mix all ingredients together. Roll into 1-inch balls and place on greased cookie sheet. Press with fork. Bake at 425° for 10 minutes. Yield: 3 to 4 dozen.

SUGARED PEANUTS

1 cup granulated sugar
½ cup water
2 cups raw shelled peanuts (with skin)

Dissolve sugar in water in saucepan over medium heat. Add peanuts and continue cooking over medium heat, stirring frequently. Cook until peanuts are completely coated and no syrup is left. Pour onto ungreased cookie sheet, spreading so that peanuts are separated as much as possible. Bake at 300° for 30 minutes, stirring at 5 minute intervals. Yield: 3 cups.

24 APPETIZERS

DRY ROASTED PECANS

1 egg white, beaten until stiff
1 teaspoon salt
1 teaspoon water
1 teaspoon sugar
1 quart pecan halves

Line a 13x9x2-inch baking dish with foil and spray with vegetable oil. Add salt, water and sugar to beaten egg white. Fold nuts into egg white mixture. Pour nuts into baking dish and bake 1 hour at 250°, uncovered. Stir every 15 minutes. Remove from oven and cool in one layer on paper towel. When cool, store in airtight container. May be frozen. Yield: 1 quart.

ITALIAN WHEAT SNACK

6 tablespoons unsalted margarine
¼ teaspoon oregano
¼ teaspoon thyme
¼ teaspoon parsley flakes
¼ teaspoon basil leaves
½ teaspoon garlic powder
½ teaspoon onion powder
⅛ teaspoon hot pepper sauce
3 cups spoon-size wheat cereal (no salt added variety)
1 cup dry roasted unsalted peanuts or sunflower nuts

Preheat oven to 300°. In a medium saucepan, over medium heat, melt margarine. Stir in seasonings. Mix well. Add cereal and nuts, mixing well. Spoon cereal mixture onto 15x10-inch baking pan and bake 15 minutes, stirring occasionally. Yield: 4 cups.

TOASTED PECANS

12 cups pecan halves
½ cup butter, softened
salt

Spread pecans in a 17x12-inch pan. Place in a 250° oven. Toast at least 30 minutes to dry. Add butter. Coat pecans with butter as it melts. After pecans and butter have been mixed well, sprinkle generously with salt. Stir often, sprinkling with salt each time. Toast pecans 1 hour or more, or until butter has been absorbed and pecans are crisp. Yield: 12 cups.

BEVERAGES

BRANDY ICE

6 scoops vanilla ice cream
6 ounces brandy
3 ounces white crème de cacao
1½ ounces white crème de menthe (optional)
9 ice cubes

Place in blender and blend on high speed, until smooth. Yield: 4 to 6 servings.

FROZEN FRUIT DAIQUIRI

1 (6-ounce) can frozen limeade concentrate
6 ounces light rum
1 banana
15 ice cubes
1 (10-ounce) package frozen strawberries

Place ingredients in blender. Blend until smooth. Yield: 6 servings.

CHAMPAGNE PUNCH

4 (6-ounce) cans frozen lemonade concentrate
6 cups unsweetened pineapple juice
3 cups water
2 quarts ginger ale, chilled
1 quart soda water, chilled
1 bottle dry champagne, chilled

Mix lemonade, pineapple juice and water; chill. At serving time, add remaining ingredients. Yield: 50 servings. *Delicious.*

PARTY STYLE MINT JULEPS

1 quart bourbon
1 pint finely chopped mint leaves
8 sprigs mint

Steep mint leaves in bourbon for 1 hour at room temperature. Fill sixteen 8-ounce glasses with finely cracked ice. Strain bourbon and pour into glasses, allowing 2 ounces minted bourbon per glass. Stir. Add more ice to fill glasses to rim. Garnish each glass with mint sprigs. Juleps may be prepared ahead and frozen until serving time. Yield: 16 servings.

SYLLABUB

¾ cup sugar
½ cup bourbon
1 quart milk
1 pint whipping cream

In large mixing bowl, stir sugar into bourbon until dissolved. Add milk, stirring constantly. Add cream and whip at high speed until foamy. Yield: 6 servings. *A Christmas Eve tradition.*

PINA COLADA

1 (8-ounce) can crushed pineapple, undrained
1 (8½-ounce) can cream of coconut milk
1 large ripe banana
½ cup nonfat dry milk
¼ cup water
¼ cup white rum
1 teaspoon lemon juice
1 tablespoon sugar
15 ice cubes

Mix in a blender and serve. Yield: 4 servings.

STRAWBERRY SPRITZERS

1 (10-ounce) package frozen strawberries, thawed
1 (.750 liter) bottle white wine, chilled
14 ounces soda water, chilled
fresh strawberries

Place undrained strawberries in blender and blend until smooth. In a large glass pitcher, combine strawberries, wine and soda water. Pour into wine glasses and garnish with strawberries. Yield: 12 (4-ounce) servings.

WATERMELON SCREWDRIVERS

1 small round watermelon
2 tablespoons fresh lemon juice
¾ cup vodka
4 cups orange juice
4 sprigs of mint for garnish

Cut watermelon in chunks and discard rind and seeds. In a food processor or blender, purée melon chunks with lemon juice. Pour purée into divided ice trays and freeze. When ready to serve, divide melon cubes among four glasses. Pour 1 jigger of vodka and 1 cup of orange juice in each glass. Stir and garnish with mint sprigs. Yield: 4 servings.

BEVERAGES

TOMATO WOW

1 (46-ounce) can tomato juice
3 ounces orange juice concentrate
juice of 2 lemons
juice of 1 lime
2 tablespoons Worcestershire sauce
2 teaspoons salt

Blend all ingredients and refrigerate. Serve in frosted glasses. Yield: 6 to 8 servings.

FRUIT MILK SHAKE

1 small banana
½ cup unsweetened apple juice
6 tablespoons low fat plain yogurt
⅔ cup low fat milk
½ teaspoon vanilla
¼ teaspoon ground cinnamon
4 ice cubes

Combine all ingredients in blender and blend on high speed for one minute. Yield: 2 servings.

TROPICAL MILK

1 cup orange juice
1 cup crushed pineapple
1 cup milk
1 banana, peeled and sliced
1 tablespoon sugar
1 teaspoon vanilla extract
½ teaspoon coconut extract
8 ice cubes
mint leaves for garnish

Chill 4 glasses. Place ingredients, except mint, in blender and process until smooth and frothy. Pour into chilled glasses and garnish each with mint leaves. Yield: 4 servings.

PEACH SOUR

4 ounces peach flavored brandy
1 teaspoon powdered sugar
juice of 1 lemon
4 ice cubes

Place ingredients in a blender and blend until smooth. Pour in sour glasses. Yield: 2 servings.

ORANGE JEWEL

1 (6-ounce) can orange juice
    concentrate
1 cup milk
¼ cup sugar

1 cup water
8 to 10 ice cubes
1 teaspoon vanilla extract

Put all ingredients in blender and blend until smooth. Yield: 4 to 6 servings.

MIMOSA HAWAIIAN

1 (12-ounce) can apricot nectar
1 (12-ounce) can pineapple juice
1 (6-ounce) can frozen orange
    juice concentrate, thawed

¾ cup water
1 (25.4-ounce) bottle dry white
    champagne, chilled

Combine first 4 ingredients in a large pitcher; stir well. Chill. Stir in champagne immediately before serving. Yield: 10 servings.

SUMMER PUNCH

1 (6-ounce) can frozen orange
    juice concentrate
1 (6-ounce) can frozen lemonade
    concentrate

1 (20-ounce) can apricot nectar
1 (12-ounce) can pineapple juice

Add water to frozen concentrates as directed on cans. Combine with apricot nectar and pineapple juice. Chill and serve. Yield: 3 quarts.

STRAWBERRY PUNCH

3 (0.2-ounce) packages
    strawberry-flavored instant
    drink mix
1 (12-ounce) can frozen orange
    juice concentrate

3 cups sugar
4 quarts water

Combine powdered drink mix, orange juice, and sugar. Add 1 quart water and freeze. Before serving, add 3 quarts water to frozen mixture and stir until thawed. Yield: 20 to 24 servings.

WHISKEY PUNCH

1 cup strong tea
1 cup granulated sugar
1 cup orange juice

½ cup lemon juice
¾ cup whiskey
1 pint orange sherbet

Combine first 5 ingredients. Chill. Pour into punch bowl. Immediately before serving, stir in sherbet. Yield: 10 to 15 servings.

EASY COFFEE LIQUEUR

2 cups boiling water
¾ cup instant coffee
6 cups water

5½ cups sugar
1 tablespoon vanilla extract
1 quart vodka

Bring water to a boil; add instant coffee and steep for one minute. Add remaining ingredients and simmer for one hour. Cool. Serve over ice or with equal parts of cream or milk. Yield: 1 gallon.

RUSSIAN COFFEE

1½ ounces coffee liqueur
1½ ounces vodka

1½ ounces cream
⅔ cup crushed ice

Put all ingredients into blender. Blend at low speed for 30 seconds. Serve in saucer-shaped champagne glasses. Yield: 2 servings.

IRISH CREAM

8 ounces Irish whiskey
8 ounces whipping cream
4 ounces milk
1 teaspoon chocolate syrup

1 teaspoon instant coffee
1 (14-ounce) can sweetened
    condensed milk

Combine all ingredients. Refrigerate and enjoy. Yield: 8 servings.

HOT BUTTERED RUM

1 pound butter
1 pound dark brown sugar
1 pound powdered sugar
1 quart vanilla ice cream

½ teaspoon ground cloves
2 teaspoons cinnamon
rum
hot water

Cream together first 6 ingredients. Pour into ½ gallon container and freeze. Place 1 tablespoon of frozen mixture and 1 ounce of rum in a mug and add hot water. Yield: 50 servings. *Good to serve during cold weather in front of the fireplace.*

HOT MULLED CIDER

1 teaspoon whole allspice
1 teaspoon whole cloves
dash nutmeg
1 (3-inch) cinnamon stick

½ cup brown sugar
2 quarts apple cider
orange wedges for garnish

Tie allspice and cloves in a cheesecloth bag. Place spice bag, nutmeg, cinnamon stick, brown sugar and cider in a large kettle. Slowly bring to a boil; cover and simmer for 20 minutes. Remove spice bag. Pour into mugs and garnish with orange slices. May be made ahead and reheated. Yield: 10 servings.

AUTUMN PUNCH

½ gallon apple juice
1½ quarts cranberry juice
2 cups water

¼ cup brown sugar
2 cinnamon sticks
½ teaspoon whole cloves

Combine all ingredients. Bring to a boil. Lower heat and simmer 30 minutes. Yield: 1 gallon. *Smells wonderful and tastes great. Perfect for holiday open house. May be kept warm in crock pot.*

BEVERAGES

MONTGOMERY CHRISTMAS PUNCH

3 dozen oranges
2 dozen lemons
2 (10-ounce) cans crushed pineapple
2 (12-ounce) jars cherries, chopped

2 quarts grape juice
1 quart strong tea
2 cups sugar

Squeeze oranges and lemons and remove seeds from juice. Combine juices with remaining ingredients. Age at least 5 days in a covered, refrigerated container. Yield: 6 quarts. *This punch is said to "settle the stomach" following large holiday meals.*

HOT EGGNOG

1 egg
dash of salt
1 tablespoon sugar
6 ounces hot milk

2 ounces hot cognac
1 teaspoon dark rum
ground nutmeg

Beat egg and salt together until egg is thick and lemon yellow. Add sugar and beat until sugar is blended. Add hot milk, cognac and rum. Stir well. Pour into mug and sprinkle with ground nutmeg. Yield: 1 serving.

EGGNOG BOWL

12 eggs
½ cup sugar
1 fifth cognac
½ cup dark rum

3 quarts milk
1 cup cream
grated nutmeg

Separate eggs. In punch bowl, combine egg yolks and sugar. Beat well with wire whisk. Gradually add cognac, rum, milk and cream. Beat well. Place bowl in refrigerator for at least 2 hours. Just before serving, beat egg whites until stiff. Fold whites into punch until thoroughly blended. Ladle into cups and sprinkle with nutmeg. Yield: 24 servings.

SOUPS AND SAUCES

BLACK BEAN GAZPACHO

2 cups black beans
8 cups water
2 cups chopped onions
1 cup chopped celery
½ cup chopped carrots
1 teaspoon salt
1 bay leaf
½ cup dry Madeira

Place beans and water in large saucepan; bring to a boil. Boil 2 minutes; cover and set aside for one hour. Add onions, celery, carrots, salt and bay leaf. Simmer, covered, for 2 hours. Allow soup to cool. Remove bay leaf and purée soup with the liquid. Bring soup to a simmer and add Madeira. Simmer 5 minutes. Ladle into bowls and garnish with one or more of the following: chopped cucumbers, chopped hard-boiled eggs, diced green peppers, minced onions, chopped tomato, toasted croutons, crumbled crisp bacon. Yield: 6 servings.

HEARTY BEAN SOUP

Bean Mix:
1 pound dried navy beans
1 pound dried split peas
1 pound dried pinto beans
1 pound dried lentils
1 pound dried black-eyed peas
1 pound dried kidney beans

Layer ⅓ cup of each kind of bean in glass pint jars. Makes 6 (2-cup) jars for use in bean soup as follows:

2 cups bean mix
8 cups water
1 (8-ounce) package bacon
1 large onion, chopped
1 bay leaf
2 cloves garlic, minced
⅛ teaspoon pepper
1 (14-ounce) can taco sauce
16 ounces ham, cubed

Rinse beans and remove imperfects. Combine beans and water in a large stock pot. Cover and bring to a boil. Boil 2 minutes. Remove from heat; let stand 1 hour. Add whole bacon strips, onion, bay leaf, garlic, and pepper. Bring to a boil; lower heat, cover and simmer for 1½ to 2 hours or until beans are tender, stirring occasionally. Add remaining ingredients. Simmer 15 minutes. Remove bacon strips. Yield: 6 to 8 servings. *Note: Bean Mix may be doubled. Any 6 varieties of beans may be used. Bean Mix makes an unusual, useful and tasty gift.*

BUTTERMILK BROCCOLI SOUP

1¾ pounds broccoli
2 Idaho potatoes
2 tablespoons butter
1 cup finely chopped onions
1 clove garlic, minced

7 cups chicken broth
3 cups buttermilk
½ teaspoon ground nutmeg
1 dash hot sauce

Cut broccoli into flowerets. Cut tender part of stems into one-inch pieces. Remove one cup of smallest flowerets for garnish. Drop garnish pieces in boiling water and cook 30 seconds. Drain; rinse in cold water. Drain and set aside. Peel and cut potatoes into cubes. Heat the butter in a large stock pot. Add onions and garlic. Cook, stirring until onions are transparent. Add potatoes, broccoli and chicken broth. Bring to a boil; reduce heat, and simmer 20 minutes or until potatoes are tender. Spoon mixture into a blender or food processor. Blend thoroughly in small batches until all liquid and vegetables have been puréed. Return soup to kettle; add buttermilk, nutmeg and hot sauce. Heat soup thoroughly. Garnish with reserved flowerets. Yield: 6 to 8 servings.

FRENCH CARROT SOUP

6 medium carrots, peeled and
    chopped
4 cups chicken broth
1 small onion, chopped
1 small bay leaf
1 teaspoon salt

dash white pepper
1 tablespoon butter
1½ cups milk
2 teaspoons sugar
chopped chives

Combine carrots, broth, onion, bay leaf, salt and pepper. Cook 10 minutes or until carrots are tender. Remove bay leaf and set soup aside to cool. When cool, purée in a food processor or blender. Melt butter in the same saucepan in which the carrots were cooked. Add the milk and sugar; stir until sugar is dissolved. Add the puréed mixture and heat through. Do not boil. Serve hot and garnish with chopped chives. Yield: 6 servings.

CRÈME CRÉCY

10 carrots, peeled and sliced
4 medium potatoes, peeled and cubed
1 cup chopped onion
6 cups chicken broth, fresh or canned
½ teaspoon dried thyme

1 bay leaf
1 cup half-and-half
¼ teaspoon white pepper
½ teaspoon sugar
1 teaspoon salt
1 cup cold milk

Combine carrots, potatoes and onions in broth in a large saucepan. Bring to a boil; add thyme and bay leaf. Lower heat and simmer 30 minutes. Remove from heat and allow to come to room temperature. Purée mixture in blender or food processor. Add remaining ingredients; stir well. Chill. Flavor improves if made the day before. Yield: 6 to 8 servings.

FRESH CANTALOUPE SOUP

1 medium cantaloupe
3 cups orange juice
½ teaspoon ground cinnamon

1 tablespoon lemon juice
1 tablespoon lime juice
mint leaves for garnish

Cut cantaloupe into 8 sections. Remove seeds and cut pulp away from rind. Place pulp and remaining ingredients in food processor or blender and process until smooth. Chill before serving. Serve in long-stemmed glasses and garnish with mint leaves. Yield: 8 servings.

CORN CHOWDER

4 slices bacon
½ cup chopped onion
3 cups diced potatoes
2 cups water
2 cups corn, fresh, canned or frozen

1 teaspoon salt
1 teaspoon white pepper
4 cups hot milk

Cook bacon until crisp. Drain, crumble and set aside. In a large pot, cook onions in bacon grease. Add remaining ingredients, except milk. Cook until potatoes are tender. Add milk and heat thoroughly. Serve hot, garnished with crumbled bacon. Yield: 6 to 8 servings.

GAZPACHO

½ cup diced celery
½ cup diced onion
1 cup peeled, diced tomatoes
½ cup diced green peppers
½ cup chopped cucumber
1 (10¾-ounce) can tomato soup
1 (10¾-ounce) soup can water
1½ cups cocktail vegetable juice

1 tablespoon wine vinegar
1 tablespoon Italian dressing
pinch garlic salt
¼ teaspoon salt
⅛ teaspoon pepper
4 dashes hot sauce
dash Worcestershire sauce
chopped black olives for garnish

Combine all ingredients, except olives, in large bowl. Cover and refrigerate at least 4 hours. Stir gently. Serve in chilled bowls, mugs, or long-stemmed glasses. Garnish with chopped black olives. Yield: 6 to 8 servings.

FRENCH ONION SOUP

1½ pounds onions
¼ cup butter or margarine
2 tablespoons sugar
2 tablespoons all-purpose flour
6 cups chicken broth
½ to 1 cup dry wine, red or white

salt and pepper to taste
6 slices mozzarella cheese
½ cup grated Parmesan cheese
toasted French bread

Peel onions and slice thin. Brown lightly in butter. Add sugar and flour to onions. Add to chicken broth, cover and simmer for about 30 minutes. Add wine and season to taste with salt and pepper. Put one slice of mozzarella cheese in each soup bowl or small casserole. Add hot soup mixture. Top with toasted French bread and a slice of mozzarella cheese. Bake at 350° for 30 minutes. Sprinkle with grated Parmesan before serving. Yield: 4 to 6 servings.

PRACTICALLY NO-CALORIE SOUP

6 medium onions
2 green peppers
1 bunch of celelry
1 medium head of cabbage

2 (16-ounce) cans tomatoes
water
2 envelopes dried onion soup mix

Chop vegetables. Place in large pot and cover with water. Bring to a boil and continue boiling 10 minutes. Add onion soup mix. Reduce heat and simmer until vegetables are tender. Yield: 8 to 10 servings.

SOUPS

HOT AND SOUR SOUP

1 quart chicken stock
1 teaspoon salt
1 tablespoon soy sauce
4 dried Chinese mushrooms, soaked in water and sliced
½ cup bamboo shoots, thinly sliced
½ pound pork, thinly sliced
1 cake bean curd, cut in strips
¼ teaspoon white pepper
2 tablespoons white vinegar
2 tablespoons cornstarch
water
1 egg, slightly beaten
2 tablespoons sesame oil

In large soup pot, combine chicken stock, salt, soy sauce, mushrooms, bamboo shoots and pork. Bring to a boil and reduce heat to simmer for 10 minutes. Drop in bean curd, pepper and vinegar. Bring to a boil again. Stir water into cornstarch to make a paste. Stir paste into pot then slowly stir in the egg. Remove pot from heat. Stir in sesame oil. Yield: 4 to 6 servings.

Magic Wok Restaurant
Augusta, Georgia

POTATO SOUP

2 medium onions, finely chopped
water
4 large potatoes, diced
3 tablespoons butter or margarine
4 cups milk
salt and pepper to taste
chopped chives for garnish

Cook onions in a small amount of boiling water. Add potatoes and enough water to cover potatoes; simmer until potatoes are tender. Drain onions and potatoes, reserving 4 tablespoons of liquid. Add butter or margarine, milk, salt and pepper. Simmer for 15 minutes. Serve in heated bowls and garnish with chopped chives. Yield: 4 to 6 servings.

CREAMY SQUASH SOUP

2 pounds yellow squash, chopped
1 cup chopped onion
1 cup water
½ teaspoon salt
2 tablespoons butter
2 tablespoons all-purpose flour
2 cups chicken broth
1 teaspoon dried thyme
dash white pepper
1 cup sour cream
chopped pimento for garnish

Cook squash and onion in water with salt until squash is tender. Place squash and liquid in blender or food processor and purée. Melt butter in saucepan. Add flour and cook until golden. Slowly add broth, stirring constantly. Add puréed mixture to broth; add thyme and pepper. Simmer 10 minutes. Cool to room temperature. Add sour cream; blend well. Chill well. Serve garnished with pimento. Yield: 6 servings. *Soup may be served warm. Do not boil.*

BRUNSWICK STEW

1 (3 to 4 pound) hen
2 pounds beef cubes
water
2 cups cubed potatoes
4 cups cut corn
1 cup chopped onion
2 cups lima beans
4 cups canned tomatoes
1 tablespoon salt
1 tablespoon liquid hot sauce
1 tablespoon black pepper
1 tablespoon Worcestershire sauce
rice

Place chicken and beef in a large saucepan. Add enough water to cover. Cook over medium heat until meat is tender. When done, remove meat from broth, reserving liquid. Remove chicken from bones. Chop meat in food processor or shred with a fork. Skim fat from broth. Return meat to broth. Add remaining ingredients. Simmer slowly for several hours to blend flavors and thicken. Serve hot over white rice. Yield: 18 servings.

CHICKEN NOODLE SOUP

6 chicken breast halves
6 cups water
1 cup chopped onion
1 cup chopped celery
1 cup cubed carrots
1 tablespoon dried parsley flakes
½ teaspoon sage
¼ teaspoon garlic powder
dash liquid pepper sauce
salt and pepper to taste
½ cup thin egg noodles, uncooked
½ cup frozen peas

Boil chicken in water in covered stock pot until done. Remove chicken from bones and cube. Return chicken to broth. Add remaining ingredients except peas. Cover and simmer 30 minutes. Add peas and cook 10 minutes longer. Yield: 6 servings.

COUNTRY SOUP

½ cup chopped carrots
½ cup chopped celery
½ cup chopped onion
¼ cup butter
4 teapoons instant chicken bouillon
3½ cups water
1 cup instant potato buds
1 cup milk
2 tablespoons cream
½ teaspoon lemon juice
1 (8-ounce) can early peas, drained
chives

In a large saucepan, sauté carrots, celery and onion in butter until tender. Add bouillon and water. Bring to a boil; reduce heat and simmer for 15 minutes. Add potato buds and milk. Mix thoroughly. Add cream, lemon juice and peas. Heat through. Garnish with chives. Yield: 6 to 8 servings.

VEGETABLE-BURGER SOUP

1 pound ground beef
1 (1-pound) can stewed tomatoes, about 2 cups
1 (8-ounce) can tomato sauce
2 cups water
1 (10-ounce) package frozen mixed vegetables
½ envelope (¼ cup) dry onion-mushroom soup mix
1 teaspoon sugar

In large heavy saucepan, brown ground beef lightly; drain excess fat. Stir in tomatoes, tomato sauce, water, vegetables, soup mix, and sugar. Bring to a boil. Reduce heat, cover, and simmer at least 30 minutes. Yield: 4 servings.

OLD FASHIONED VEGETABLE SOUP

3 pounds beef shank
1 (18-ounce) can tomato juice
6 cups water
1 cup chopped onion
3 teaspoons salt
2 teaspoons Worcestershire sauce
¼ teaspoon chili powder
2 bay leaves
1 (1-pound) can tomatoes
1 cup chopped celery
1 (8¾-ounce) can whole kernel corn
1 cup sliced carrots
1 cup cubed potatoes
1 (10-ounce) package frozen lima beans

Combine meat, tomato juice, water, onion, and seasonings in soup kettle. Cover and simmer 2 hours. Remove shank and cut meat from bones in large cubes. Skim excess fat from broth. Add meat and vegetables to broth; cover and simmer 1 hour. Remove bay leaf and serve. Yield: 8 servings.

CURRIED TUNA-MUSHROOM SOUP

1 (4-ounce) can mushrooms, drained
½ cup finely chopped onion
2 tablespoons butter
1 (10½-ounce) can cream of mushroom soup
3 to 4 cups milk
1 (7-ounce) can tuna, drained and flaked
1 tablespoon chopped parsley
½ teaspoon salt
1 teaspoon curry powder
1 (2-ounce) can pimento, chopped

Sauté mushrooms and onions in butter. Add remaining ingredients. Simmer over low heat 10 minutes. Yield: 6 servings.

SEAFOOD GUMBO

½ cup plus 2 tablespoons butter
1 pound fresh okra, sliced
1 pound ham, cubed
1½ cups chopped onion
1 cup chopped green pepper
1 cup sliced celery
2 cloves garlic, minced
2 tablespoons all-purpose flour
4 cups chicken stock, fresh or canned
1 (6-ounce) can tomato paste
2 cups canned or fresh tomatoes, chopped
2 bay leaves
1 teaspoon dried parsley
½ teaspoon dried thyme
1 tablespoon Worcestershire
½ teaspoon liquid pepper sauce
1 pound raw shrimp, shelled and deveined
1 pound fresh lump crab meat
1 pound raw scallops
hot white rice

In a large skillet, melt ½ cup butter. Add okra, ham, onion, green pepper, celery and garlic. Sauté 5 minutes. In a large soup pot, melt 2 tablespoons butter; stir in flour and cook until golden brown. Add cooked vegetables and ham to roux; mix well. Slowly add chicken stock; mix thoroughly. Add tomato paste, tomatoes, and seasonings. Bring to a boil; reduce heat and simmer 1 hour. Add raw shrimp, crab and scallops. Cook 5 to 7 minutes or just until shrimp are pink. Serve over hot white rice. Yield: 10 to 12 servings.

SHRIMP BISQUE

2 quarts water
2 pounds shrimp
2 bay leaves
4 stalks celery
2 cups flour
1 cup butter
1 large onion, chopped
2 cups chopped celery
½ teaspoon thyme
½ cup sherry
1 cup heavy cream
juice of 1 lemon
dash cayenne

Combine water, shrimp, bay leaves and 4 celery stalks. Boil until shrimp turn pink; drain shrimp reserving liquid. Peel and chop shrimp. Melt butter and add flour to make a roux. Add chopped celery and onion and cook until vegetables are transparent. Add stock to roux and cook until thick. Stir in chopped shrimp, seasonings, sherry, cream, and juice. Heat through but do not boil. Yield: 8 to 10 servings.

SALMON POTATO CHEESE SOUP

1 large onion, thinly sliced (2 cups)
1¼ cups diced celery
¼ cup margarine
3½ cups potatoes, peeled and thinly sliced
1 cup chicken broth
3 cups milk
1 cup half-and-half
2 cups shredded sharp Cheddar cheese
1 teaspoon thyme
1 tablespoon Worcestershire sauce
1 (15½-ounce) can salmon, broken into chunks
salt and pepper to taste
2 tablespoons fresh parsley, minced

Sauté onion and celery in margarine until tender. Add potatoes and broth; cook covered until potatoes are tender, about 20 minutes. Add milk, half-and-half, cheese, thyme, Worcestershire sauce, and salmon. Season with salt and pepper. Cook, stirring constantly, until salmon is hot and cheese is melted. Serve hot, garnished with fresh parsley. Yield: 8 servings.

GROUPER SOUP

1 pound grouper fillets
½ teaspoon salt
¼ teaspoon white pepper
1 cup chopped onion
2 cups potatoes, cubed
2 cups chicken broth, fresh or canned
1 cup heavy cream
chopped fresh parsley for garnish

Cut grouper into bite-size pieces. In a saucepan, combine fish, seasonings, onion, potatoes and broth. Cook until fish flakes easily with fork. Remove from heat. Stir in cream. Serve hot with parsley garnish. Yield: 4 servings.

SEAFOOD BISQUE

2 cups white sauce (See Index)
1 (10-ounce) can cream of shrimp soup
1 (10-ounce) can Manhattan style chowder

Combine all ingredients. Cook over low heat stirring constantly. Serve with crackers for a hearty supper. Yield: 6 servings.

OYSTER STEW

1 medium onion, chopped
water
8 cups milk

1 pint stewing oysters
¼ cup butter
salt and pepper to taste

Chop one medium onion; place in 2-quart saucepan with enough water to cover onion. Cook until onion is tender. Add milk and bring to a boil. Add oysters. Return to boil; when mixture boils remove from heat. Add butter and salt and pepper. Cover and let stand 10 minutes before serving. Serve with saltines or oyster crackers. Yield: 4 to 6 servings.

BASIC WHITE SAUCE

Thin:
1 tablespoon butter
1 tablespoon all-purpose flour
¼ teaspoon salt

dash white pepper
1½ cups milk

Medium:
2 tablespoons butter
2 tablespoons all-purpose flour
¼ teaspoon salt

dash white pepper
1 cup milk

Thick:
3 tablespoons butter
4 tablespoons all-purpose flour
¼ teaspoon salt

dash white pepper
1 cup milk

Melt butter in saucepan over low heat. Blend in flour, salt, and pepper. Add milk, stirring constantly. Cook quickly until mixture thickens and bubbles. Yield: 1 to 1½ cups.

BEARNAISE SAUCE

3 egg yolks
3 tablespoons tarragon vinegar
¼ teaspoon salt
¼ teaspoon coarsely ground pepper
⅔ cup butter, melted
2 tablespoons dry white wine
1 teaspoon dried whole tarragon
2 teaspoons minced green onions

Combine egg yolks, vinegar, salt, and pepper in container of electric blender; process 3 seconds at high speed. Turn blender to low speed and carefully add hot butter to yolk mixture in a very slow, steady stream. Turn blender to high speed and process until thick. Combine wine, tarragon, and green onions in a small saucepan and cook over high heat until almost all liquid evaporates. Add to mixture in blender and process 4 seconds at high speed. Yield: 1⅓ cups.

EASY HOLLANDAISE SAUCE

1 egg, beaten
2 tablespoons white vinegar
1 teaspoon sugar
water
1 tablespoon butter
1 tablespoon all-purpose flour
2 heaping tablespoons mayonnaise

In a measuring cup, place beaten egg, vinegar and sugar. Mix well and fill measuring cup to half-cup mark with water. Set aside. In small saucepan, melt butter over low heat and slowly add flour; mix well. Gradually add egg mixture. Cook, stirring continuously over low heat. When mixture thickens, remove from heat and allow to cool. Before serving add mayonnaise and blend well. *Great over asparagus!* Yield: 1¼ cups.

MICROWAVE CHEESE SAUCE

2 tablespoons butter
2 tablespoons all-purpose flour
½ teaspoon salt
1 cup whole milk
1 cup sharp cheese, shredded
dash cayenne pepper

In a 1-quart glass measuring cup, place butter, flour, and salt. Microwave at high for 1 minute, stirring after 30 seconds. Gradually stir in milk. Microwave at high 3½ to 4½ minutes, stirring every minute until thick and bubbly. Add cheese and cayenne pepper. Microwave at high 1 to 2 minutes to melt cheese. Yield: 2 cups.

BARBECUE SAUCE

1½ cups apple cider vinegar
juice of 2 lemons
2 tablespoons Worcestershire sauce
1 tablespoon peanut butter
1 teaspoon salt
1 teaspoon pepper
2 tablespoons chili powder
2 teaspoons celery seed
½ cup margarine

Combine all ingredients and bring to boil over medium heat. Cook until all peanut butter is dissolved. If sauce is too thin, add a little more peanut butter, one teaspoon at a time. Stir to avoid sticking. Great with chicken and pork chops. Yield: 2 cups.

HICKORY BARBECUE SAUCE

1 (20-ounce) bottle ketchup
½ cup water
¼ cup cider vinegar
1 tablespoon brown sugar
1 tablespoon Worcestershire sauce
1 teaspoon salt
1 teaspoon minced onion
½ teaspoon liquid smoke
⅛ teaspoon garlic powder

Blend all ingredients in blender or food processor until smooth. Store in refrigerator. Use on ribs, chicken, pork chops or beef brisket. Yield: 3 cups. *Good on sandwiches!*

HAM GLAZE

1 (6-ounce) can frozen orange juice concentrate, thawed
¼ teaspoon ground cloves
¼ cup dark brown sugar
¼ teaspoon ground cinnamon

Combine all ingredients and spoon over ham while baking. Yield: 1 cup.

CRANBERRY SAUCE

1 (1-pound) package fresh whole cranberries
2 oranges, seeded
2 or 3 apples, cored
2 cups sugar

Place cranberries, oranges, and apples in food processor. Process until smooth. Add sugar, stirring to dissolve. Good with turkey and ham. Sauce may be frozen for future use. Yield: 4 cups.

MUSTARD SAUCE

4 tablespoons butter
4 tablespoons minced onions
½ cup dry white wine
1 cup heavy cream
2 tablespoons Dijon mustard

Melt butter; add onions and sauté until transparent. Add wine; cook until liquid is almost evaporated. Add cream and mustard, stirring constantly and cook 1 minute. Yield: 1 cup.

LEMON DILL HORSERADISH SAUCE

1 cup mayonnaise
juice of 1 lemon
1 tablespoon grated onion
2 tablespoons prepared horseradish
½ teaspoon salt
dash of liquid pepper sauce
½ teaspoon dried dill weed

Mix ingredients. Store in refrigerator. Serve cold or hot. Excellent on fish and vegetables. Yield: 1 cup.

GRANNY'S GIBLET GRAVY

¼ cup butter
¼ cup all-purpose flour
½ teaspoon salt
2 cups chicken broth

1 chopped chicken gizzard
1 chopped chicken liver
2 hard-boiled eggs, diced

In saucepan, melt butter; blend in flour and salt. Add chicken broth, gizzard, liver and eggs. Cook over medium heat until thick, stirring constantly. Yield: 3 cups.

GAME SAUCE

½ cup red currant jelly
¼ cup ketchup
¼ cup port wine

½ teaspoon Worcestershire sauce

Combine all ingredients in a small saucepan. Cook over medium heat, stirring frequently, until smooth and jelly is melted. Good over any roasted wild game. Yield: 1 cup.

BETTER-FOR-YOU SOUR CREAM

1 cup low-fat cottage cheese
½ cup buttermilk

2 teaspoons fresh lemon juice
¼ teaspoon salt

Place all ingredients in a blender and process at highest speed for 60 seconds. Stop blender every 15 seconds and push mixture down with a spatula. Store in refrigerator. Consistency firms as mixture is stored. Yield: 1½ cups.

SWEETENED CONDENSED MILK

1 cup boiling water
½ cup margarine

2 cups powdered milk
2 cups sugar

Combine all ingredients in electric blender. Process until smooth. Refrigerate until ready to use. Yield: 3 cups.

FONDUE SAUCES

CHILI SAUCE

½ cup chili sauce (prepared)　　½ teaspoon steak sauce
1 teaspoon horseradish

Combine all ingredients. Cover and refrigerate at least one hour. Serve with beef. Yield: ½ cup.

RED DEVIL SAUCE

1 (15-ounce) can or 2 (8-ounce) cans tomato sauce with tomato bits
4 teaspoons sugar
2 tablespoons chopped green onions
2 tablespoons red wine vinegar
1 clove garlic, crushed
hot pepper sauce to taste

Combine ingredients; chill. Serve with beef, chicken or shrimp. Yield: 2 cups.

HOT MUSTARD SAUCE

½ cup dry mustard　　　1 teaspoon oil
½ cup hot water　　　　1 teaspoon salt

Combine ingredients and allow to stand at room temperature 15 minutes. Yield: 1 cup.

CURRY SAUCE

1 cup sour cream
½ cup mayonnaise
1 tablespoon chopped fresh parsley
2 teaspoons curry powder
1 teaspoon lemon juice
½ teaspoon Worcestershire sauce
½ clove garlic, crushed
¼ teaspoon salt

Blend ingredients until smooth. Chill. Serve with beef, chicken or shrimp. Yield: 1½ cups.

BARBECUE SAUCE

2 (8-ounce) cans tomato sauce
2 tablespoons brown sugar
¼ cup cider vinegar
2 tablespoons Worcestershire sauce
1 teaspoon salt
1 teaspoon dry mustard
1 teaspoon chili sauce
1 tablespoon paprika

Combine all ingredients. Simmer 15 minutes, stirring occasionally. Yield: 2½ cups.

SALADS AND SALAD DRESSINGS

COCONUT CHICKEN SALAD

4 chicken breast halves
1 stalk celery, sliced
¼ cup mayonnaise
¼ teaspoon curry
juice of ½ lime
1 cup pineapple chunks
½ cup coarsely chopped pecans
½ cup shredded coconut

Boil chicken until fork tender. Remove bones and skin; chop chicken in large chunks. Add remaining ingredients; mix well. Chill before serving. Yield: 4 servings.

TARRAGON CHICKEN SALAD

4 quarts water
3 pounds chicken breasts
½ cup sour cream
½ cup mayonnaise
2 celery ribs, chopped
2 green onions, thinly sliced
½ cup chopped pecans
2 teaspoons dried tarragon flakes
salt and pepper to taste

Cook chicken breasts in boiling water for 20 minutes, until done. Remove from water; cool and bone. Cut meat into bite-size chunks and put in a medium-sized mixing bowl. In a small bowl, whisk together sour cream and mayonnaise. Pour over chicken. Add celery, onions, pecans, tarragon, salt and pepper. Toss well. Cover and refrigerate at least 4 hours. Yield: 4 to 6 servings.

PAELLA SALAD

1 (7-ounce) package yellow rice
2 tablespoons tarragon vinegar
⅓ cup oil
1 tablespoon prepared mustard
¼ teaspoon monosodium glutamate
2 cups cooked cubed chicken
1 cup peeled cooked shrimp
1 large tomato, peeled and chopped
1 green pepper, chopped
1 large onion, chopped
1 stalk celery, sliced
1 (2-ounce) jar diced pimento
1 teaspoon salt
⅛ teaspoon dried oregano
⅛ teaspoon dried basil

Cook rice according to package directions and cool. Combine all ingredients and toss gently. Cover and chill before serving. Yield: 8 servings. *May be prepared the night before.*

SHRIMP SALAD

1 pound shrimp, cooked, shelled, deveined, and chopped
1 cup celery, chopped
2 hard-boiled eggs, chopped
½ cup mayonnaise
salt and pepper to taste

Mix ingredients thoroughly. Serve on lettuce leaves or stuffed into hollowed tomatoes. Yield: 4 servings.

SALADE NIÇOISE

Salad:
5 small new potatoes
¼ pound green beans
1 small head romaine, Boston, or Bibb lettuce
2 (7-ounce) cans white, water-packed tuna
3 tomatoes, quartered
1 green pepper, cut in 1-inch pieces
1 small red onion, cut in thin rings
12 pitted black olives
3 hard-boiled eggs, quartered lengthwise
12 drained anchovy fillets, optional
capers, optional

Vinaigrette Dressing:
¼ cup tarragon vinegar
½ cup light olive or vegetable oil
1 chopped garlic clove
¼ teaspoon dry mustard or ½ teaspoon Dijon style mustard

Peel, boil, slice, and refrigerate potatoes. Cut green beans into 1-inch pieces. Boil 5 minutes, drain and refrigerate. Tear lettuce in bite-size pieces and place in bottom of large salad bowl. On top of lettuce, in pie-shaped patterns, place potatoes, tuna, tomatoes, beans, green peppers, onion, and olives. Decorate middle and around the edge with eggs and anchovies (if used). Sprinkle on capers. Combine dressing ingredients; blend well. Pour dressing over salad and toss. Serve immediately. Yield: 10 servings.

TUNA SALAD

1 (7-ounce) package macaroni rings
1½ cups frozen peas, thawed
1 (12½-ounce) can water-packed tuna
1 cup chopped celery
1 medium onion, chopped
1¼ cups mayonnaise

Cook macaroni rings according to package directions; drain and cool. Combine rings with remaining ingredients. Chill for 1 hour. Serve on a bed of lettuce. Yield: 4 to 6 servings. *Great light dinner on hot evening!*

TUNA SALAD WITH CHINESE NOODLES

1 (9¼-ounce) can tuna
2 tablespoons pimento
3 tablespoons chopped olives
3 tablespoons chopped green pepper
½ cup chopped onion
1 teaspoon white vinegar
½ cup salad dressing or mayonnaise
dash of Worcestershire sauce
1 (3-ounce) can Chinese noodles
cherry tomatoes for garnish

Combine all ingredients except noodles and tomatoes. Spoon ingredients over Chinese noodles and garnish with tomatoes. Yield: 4 servings.

SUMMER PASTA SALAD

2 cups broccoli flowerets
2 cups cauliflower flowerets
12 pitted black olives, sliced
1 small zucchini, cubed
1 small yellow squash, cubed
1 small onion, sliced in rings
1 cup sliced fresh mushrooms
8 cherry tomatoes, cut in fourths
1 (10-ounce) package snow peas, cooked and drained
2 cups cooked "twist" noodles
1 cup "Excellent Vinaigrette" (See index), or Italian dressing

Combine vegetables and noodles. Toss with 1 cup of viniagrette or Italian dressing. Yield: 6 servings.

COLORFUL PASTA SALAD

Salad:
½ cup cooked shell macaroni
½ cup cooked twist macaroni
½ cup cooked spring macaroni
1 cup cherry tomatoes
½ cup sliced carrots
½ cup coarsely chopped green pepper
½ cup sliced yellow squash
½ cup sliced zucchini squash
½ cup whole black olives
grated Parmesan cheese

Dressing:
⅓ cup olive oil
⅓ cup vegetable oil
4 tablespoons tarragon vinegar
2 tablespoons prepared wine mustard
½ teaspoon monosodium glutamate

Place salad ingredients in a large bowl. Combine dressing ingredients and pour over salad. Toss and serve with grated Parmesan cheese. Yield: 4 to 6 servings.

LINGUINI SALAD

Salad:
⅓ pound linguini
1 (12-ounce) can marinated artichoke hearts
2 large tomatoes, chopped
½ cup walnuts, chopped
2 tablespoons chopped parsley
1 cup fresh mushrooms, sliced

Dressing:
juice from can of artichoke hearts
½ cup vegetable oil
¼ cup red wine vinegar
1 clove garlic, crushed
basil
salt and pepper

Cook linguini according to package directions; drain. Drain and chop artichoke hearts; reserve liquid. Mix salad ingredients in a large bowl. Combine dressing ingredients and pour over salad. Cover and refrigerate 2 hours. Yield: 8 servings.

AUGUSTA'S FAVORITE SALAD

½ cup salad oil
¼ cup red wine vinegar
1 teaspoon monosodium glutamate
1 teaspoon seasoned salt
½ teaspoon oregano leaves
1 tomato, chopped
2 teaspoons green onion tops or chives
2 teaspoons fresh chopped parsley
1 medium head lettuce, torn or chopped in small pieces
croutons, optional

Mix all ingredients, except lettuce. Add chopped lettuce and toss. Toss with croutons or toasted pita bread chips. Yield: 6 servings.

ASHEVILLE SALAD

1 (10¾-ounce) can tomato soup
1 cup mayonnaise
3 (3-ounce) packages cream cheese, softened
2 envelopes unflavored gelatin
½ cup hot water
2 cups chopped celery
1 green pepper, chopped
1 medium onion, chopped
1 (7-ounce) can tuna
1 (6½-ounce) can crab meat

Heat soup. Add mayonnaise and cream cheese; cook until cheese dissolves. Dissolve gelatin in water. Add gelatin to soup mixture and cool. Add remaining ingredients. Pour into 1½-quart container. Chill. Yield: 6 servings.

BORSCHT SALAD

1 (1¼-pound) can crushed pineapple
1 (6-ounce) package raspberry-flavored gelatin
1½ cups boiling water
1 cup shredded beets
2 tablespoons vinegar
dash salt
2 teaspoons dill seed
1 cup chopped celery
sour cream

Drain pineapple; reserve juice. Dissolve gelatin in boiling water; add beets, pineapple juice, vinegar, salt and dill seed. Chill until mixture thickens. Fold in chopped celery and pineapple. Chill until firm. Top with sour cream. Yield: 6 to 8 servings.

THREE BEAN SALAD

1 (16-ounce) can each of cut green beans, waxed beans, and kidney or pinto beans
1 medium onion, sliced and separated into rings
½ teaspoon dry mustard
½ cup sugar
½ teaspoon salt
dash of pepper
½ cup white vinegar
½ cup oil
1 green pepper, optional for garnish
1 small chopped onion, optional for garnish

Drain beans well. Mix together beans with onion rings in a covered container. Set aside. Mix dry ingredients. Add vinegar; stir until sugar dissolves. Add oil. Pour mixture over beans and onions. Cover and marinate several hours or overnight, stirring mixture occasionally. Drain liquid before serving. Decorate, if desired, with thin slices of green pepper and chopped onion. Will keep for three weeks in a covered container in the refrigerator. Yield: 12 servings.

MARINATED COLE SLAW

1 large head of cabbage
1 large onion
1 large green pepper
1 large carrot
1 cup sugar
1 cup cider vinegar
1 teaspoon celery seed
1 teaspoon dry mustard
½ cup salad oil

Shred cabbage, onion, green pepper and carrot in food processor (or by hand) and place in large container. Combine remaining ingredients and boil. Cool dressing slightly; pour over vegetables; toss. Refrigerate in covered container at least 4 hours. Will keep several weeks in refrigerator. Yield: 8 to 10 servings. *Good for eggless diets—no mayonnaise.*

CAULIFLOWER SALAD

Salad:
1 head lettuce, torn into small pieces
1 head cauliflower, grated
1 large red onion, sliced and separated into rings
1 (10-ounce) box frozen peas, uncooked
1 pound bacon, cooked and crumbled
1 cup water chestnuts, sliced

Dressing:
2 cups mayonnaise
½ cup shredded Cheddar cheese
2 teaspoons sugar

Layer ingredients in order listed. Thoroughly combine ingredients for dressing. Spread dressing over top layers. DO NOT TOSS. Cover and refrigerate overnight. Toss just before serving. Yield: 6 to 8 servings.

✓ SWEET AND SOUR CARROT SALAD

1½ pounds carrots, pared and thinly sliced
1 medium red onion, thinly sliced
½ cup chopped green pepper
1 (10¾-ounce) can tomato soup
¾ cup sugar
½ cup vegetable oil
½ cup red wine vinegar
½ teaspoon salt
1 teaspoon Worcestershire sauce

Cook carrots for 5 minutes in enough boiling water to cover carrots. Drain and cool. Combine carrots, onion and green peppers in a serving bowl. Combine soup, sugar, oil, vinegar, salt and Worcestershire sauce; pour over the vegetables. Stir gently to combine. Cover; refrigerate at least 24 hours to blend flavors. Yield: 12 servings. *Good with deli sandwiches or with roasted and barbecued meats.*

FAUCON SALAD

1 clove garlic
1 head lettuce, torn in small pieces
4 hard-boiled eggs, sliced
3 tablespoons oil
1 teaspoon dry mustard
1 tablespoon white vinegar
1 teaspoon cayenne
2 teaspoons salt
¼ pound Roquefort cheese

Rub salad bowl with garlic. Put lettuce in bowl and top with eggs. Mix oil, mustard, vinegar, cayenne, salt and Roquefort cheese. Pour over lettuce and eggs. Yield: 4 to 6 servings.

MOLDED CHEESE SALAD

1 envelope unflavored gelatin
¼ cup water
1½ cups cottage cheese
1 (3-ounce) package cream cheese, softened
⅓ cup chopped celery
2 tablespoons chopped chives
¼ teaspoon salt
½ cup milk

Soften gelatin in water. Add cottage cheese to cream cheese; beat until fluffy. Blend in celery, chives and salt. Fold in gelatin. Add milk and pour into 6 individual molds or 1-quart ring mold. Chill until firm. Yield: 6 servings.

CORN SALAD

1 (12-ounce) can whole kernel corn, drained
2 small green onions, chopped
¼ cup chopped celery
¼ cup chopped green pepper
1 tablespoon fresh parsley, minced
2 tablespoons cider vinegar
1 tablespoon oil
¼ teaspoon salt
¼ teaspoon fresh ground pepper
lettuce leaves or tomato cups

Combine all ingredients except lettuce and tomatoes. Chill at least 4 hours or overnight. Serve on lettuce leaves or in tomato cups. Yield: 4 to 6 servings. *Colorful! Delicious!*

CUCUMBER SALAD

2 cucumbers
½ teaspoon dried dill weed
¾ cup water
1 teaspoon sugar
½ teaspoon salt
3 tablespoons white vinegar
lettuce leaves
chopped pimento, optional

Wash but do not peel cucumbers; slice very thin. Sprinkle with dill weed. Combine water, sugar, salt and vinegar in a jar; shake to blend. Pour over cucumbers and refrigerate. Allow cucumbers to marinate for 2 hours. Drain and serve on a bed of lettuce leaves. Garnish with chopped pimento, if desired. Yield: 4 servings.

MOLDED GAZPACHO SALAD

1 (13-ounce) can red consommé madrilene
2 envelopes unflavored gelatin
½ cup cold water
1 small clove garlic, minced
1 tablespoon olive or salad oil
1 tablespoon white wine vinegar
¼ cup onion, finely chopped
¼ cup celery, finely chopped
1 small cucumber, peeled, seeded and finely chopped
lettuce leaves for serving

Heat consommé in saucepan. Soften gelatin in water and dissolve in heated consommé. Remove consommé from heat; add garlic, oil and vinegar. Refrigerate until thick, but not set. Fold in remaining ingredients. Pour into 6-cup mold or 8 individual molds. Refrigerate overnight. Unmold on lettuce leaves. Yield: 6 to 8 servings.

GREEK SALAD

2 heads Boston lettuce, shredded
1 head romaine lettuce, shredded
3 celery ribs diced
6 radishes sliced
1 bunch scallions, sliced
1 cucumber, sliced thin
1 green pepper, sliced in thin strips
12 oil cured olives
½ pound feta cheese, diced
3 tomatoes cut in wedges

Dressing:
½ cup olive oil
juice of 2 lemons
½ teaspoon oregano
1 tablespoon parsley

Place salad ingredients in large salad bowl. Beat dressing ingredients together and pour over salad. Toss and serve. Yield: 12 servings.

GREEN PEA SALAD

1 (17-ounce) can small English peas
2 tablespoons chopped green pepper
2 tablespoons chopped onion
1 teaspoon chopped pimento
2 tablespoons sliced celery
¼ cup diced Cheddar cheese
1 tablespoon pickle relish
1 hard-boiled egg, diced
2 tablespoons mayonnaise

Drain peas. Add remaining ingredients; mix gently. Chill. Serve on lettuce leaves. Yield: 4 to 6 servings.

GERMAN POTATO SALAD

6 white potatoes, cubed
water
4 strips of raw bacon
1 medium onion, chopped
¼ to ½ cup white vinegar

1 tablespoon sugar
½ teaspoon salt
¼ teaspoon pepper
¼ cup parsley flakes

Boil potatoes in water to cover until almost done, about 20 minutes. Drain; reserve 1 cup water. Cut raw bacon into 1-inch strips; fry in skillet until done. Add onion to pan and sauté about 5 minutes. Add potatoes and reserved water; add remaining ingredients. Simmer until almost dry, about 20 minutes. Yield: 6 servings.

NEW POTATO SALAD

8 to 10 small new potatoes
water
1 cup mayonnaise
1 cup sour cream

1 teaspoon celery seed
1 teaspoon parsley flakes
2 green onions, thinly sliced

Wash potatoes, but do not peel. Boil potatoes in lightly salted water 10 to 15 minutes or until tender. Drain thoroughly. Combine remaining ingredients. Gently stir mayonnaise mixture into potatoes. Cover and refrigerate at least 4 hours. Best if prepared the day before. Yield: 4 to 6 servings.

YUGOSLAVIAN POTATO SALAD

1½ pounds firm potatoes, cooked, peeled, and sliced ¼-inch thick
¾ cup olive oil
2 tablespoons white wine vinegar
2 tablespoons lemon juice
2 tablespoons fresh parsley, chopped

2 teaspoons Dijon-style mustard
1 clove garlic, minced
½ teaspoon salt
¼ teaspoon freshly ground black pepper
garnish: chopped scallions, sliced radishes, and tomato wedges

Prepare potatoes and set aside. Mix remaining ingredients, except garnish, and pour over potatoes. Refrigerate 3 hours or overnight. Garnish with scallions, radishes and tomatoes. Yield: 8 servings.

CRUNCHY RICE SALAD

2 cups cooked rice
1 (11-ounce) can mandarin
　oranges, drained
1 cup chopped green onion
1 cup diagonally sliced celery
1 (8-ounce) can sliced water
　chestnuts, drained
1 (3½-ounce) can sliced
　mushrooms, drained
¼ cup rice vinegar
¼ cup vegetable oil
¼ cup soy sauce
lettuce leaves

Combine rice, oranges, onion, celery, water chestnuts and mushrooms; toss slightly. Combine vinegar, oil, and soy sauce; pour over rice and toss. Chill thoroughly. Serve on lettuce leaves. Yield: 10 to 12 servings.

CURRIED RICE SALAD

1½ cups cooked rice
¼ cup minced onion
1 tablespoon vinegar
2 tablespoons salad oil
1 teaspoon curry powder
2 teaspoons salt
1 cup chopped celery
1 cup cooked green peas
½ cup mayonnaise

Combine first 6 ingredients. Chill several hours or overnight. Add remaining ingredients; stir and serve. Yield: 4 to 6 servings.

SAUERKRAUT SALAD

1 (1-pound 11-ounce) can
　sauerkraut
½ cup chopped onion
½ cup chopped celery
½ cup chopped green pepper
1 teaspoon celery seed
1 (4-ounce) jar chopped pimento
1 cup sugar
1 tablespoon white vinegar

Drain sauerkraut and chop fine. Combine sauerkraut with remaining ingredients; mix well and chill. Yield: 6 to 8 servings. *Good for picnics.*

HOT SPINACH SALAD

1 pound fresh spinach
5 strips bacon
2 tablespoons olive oil
½ teaspoon Worcestershire sauce
½ teaspoon salt
½ teaspoon black pepper
⅓ cup tarragon vinegar
½ teaspoon dry mustard
½ teaspoon sugar
juice of ½ lemon
1 cup chopped hard-boiled eggs

Wash and dry spinach leaves. Put leaves in a wooden salad bowl and place in warm oven (warm serving plates, also). Cook bacon until crisp; drain, crumble and set aside. Pour off all but 2 tablespoons bacon fat. Add olive oil and heat. Add Worcestershire sauce, salt, pepper, vinegar, mustard, sugar and lemon juice. Whisk to thoroughly blend. Heat dressing while whisking. Remove from heat; add chopped eggs and mix. Pour hot mixture over warm spinach; toss. Sprinkle crumbled bacon over salad. Serve on warmed plates. Yield: 4 to 6 servings.

TACO SALAD

1 head lettuce, shredded
1 onion, minced
2 cups diced Cheddar cheese
3 tomatoes, chopped
1 pound ground beef, browned and drained
1 (16-ounce) can chili beans, drained
1 medium bag nacho cheese flavored chips, crushed
½ cup taco sauce
1 (8-ounce) bottle spicy French style dressing

In a large salad bowl, layer first 7 ingredients. Combine taco sauce and dressing. Pour over salad; toss and serve immediately. Yield: 6 to 8 servings.

MARINATED ZUCCHINI SALAD

1 large zucchini
1 large yellow crooked-neck
  squash
1 large onion
1 small green pepper
1 large tomato
1 (8-ounce) bottle diet Italian
  dressing
romaine lettuce leaves
Parmesan cheese

Slice zucchini, squash, onion and pepper in thin rings. Cube tomatoes. Place in shallow dish; pour on dressing. Marinate at least 1 hour. Stir occasionally. Serve on lettuce leaves; sprinkle with Parmesan cheese. Yield: 4 servings.

BROKEN GLASS SALAD

1 (3-ounce) package each lime,
  lemon, and strawberry
  flavored gelatin
3¾ cups hot water
1 envelope unflavored gelatin
¼ cup cold water
1 cup unsweetened pineapple
  juice
1 pint whipping cream
½ cup sugar (or 3 teaspoons
  sugar substitute)
1 teaspoon vanilla extract
graham cracker crumbs

Pour flavored gelatin in 3 separate bowls. Add 1¼ cups hot water to each bowl and stir to dissolve gelatin. Chill until set. Cut in small pieces and mix all flavors together. Soften unflavored gelatin in ¼ cup cold water. Heat pineapple juice and add to unflavored gelatin. Cool. Whip cream; add sugar and vanilla. Fold into gelatin mixture. Fold gelatin squares into gelatin mixture. Pour into 13x9-inch pan. Top with graham cracker crumbs. Chill. Yield: 10 to 12 servings. *Children really like this salad.*

FIVE CUP SALAD

1 cup sour cream
1 cup coconut
1 cup mandarin oranges
1 cup chunked pineapple
1 cup miniature marshmallows
chopped nuts, optional
1 cup maraschino cherries,
  optional

Mix all ingredients one day in advance and refrigerate. Yield: 10 to 12 servings.

APPLE SALAD

4 large apples
½ cup raisins
½ cup coconut
½ cup pecans
1 cup celery
½ cup mayonnaise
½ cup sour cream

Peel, core, and chop apples. Add remaining ingredients to apples after chopping coconut, pecans, and celery. Mix well; serve on lettuce leaves. Yield: 6 servings.

FROZEN BANANA SALAD

2 cups crushed pineapple
2 cups cottage cheese
1 (7-ounce) jar marshmallow
  creme
4 mashed bananas
1 cup frozen whipped topping
½ cup chopped pecans, optional
lettuce leaves
cupcake papers

Drain pineapple; reserve 2 to 4 tablespoons juice. Combine cottage cheese with juice in blender until smooth. Mix pineapple, marshmallow creme, bananas, topping and pecans in a large bowl. Add blender mixture. Spoon into cupcake papers in a cupcake pan. Freeze. To serve, remove paper; place on lettuce leaves. Yield: 24 servings.

BLUEBERRY SALAD

1 (16-ounce) can blueberries
1 (8¼-ounce) can crushed
  pineapple
2 (3-ounce) packages blackberry
  flavored gelatin
2 cups boiling water
1 cup sour cream
1 (8-ounce) package cream
  cheese
½ cup sugar
1 teaspoon vanilla extract
finely chopped pecans or grated
  nutmeg

Drain blueberries and pineapple and reserve juice. Add enough cold water to make 1 cup liquid. Dissolve gelatin in boiling water; add reserved juice and cold water mixture. Stir in blueberries and pineapple. Pour into 13x9-inch dish. Refrigerate until congealed. Mix sour cream, cream cheese, sugar and vanilla until smooth. Spread over congealed mixture; sprinkle with pecans or nutmeg. Yield: 12 servings.

FROZEN CHERRY SALAD

1 (16-ounce) container non-dairy
  topping
1 (14-ounce) can sweetened
  condensed milk
1 (16-ounce) can cherry pie
  filling
1 (8¼-ounce) can crushed
  pineapple, undrained

Combine all ingredients. Pour into 9½x13½-inch pan or two 8-inch square pans. Freeze. Yield: 12 servings.

CRANBERRY CREAM SALAD

1 (3-ounce) package
  cherry-flavored gelatin
3 tablespoons sugar
1 cup boiling water
1 (8-ounce) can whole cranberry
  sauce
⅓ cup chopped celery
⅓ cup chopped walnuts
1 cup sour cream
lettuce leaves

Dissolve gelatin and sugar in boiling water. Add cranberry sauce; chill until thickened, but not firm. Add remaining ingredients; mix well. Pour into gelatin mold or 8-inch square pan. To serve, unmold on lettuce leaves. Yield: 6 to 8 servings.

SUMMER FRUIT SALAD

1 cantaloupe
2 peaches
2 bananas
1 (20-ounce) can pineapple chunks, undrained
1 unpeeled red apple, cubed
1 cup fresh halved strawberries
1 (6-ounce) can frozen orange juice concentrate, thawed and undiluted

Peel cantaloupe and cut into ¾-inch cubes; peel peaches and cut into wedges. Cut bananas into ¼-inch slices. Layer fruits in same order in large bowl; spoon concentrate over fruit. Cover and chill 6 to 8 hours. Yield: 8 to 10 servings.

ORANGE SALAD CUPS

6 medium oranges
1 banana, halved and sliced
1 apple, peeled and shredded
1 cup miniature marshmallows
⅓ cup seedless green grapes, halved
⅓ cup seedless red grapes, halved
1 cup commercial sour cream, divided
2 tablespoons honey
¼ teaspoon salt
additional red grape halves
Boston lettuce leaves

Cut oranges in half crosswise. Clip membranes and carefully remove pulp, being careful not to puncture the bottom of the orange. Using kitchen shears, cut the edges of the oranges into scallops. Set orange cups aside. Dice orange pulp; drain. Combine orange pulp, banana, apple, marshmallows, and grapes in a medium bowl. In a separate bowl, combine ¼ cup sour cream and honey; mix well. Stir in remaining sour cream and salt. Add ¾ cup sour cream mixture to the fruit mixture and toss gently. Fill each orange cup with the fruit mixture then garnish tops with remaining sour cream mixture and extra red grape halves. Place orange cups on serving platter lined with Boston lettuce leaves. Yield: 12 servings.

PINEAPPLE CHEDDAR SALAD

1 (3-ounce) package
  lemon-flavored gelatin
1 cup boiling water
1 (8½-ounce) can crushed
  pineapple, undrained

¾ cup sugar
1 cup whipping cream, whipped
1 cup shredded Cheddar cheese
½ cup chopped pecans

Dissolve gelatin in 1 cup boiling water. Stir in pineapple and sugar; cool. Fold in whipped cream, Cheddar cheese and pecans. Spoon into a 9-inch square pan. Chill until firm. Cut into squares for serving and place on lettuce leaves, if desired. Yield: 6 servings.

MANDARIN SALAD MOLDS

1 envelope unflavored gelatin
2 cups unsweetened orange
  juice, divided
1 (11-ounce) can mandarin
  oranges in light syrup,
  drained

vegetable cooking spray
lettuce leaves
additional mandarin orange
  sections, optional
1 tablespoon plus 1 teaspoon
  orange-flavored liqueur

Sprinkle gelatin over ½ cup orange juice; let stand 1 minute. Bring remaining 1½ cups orange juice to a boil; add to gelatin mixture and stir until gelatin dissolves. Chill until consistency of unbeaten egg whites. Stir drained mandarin oranges into gelatin mixture; pour into four 6-ounce custard cups coated with cooking spray. Chill until firm. Unmold on lettuce leaves and garnish with additional mandarin oranges. Pour 1 teaspoon orange liqueur over each mold before serving. Yield: 4 servings.

CREAMY ORANGE-LIME MOLD

3 cups unsweetened orange
  juice, divided
1 (6-ounce) package
  lime-flavored gelatin

1 (8-ounce) package cream
  cheese, softened
½ cup mayonnaise
1 tablespoon lemon juice

Bring 1 cup of orange juice to a boil. Remove from heat; add gelatin and stir until dissolved. Stir in remaining juice. Beat softened cream cheese with mayonnaise and lemon juice until smooth. Gradually add gelatin mixture to cream cheese; continue beating until smooth. Pour into 6-cup mold or 10 individual molds. Chill until firm. Yield: 8 to 10 servings.

PEAR GELATIN SALAD

1 (16-ounce) can pears
1 (3-ounce) package
   lime-flavored gelatin
1 (3-ounce) package cream
   cheese, softened

⅛ teaspoon salt
½ pint cream, whipped

Drain pears; reserve juice. Chop pears. Add enough water to reserved juice to make 1 cup. Heat juice; add gelatin and stir. Blend cream cheese into hot pear juice and mix well. Add salt. Refrigerate until almost set. Add chopped pears and whipped cream. Pour into 5-cup mold. Refrigerate until set. Yield: 4 to 6 servings.

RASPBERRY ORANGE MOLD

1 navel orange
1 (16-ounce) can whole berry
   cranberry sauce
2 (3½-ounce) packages
   raspberry-flavored gelatin
1 (3½-ounce) package
   strawberry-banana-flavored
   gelatin

1 cup boiling water
1 (6-ounce) can crushed
   pineapple, drained
½ cup sugar
¾ cup chopped nuts

Place whole orange in food processor or blender and blend. Add cranberry sauce; blend. Add gelatins to boiling water; stir until dissolved. Combine remaining ingredients; place in lightly greased mold. Chill until firm. Yield: 6 servings.

SCREWDRIVER SALAD

2 (11-ounce) cans mandarin oranges
¾ cup vodka, divided
2 (3-ounce) packages orange-flavored gelatin
2 cups boiling water
1 (6-ounce) can orange juice concentrate
1 (6-ounce) can crushed pineapple
1 (3-ounce) package instant lemon pudding
1 cup milk
1 (9-ounce) container whipped dairy topping

Drain 1 can mandarin oranges and cover with ½ cup vodka. Set aside. Dissolve gelatin in boiling water; add orange juice and stir. Drain second can of mandarin oranges; add to gelatin. Add ¼ cup vodka and pineapple with juice to gelatin. Mix; pour into 13x9-inch dish. Chill until firm. Combine pudding with milk and spread over chilled gelatin. Refrigerate until firm. Spread whipped dairy topping over pudding layer; drain marinated oranges and place on topping. Yield: 12 to 16 servings.

STRAWBERRY NUT SALAD

2 (3-ounce) packages strawberry-flavored gelatin
1 cup boiling water
2 (10-ounce) packages frozen sliced strawberries, thawed and undrained
1 (20-ounce) can crushed pineapple, drained
3 medium bananas, mashed
1 cup coarsely chopped nuts
1 pint sour cream
lettuce leaves

In a large bowl, combine gelatin with boiling water; stir until dissolved. Fold in strawberries, pineapple, bananas and nuts. Pour half of the strawberry mixture into a 12x8-inch dish. Refrigerate until firm. Top with sour cream and gently spoon on rest of strawberry mixture. Refrigerate. Cut into squares and serve on lettuce leaves. Yield: 12 servings.

BLUE CHEESE DRESSING

½ cup evaporated milk
2 tablespoons lemon juice
1 clove garlic, minced

¼ pound blue cheese, crumbled
1 cup mayonnaise

Blend and refrigerate. Yield: 1½ cups.

CELERY SEED DRESSING

½ cup sugar
1 teaspoon dry mustard
1 teaspoon salt
2 teaspoons celery seed

2 teaspoons grated onion
⅓ cup cider vinegar
2 teaspoons horseradish
1 cup salad oil

Combine all ingredients in blender. Blend well. Chill. Yield: 1½ cups.

THOUSAND ISLAND DRESSING

1 cup mayonnaise
¼ to ½ cup chili sauce

1 hard-boiled egg, grated
pickle relish to taste

Combine all ingredients. Chill. Yield: 1½ cups.

FRESH TOMATO DRESSING

¼ cup vegetable oil
¾ cup diced fresh tomatoes
2 tablespoons tarragon vinegar
2 tablespoons sliced green onion

¾ teaspoon dried basil
¼ teaspoon sugar
¼ teaspoon paprika
fresh ground pepper to taste

Place all ingredients in blender. Blend at high speed until smooth, about 10 seconds. Scrape down sides of container, if necessary, and blend 5 additional seconds. Serve over green salad. Refrigerate unused portion. Yield: ¾ cup.

EXCELLENT VINAIGRETTE

1 tablespoon Dijon-style mustard
4 tablespoons red wine vinegar
1 teaspoon granulated sugar
½ teaspoon ground pepper
1 teaspoon minced parsley
½ teaspoon snipped chives
½ cup olive oil

Spoon mustard into bowl; whisk in vinegar, sugar, pepper and herbs. Slowly dribble oil into mustard mixture, whisking continuously. Adjust seasoning to taste. Vinaigrette is best if made just before serving. To store vinaigrette, cover until ready to serve; whisk again before serving. Serve over salads or freshly steamed vegetables. Yield: ½ cup.

SALAD NOTES

Buy fluffy, firm bundles of parsley. Rinse and store in glass or vase of water in refrigerator.

Chewing parsley will instantly freshen the breath of even the most avid garlic eater.

To store garlic, separate and peel all cloves. Place cloves in a wide-mouthed glass jar (baby food jars are excellent) and cover with a light safflower or sesame oil. The oil will seal air from the cloves for up to 6 weeks. The garlic flavored oil may be used in other dishes. Just keep refilling the jar with oil.

BREADS

ENGLISH MUFFIN LOAVES

6 cups all-purpose flour, divided
2 packages dry yeast
1 tablespoon sugar
1½ teaspoons salt
¼ teaspoon soda
2 cups milk
½ cup water
cornmeal

Combine 3 cups flour, yeast, sugar, salt and soda in a large mixing bowl; set aside. Combine milk and water in a small saucepan; heat until very warm (120°). Gradually add milk mixture to dry ingredients mixing on low speed of electric mixer 2 to 3 minutes. Stir in enough remaining flour to make a soft dough. Divide dough in half; shape each half into a loaf. Grease two 8½x4x3-inch loaf pans; sprinkle bottom and sides with cornmeal. Cover and let rise in a warm place, free from drafts, until doubled in bulk (about 45 minutes). Bake at 400° for 25 minutes. Yield: 2 loaves.

BEAUTIFUL BREAD

2 cups boiling water
1 cup dry rolled oats
2 (¼-ounce) packages dry yeast
⅓ cup lukewarm water
1 tablespoon salt
½ cup honey
2 tablespoons melted butter
4 to 5 cups all-purpose flour
water and egg yolk

Pour 2 cups boiling water over 1 cup dry rolled oats. Allow mixture to stand for ½ hour or until oats are thoroughly soft. Dissolve yeast in ⅓ cup lukewarm water. Add 1 tablespoon salt, ½ cup honey and two tablespoons melted butter to oats; stir in yeast. Gradually add enough flour to make soft dough. Knead 7 to 10 minutes. Add enough additional flour to make dough smooth and elastic. Place dough in a large bowl which has been oiled. Turn dough in bowl to completely oil surface of dough. Cover bowl with towel and let rise until dough is double in size. Punch down; let rest 5 minutes. Divide dough into two loaves. Place in two 8x4-inch loaf pans which have been greased and floured. Let dough rise again until doubled. Heat oven to 325°. Mix a few drops of water with one egg yolk. Brush tops of loaves. Bake for 40 minutes or until loaves sound hollow when tapped on bottom. Remove from pans and cool on racks. Yield: 2 loaves.

WHITE BATTER BREAD

1 cup milk
3 tablespoons sugar
1 tablespoon salt
2 tablespoons margarine

1 cup warm water
2 (¼-ounce) packages active dry yeast
4¼ cups unsifted flour

Scald milk; stir in sugar, salt and margarine. Cool to lukewarm. Measure warm water into large bowl. Sprinkle with yeast; stir to dissolve. Add lukewarm milk mixture. Stir in flour (batter will be stiff). Beat until well blended (about 2 minutes). Cover and let rise in warm place, free from draft until doubled in bulk (about 40 minutes). Stir batter down. Beat vigorously for 30 seconds. Turn into 1 greased 9x5x3-inch loaf pan. Bake at 375° for 50 minutes. Remove from pan and cool on cooling rack. Yield: 1 loaf.

DILL COTTAGE CHEESE BREAD

1 (¼-ounce) package active dry yeast
¼ cup warm water
1 cup cream-style cottage cheese
¼ cup shortening
2 tablespoons sugar
1 tablespoon minced onion

2 teaspoons dill seed
1 teaspoon salt
¼ teaspoon soda
1 egg, well beaten
2¼ to 2½ cups all-purpose flour
melted butter or margarine

Soften yeast in warm water. In saucepan, heat cottage cheese to lukewarm. Stir in shortening, sugar, onion, 2 teaspoons dill seed, salt, soda and softened yeast. Beat in egg. Add flour, a little at a time, stirring to make a soft dough. Knead on lightly floured surface until smooth and elastic, about 5 minutes. Place in greased bowl, turning once to grease surface. Cover and let rise in warm place 1 hour. Punch down; cover and let rest 10 minutes. Shape and place in greased 9x5x3-inch pan. Cover and let rise until doubled in bulk (35 to 45 minutes). Bake at 350° for 40 minutes. Remove from pan and brush with melted butter or margarine. Yield: 1 loaf.

CORN SPOON BREAD

1 (17-ounce) can cream style corn
1 (17-ounce) can whole kernel corn, drained
½ cup margarine, melted
1 cup sour cream
1 egg, beaten
1 (7-ounce) box cornbread mix

Combine first 3 ingredients. Add sour cream and egg and blend well. Add cornbread mix and stir. Pour into 9x13-inch greased pan and bake at 350° for 45 minutes to 1 hour or until inserted knife comes out clean. (Dough may be prepared ahead of time and refrigerated until ready to bake.) Yield: 8 to 10 servings.

ZUCCHINI BREAD

3 cups all-purpose flour
1 teaspoon baking powder
1 teaspoon soda
1 teaspoon ground cinnamon
1 teaspoon ground nutmeg
1½ cups pecans, chopped
¾ cup safflower or vegetable oil
3 eggs
2 cups sugar or 1⅓ cups honey
2 teaspoons vanilla extract
3 cups unpeeled shredded zucchini

Combine first 6 ingredients in a mixing bowl. Make a well in the center of mixture. Combine oil, eggs, sugar, vanilla and shredded zucchini. Add liquid mixture to dry ingredients; stir until moistened. Spoon mixture into 2 greased and floured 9x5x3-inch loaf pans or 4 mini-loaf pans. Bake at 350° for 1 hour. Cool loaves 10 minutes in pan. Remove from pans and cool on wire racks. Freezes well. Yield: 2 large loaves or 4 small loaves.

CHEESE AND ONION BREAD

2 cups mayonnaise
1½ cups sharp Cheddar cheese, shredded
1 bunch scallions, finely chopped
1 cup Parmesan cheese, divided
1 (12-inch) loaf French bread
1 cup cooked and crumbled bacon

Cut bread in half horizontally. Combine mayonnaise, Cheddar cheese, onions and ½ cup Parmesan. Spread on bread halves. Sprinkle on bacon and remaining Parmesan. Bake at 350° for 5 minutes. Broil for 3 to 5 minutes. Yield: 8 servings.

SOFT BREAD STICKS

6 tablespoons butter
2 cups biscuit mix

1 tablespoon sugar
½ cup milk

In oven, melt butter in 13x9-inch pan. Combine biscuit mix, sugar and milk. Stir with fork until a soft dough is formed. Beat vigorously 20 strokes. On a lightly floured surface, knead dough 12 times. Roll out to an 8x12-inch rectangle. Cut dough in half lengthwise. Cut each half into 16 strips. Dip each strip in melted butter. Arrange lengthwise in baking dish. Bake 10 to 12 minutes at 400°. Sprinkle with sugar or cinnamon, if desired. Serve warm. Yield: 32 servings.

CHEESE BISCUITS

1 pound Cheddar cheese, shredded
1 pound butter, softened

4 cups self-rising flour
pecan halves

Allow shredded cheese and butter to come to room temperature. Blend softened shredded cheese and butter. Gradually stir in flour until well mixed. Roll dough very thin on floured surface. Cut with small biscuit cutter. Top each biscuit with a pecan half and bake at 400° for 12 minutes. Remove from pan and cool on paper towels. Biscuits will be very "short." Yield: 4 dozen.

BEER BISCUITS

2 cups biscuit mix
2 teaspoons sugar

¾ cup hot beer

Mix ingredients thoroughly. Pour batter into miniature muffin tins. Fill each cup ½ full. Bake at 450° for 8 to 10 minutes. Yield: 24 biscuits.

MILE-HIGH BISCUITS

3 cups all-purpose flour
2 tablespoons sugar
1 tablespoon plus 1½ teaspoons baking powder
¾ teaspoon cream of tartar
¾ teaspoon salt
¾ cup shortening
1 egg, beaten
¾ cup milk

Combine flour, sugar, baking powder, cream of tartar and salt; mix well. Cut in shortening with a pastry blender until mixture resembles coarse meal. Combine egg and milk; add to flour mixture, stirring until dry ingredients are moistened. Turn dough out onto lightly floured surface; knead 8 to 10 times. Roll dough to 1-inch thickness; cut with a 2½-inch biscuit cutter. Place biscuits on ungreased baking sheet. Bake at 350° for 15 minutes or until golden brown. Yield: 15 biscuits.

ARVED'S ORANGE BISCUITS

Dough:
2 cups self-rising flour
½ cup shortening
⅔ cup milk
2 tablespoons butter, melted
⅓ cup nuts
⅓ cup plus 1 tablespoon sugar
cinnamon

Sauce:
2½ cups orange juice
3 tablespoons butter
⅓ cup sugar

DOUGH: Cut shortening into flour until mixture resembles coarse meal. Quickly stir in milk; knead dough lightly. Roll dough on floured surface into a 20x13-inch rectangle. Brush dough with melted butter and sprinkle with nuts, sugar and cinnamon. Roll up dough jellyroll style and cut into 1½-inch slices. Place in 9x13-inch pan.

SAUCE: In saucepan, mix orange juice, butter and sugar. Bring to a boil and simmer about 10 minutes. Pour sauce over biscuits and bake at 450° for 15 to 20 minutes. To serve, turn biscuits onto serving dish upside down. Yield: 10 to 12 servings.

BACON MUFFINS

12 slices bacon
1 cup self-rising flour
1 cup self-rising cornmeal
¼ cup sugar
2 eggs, well beaten
1 cup milk

Cook bacon until crisp; drain and crumble. Reserve ¼ cup drippings. Combine flour, cornmeal and sugar. Add eggs, milk and reserved bacon drippings. Stir just until moistened. Stir in crumbled bacon. Spoon batter into greased muffin tins and bake at 425° for 20 to 25 minutes. Yield: 12 servings.

BROCCOLI MUFFINS

1 (7-ounce) box sweet cornbread mix
1 (10-ounce) package frozen chopped broccoli, thawed
½ cup margarine, melted
4 eggs
1 large onion, chopped
1 teaspoon salt
1½ cups cottage cheese

Combine all ingredients and mix well. Pour into 12 greased muffin cups. Bake at 425° for 25 minutes. Yield: 12 servings. *Wonderful way to serve broccoli!*

BUTTERMILK BLUEBERRY MUFFINS

2 cups all-purpose flour
½ cup sugar
2¼ teaspoons baking powder
1 teaspoon salt
¼ teaspoon soda
1 egg, slightly beaten
1 cup buttermilk
¼ cup melted butter or margarine
1 cup blueberries

Combine dry ingredients in mixing bowl and set aside. Combine egg, buttermilk and butter; mix well. Make a well in center of dry ingredients and pour in liquid ingredients. Stir just until moistened. Fold in blueberries. Fill greased muffin pans ⅔ full. Bake at 425° for 20 to 25 minutes. Remove from pan immediately. Yield: 18 servings.

CARROT BRAN MUFFINS

1½ cups whole bran cereal
1 cup buttermilk
1 cup all-purpose flour
¼ cup packed brown sugar
2 teaspoons baking powder
½ teaspoon soda
½ teaspoon salt
1 beaten egg
2 medium carrots, finely shredded
3 tablespoons vegetable oil

Combine bran and buttermilk and let stand for 3 minutes or until liquid is absorbed. Stir together flour, sugar, baking powder, soda and salt. Combine cereal-milk mixture, egg, carrot and oil. Add all at once to dry ingredients. Stir just until moistened. Fill greased muffin pans ⅔ full. Bake at 400° for 20 to 25 minutes. Yield: 12 servings.

ICEBOX PARKERHOUSE ROLLS

½ cup shortening
1 package yeast
1½ cups lukewarm water
⅓ cup sugar
1½ teaspoons salt
4 cups all-purpose flour
1 egg

Melt shortening; cool. Dissolve yeast in lukewarm water. Combine shortening, yeast, sugar, salt and 2 cups flour; beat well. Add egg and remaining 2 cups flour. Mix well. Refrigerate 24 hours. To bake, place dough on floured surface. Knead to working consistency. Pinch and roll dough into 1-inch balls. Place 3 balls in each greased muffin cup. Let dough rise in pans 1 to 2 hours or until doubled in size. Bake at 400° until tops are brown. Yield: 2 to 3 dozen. *Note: Dough will not rise as well on humid days, but taste is not affected.*

ALMOST YEAST ROLLS

½ cup margarine
2 cups self-rising flour
2 tablespoons sugar
1 scant cup milk

Melt margarine in 9x13-inch baking dish. Mix flour and sugar with milk to make a soft dough. Roll on floured surface and cut. Place in melted butter. Bake at 450° for 15 minutes or until brown. Yield: 8 to 10 servings.

CARAMEL ORANGE COFFEE RING

Coffee Ring:
1 (13¾-ounce) package hot roll mix
⅔ cup warm milk (105° to 115°)
2 eggs, slightly beaten
2 tablespoons plus 2 teaspoons grated orange rind, divided
2 tablespoons plus 2 teaspoons butter or margarine, softened
⅓ cup firmly packed light brown sugar
1 teaspoon ground cinnamon

Glaze:
½ cup firmly packed light brown sugar
¼ cup butter or margarine, softened
2 tablespoons light corn syrup
4 tablespoons chopped nuts
1 tablespoon grated orange rind

COFFEE RING: Remove yeast package from roll mix. In a large mixing bowl, sprinkle yeast over warm milk. Stir until dissolved. Stir in eggs and 2 teaspoons orange rind. Add roll mix and blend. Shape dough into a ball. Place in mixing bowl and cover. Let rise in warm place until doubled in bulk (about 1 hour). Turn dough out onto floured surface; sprinkle dough with flour. Roll dough into a 16x12-inch rectangle and spread with melted margarine or butter. Combine sugar, 2 tablespoons orange rind and cinnamon; sprinkle over buttered surface. Beginning at long edge, roll up dough, jellyroll style. Press seam to seal. Grease a 10-inch bundt or tube pan. Combine glaze ingredients and spread evenly in bottom of pan. Cut dough into sixteen 1-inch slices. Stand 10 slices along edge of pan, cut side against side of pan. Stand remaining 6 slices against center tube of pan. Cover and let rise until doubled in bulk (about 1 hour). Bake at 375° for 30 to 35 minutes. Turn out onto serving platter. Yield: 12 servings.

STREUSEL COFFEE CAKE

Streusel:
½ cup chopped nuts
⅓ cup packed brown sugar
¼ cup all-purpose flour
½ teaspoon ground cinnamon
3 tablespoons margarine or butter

Cake:
2 cups all-purpose flour
1 cup sugar
3 teaspoons baking powder
1 teaspoon salt
⅓ cup margarine or butter, softened
1 cup milk
1 egg

Mix streusel ingredients; set aside. Heat oven to 350°. Combine cake ingredients and beat at low speed for 30 seconds. Beat at medium speed for 2 minutes, scraping sides of bowl. Pour half of batter in greased 13x9x2-inch pan. Sprinkle with half of streusel mix. Top with remaining batter; sprinkle with remaining streusel. Bake until toothpick inserted in center comes out clean (35 to 40 minutes). Yield: 10 to 12 servings.

OVERNIGHT COFFEE CAKE

¾ cup margarine or butter, softened
1 cup sugar
2 eggs
1 cup sour cream
2 cups all-purpose flour
1 teaspoon baking powder
1 teaspoon soda
½ teaspoon salt
1 teaspoon ground nutmeg
¾ cup brown sugar
1 teaspoon ground cinnamon
½ cup pecans, chopped

Combine butter or margarine and sugar; cream until light. Add eggs and sour cream, mixing well. Combine next five ingredients; add to creamed mixture and mix well. Pour batter into greased and floured 13x9x2-inch baking pan. Combine brown sugar, pecans and cinnamon and mix well. Sprinkle evenly over batter. Cover and chill overnight. Uncover and bake at 350° for 35 to 45 minutes. Yield: 12 servings.

CHRISTMAS STOLLEN

1 (¼-ounce) package active dry yeast
¼ cup warm water
⅓ cup butter or margarine
¾ cup milk
⅓ cup sugar
1 teaspoon salt
grated rind of 1 lemon
2 eggs
4 cups all-purpose flour
½ cup chopped blanched almonds
½ cup chopped mixed candied fruits
½ cup seedless raisins
2 tablespoons melted butter
½ teaspoon cinnamon
2 tablespoons sugar

In mixing bowl, dissolve yeast in ¼ cup warm water (105° to 115°). Melt ⅓ cup butter or margarine in small saucepan and add milk; heat to warm (105° to 115°). To yeast mixture add ⅓ cup sugar, salt, lemon rind, eggs and 2 cups flour. Beat with electric mixer until smooth. Cover and let rise in warm place 40 minutes. Stir in almonds, candied fruits and raisins. Beat in remaining flour ½ cup at a time. Turn out on lightly floured surface and knead until smooth and elastic. Divide in half and shape each half in 12x8-inch oval. Brush with melted butter and fold lengthwise. Press edges together. Put on large greased baking sheet and let rise 40 minutes or until doubled in bulk. Bake in preheated 350° oven for 25 to 30 minutes. Brush with melted butter and sprinkle with mixture of 2 tablespoons sugar and cinnamon. Cool on rack. Store tightly wrapped in refrigerator or freezer. Yield: 2 loaves.

ORANGE FRENCH TOAST

¼ cup margarine
⅓ cup sugar
2 teaspoons grated fresh orange rind
¼ teaspoon cinnamon
4 eggs, beaten
⅔ cup fresh orange juice
8 slices bread

Put margarine in 15x10-inch pan and melt in 400° oven. Mix sugar, rind and cinnamon in bowl. In a separate bowl, combine egg and juice. Dip each side of bread in egg mixture. Then sprinkle with sugar mixture and place sugared side down on baking sheet. Sprinkle top side of bread with remaining sugar. Bake 20 to 25 minutes at 400°. Yield: 8 servings.

STUFFED FRENCH TOAST

1 (8-ounce) package cream cheese
1 teaspoon vanilla
½ cup chopped walnuts
1 (16-ounce) loaf French bread
4 large eggs
1 cup whipping cream
½ teaspoon vanilla
½ teaspoon ground nutmeg
1 (12-ounce) jar apricot preserves
½ cup orange juice

Blend cream cheese and 1 teaspoon vanilla until fluffy; add nuts. Blend and set aside. Cut bread into 10 to 12 slices, 1½-inches thick. Cut a pocket in the top of each slice. Fill pocket with 1½ tablespoons of cheese mixture. Beat together eggs, cream, remaining vanilla and nutmeg. Dip bread into egg mixture being careful not to squeeze out filling. Brown slices on lightly greased griddle; remove to serving platter and keep warm. Combine preserves and juice and heat through. Drizzle sauce over toast and serve. Yield: 10 to 12 servings.

LEMON LOAF

¼ cup butter
⅓ cup sugar
2 cups unbleached flour
¼ teaspoon salt
1 teaspoon baking powder
1 teaspoon soda
2 eggs
2 teaspoons grated lemon peel (fresh is best)
1 teaspoon vanilla extract
1 cup plain yogurt
½ cup chopped pecans, optional

Grease one 8x4x2-inch loaf pan or 2 small 5x3x2-inch pans. Preheat oven to 350°. Cream butter and sugar. Sift together flour, salt, baking powder and soda; set aside. Add eggs to creamed mixture one at a time, mixing well after each addition. Add peel and vanilla. Add dry ingredients alternately with yogurt. Mix until moistened. Add nuts if desired. Bake for 50 minutes. Cool in pans 10 minutes. Turn out onto cooling racks and cool completely before cutting. Yield: 1 large loaf or 2 small loaves.

POPPY SEED BREAD

¼ cup poppy seeds
¼ cup water
1 (18-ounce) box yellow cake mix
1 (3½-ounce) package vanilla instant pudding
1 cup hot water
½ cup vegetable oil
4 eggs
½ teaspoon almond extract
sugar
cinnamon

Soak poppy seeds in ¼ cup water for 1 hour. Combine cake mix, pudding mix, water and oil. Mix well. Add eggs, one at a time, and almond flavoring and beat 4 minutes. Stir in poppy seeds and water. Sprinkle sugar and cinnamon in the bottom of 2 greased 9x5x3-inch loaf pans. Pour ¼ of the batter in each pan. Sprinkle with cinnamon and sugar. Pour in remaining batter and sprinkle again. Bake at 350° for 45 minutes. Yield: 2 loaves.

BOSTON BROWN BREAD

3 cups whole wheat flour
2 teaspoons soda
1 tablespoon salt
2¼ cups brown sugar
2 eggs, separated
2 cups buttermilk or sour milk
½ cup raisins

Combine dry ingredients and set aside. Mix egg yolks and buttermilk; stir into dry ingredients. Stir in raisins. Beat egg whites and fold into batter. Pour into 5 well-greased 1-pound vegetable cans. Bake at 350° for 45 minutes. Cool 10 minutes in cans; remove from cans and cool on wire racks. Yield: 5 loaves. *Small loaf pans may be used in place of vegetable cans.*

HOBO BREAD

2 cups raisins
2 cups boiling water
4 teaspoons soda
2 cups sugar
4 cups all-purpose flour
½ teaspoon salt
¼ cup oil

Combine raisins, water and soda. Stir; cover and let stand 3 hours. Combine all ingredients. Pour into two 9x5-inch loaf pans. Bake at 350° for 1 hour. Yield: 2 loaves.

STRAWBERRY BREAD

3 cups all-purpose flour
1 teaspoon salt
1 teaspoon soda
3 teaspoons cinnamon
2 teaspoons allspice
2 teaspoons nutmeg

2 (10-ounce) packages frozen strawberries, thawed
2 cups sugar
3 eggs, beaten
1¼ cups cooking oil
1¼ cups chopped pecans

Sift dry ingredients together in a large bowl. Make a well in the center. Blend strawberries in blender to remove large chunks. Add strawberries to remaining ingredients and pour into well. Stir to moisten all ingredients. Pour into 2 greased 9x5-inch loaf pans. Bake at 350° for 1 hour. Cool at least 10 minutes before removing from pans. Yield: 2 large loaves or 8 small loaves. *Freezes well and is great for gifts at Christmas.*

PRUNE BREAD

1 tablespoon vinegar
1 cup milk
2 eggs, beaten
1 teaspoon vanilla
1 cup cooking oil
2 cups all-purpose flour
1½ cups sugar
1 teaspoon allspice

1 teaspoon soda
1 teaspoon cinnamon
1 teaspoon nutmeg
½ teaspoon salt
1 cup chopped nuts
1 cup pitted cooked prunes, chopped

Combine vinegar and milk; add eggs, vanilla and oil and set aside. Mix dry ingredients, except nuts and prunes. Combine liquid and dry ingredients and beat 3 to 4 minutes with electric mixer. Stir in nuts and prunes. Pour into greased 9x5-inch loaf pan. Bake at 350° for 1 hour or until top springs back when pressed. Yield: 1 loaf.

PUMPKIN LOAF

Loaf:
3¾ cups all-purpose flour
2 teaspoons soda
2 teaspoons cinnamon
1 teaspoon salt
1 teaspoon nutmeg
½ teaspoon ground ginger
½ teaspoon ground cloves

1 cup margarine or butter, softened
2 cups sugar
4 eggs
1½ cups canned pumpkin
1 cup raisins
1 tablespoon all-purpose flour

Spice Glaze:
1 cup powdered sugar
¼ teaspoon nutmeg
¼ teaspoon cinnamon

dash of cloves
3 to 4 tablespoons hot water

LOAF: Combine 3¾ cups flour, soda, cinnamon, salt, nutmeg, ginger and cloves. Set aside. Cream margarine or butter and sugar. Add eggs and beat well. At low speed, add dry ingredients alternately with pumpkin to sugar mixture, beginning and ending with dry ingredients. Mix raisins with 1 tablespoon flour. Stir into pumpkin batter. Turn into 2 greased 9x5-inch loaf pans. Bake at 350° for 1 hour. Cool and drizzle loaf with Spice Glaze.

GLAZE: Mix dry ingredients together. Blend in hot water. Drizzle over loaf. Yield: 2 loaves.

DATE-NUT LOAF

8 ounces chopped dates
2 tablespoons butter
½ cup boiling water
½ cup orange juice
1 tablespoon orange peel
1 egg, beaten

2 cups sifted all-purpose flour
⅓ cup sugar
1 teaspoon baking powder
1 teaspoon soda
½ teaspoon salt
½ cup chopped walnuts

Heat oven to 325°. In a large mixing bowl, combine chopped dates and butter. Add boiling water and mix well. Cool to room temperature. Add orange juice and peel to dates; add eggs. Sift dry ingredients together. Add to date mixture and mix well. Stir in walnuts. Grease 4 mini-loaf pans or one 8x5x3-inch pan. Pour batter into pans. Bake small loaves 45 minutes and large loaf 1 hour. Yield: 1 large loaf or 4 small loaves. *Delicious with cream cheese.*

STRAWBERRY BUTTER

1 (10-ounce) package frozen strawberries, thawed

1 cup unsalted butter, softened
½ cup powdered sugar

Combine all ingredients in a mixing bowl or food processor. Blend until smooth. Store in refrigerator. Yield: 1¾ cups. *Gift idea: spoon butter mixture into baby food jars and give with homemade bread.*

SAUSAGE CORNBREAD STUFFING

1 cup minced onion
½ cup butter
1 green pepper, finely chopped
½ cup chopped celery
1 pound sausage
6 cups cornbread, crumbled

¼ cup chicken stock
1 teaspoon salt
1 teaspoon pepper
1 teaspoon marjoram
¼ cup chopped parsley

In a large skillet, sauté onion in butter until onion is tender. Add green pepper and celery. Cook until soft, 2 to 3 minutes. Remove from pan with slotted spoon and transfer to a bowl. In same skillet, cook sausage until browned. Drain sausage. Combine cornbread with stock. Add onion mixture, sausage and spices. Mix well. Pour into greased 13x9-inch baking dish and bake at 325° for 45 minutes. Yield: 12 servings.

HUSH PUPPIES

1 cup self-rising cornmeal
½ cup self-rising flour
1 teaspoon sugar
1 teaspoon soda

1 onion, chopped fine
½ cup buttermilk
cooking oil

Mix dry ingredients. Add onion and buttermilk. Mix well. (Batter should be a little thicker than cake batter.) Carefully drop by teaspoons into hot deep fat. Fry until golden brown. Yield: 10 servings.

CHEESE AND EGGS

CHEESE AND SAUSAGE CRÊPES

Crepes:
1 cup all-purpose flour, sifted
1 egg
1 cup milk
1 egg yolk
1 tablespoon oil
¼ teaspoon salt

Sausage Filling:
1 pound bulk pork sausage
¼ cup chopped onion
½ cup shredded Cheddar cheese
1 (3-ounce) package cream cheese, softened
½ teaspoon ground marjoram

Topping:
¼ cup butter, softened
½ cup sour cream

CREPES: Using a wire whisk, combine flour, egg and ½ cup milk in mixing bowl. Whisk in egg yolk, oil, salt and remaining milk. Refrigerate 30 minutes or up to 24 hours. Spray crepe pan or 8-inch skillet with vegetable oil spray and heat over medium heat. Pour ¼ cup of batter into skillet. Immediately tilt pan until batter covers bottom. Cook until crepe reaches desired color. Flip over and slightly brown other side. Turn crepe out onto paper towel. Do not stack crepes.

FILLING: Cook (and crumble) sausage and onion. Drain well. Combine remaining ingredients with sausage and onion and mix well.

TO ASSEMBLE: Place 2 tablespoons sausage filling in center of each crepe. Roll crepe over filling. Place, seam side down, in baking dish. Bake at 375° for 25 minutes. Combine topping ingredients and heat until warm. Serve crepes topped with warm topping. Yield: 10 to 12 servings.

EGG AND CHEESE STRATA

¾ loaf French bread (long loaf)
2 pounds sharp cheese, shredded
1 dozen eggs
6 cups milk
dash liquid hot sauce
¼ teaspoon celery salt
¼ teaspoon white pepper
¼ teaspoon dry mustard

Grease one 15x11-inch pan. Break bread into bite-size pieces and put in bottom of pan. Cover bread with shredded cheese. Beat eggs and milk together. Add seasonings to egg and milk mixture. Pour over bread and cheese and let stand in refrigerator overnight. Bake at 375° for 30 to 45 minutes or until golden brown and inserted knife comes out clean. Yield: 20 servings. *Expect eggs to fall! Good reheated next day. May be frozen.*

GREEK EGG AND SPINACH PIE

3 pounds fresh spinach or 3 (10-ounce) boxes frozen spinach
3 tablespoons butter
5 green onions, chopped
½ pound feta cheese, crumbled
6 eggs, lightly beaten
salt and white pepper to taste
12 sheets phyllo pastry
olive oil
Parmesan cheese

Clean spinach and discard blemished leaves. Steam spinach over boiling water until leaves are wilted; or, cook frozen spinach according to directions and drain thoroughly. Chop spinach coarsely. Melt butter and sauté onions until wilted. In a mixing bowl, combine spinach, onions, cheese, eggs, salt and pepper. Place one sheet of phyllo pastry in a 13x9-inch baking dish. Brush pastry with oil. Add five more sheets of pastry, brushing each layer with oil. Spread spinach mixture in baking dish. Cover with remaining pastry sheets, brushing each layer with oil. Trim off excess overhanging pastry. Sprinkle top of pastry with Parmesan. Bake for 45 to 50 minutes at 350° or until golden brown on top. Yield: 12 servings.

BACON AND EGG CAKE

½ pound bacon
1 tablespoon all-purpose flour
½ teaspoon salt
6 eggs, lightly beaten
½ cup milk
3 tablespoons chives, finely cut

Cut bacon strips in half crosswise and fry until done but not crisp. Drain strips on paper towels. Place bacon in baking dish and keep warm in 200° oven. Drain all but one tablespoon bacon drippings from skillet. In a mixing bowl, blend flour and salt into eggs. Slowly beat in milk. Warm bacon fat in skillet over medium heat. Add egg mixture; cook for 30 minutes on low heat. Do not stir. Check for overbrowning by lifting edge with knife or spatula. Arrange bacon slices and chives over top of cake and serve directly from pan. Yield: 4 servings.

BAKED SCRAMBLED EGGS

Cheese Sauce:
2 tablespoons margarine
2½ tablespoons all-purpose flour
2 cups milk
½ teaspoon salt
⅛ teaspoon pepper
1 cup shredded American cheese

Eggs:
1 cup cubed ham or Canadian bacon
¼ cup chopped onion
3 tablespoons butter, melted
12 eggs, beaten
1 (4-ounce) can sliced mushrooms, drained
¼ cup butter, melted
2¼ cups soft breadcrumbs
⅛ teaspoon paprika

CHEESE SAUCE: Melt margarine; add flour and cook 2 minutes. Slowly add milk, stirring constantly. Add remaining ingredients; stir until smooth. Set aside.

EGGS: Sauté ham and onions in 3 tablespoons butter for 3 minutes. Add eggs and cook, stirring constantly over medium-high heat until large curds form. When eggs are set, stir in mushrooms and Cheese Sauce. Spoon egg mixture into greased 13x9-inch baking dish. Combine ¼ cup butter and breadcrumbs; mix well. Spread breadcrumbs evenly over eggs. Sprinkle with paprika. Cover and chill overnight. Bake uncovered at 350° for 30 minutes. Yield: 10 to 12 servings.

ONION FRITTATA

2 tablespoons butter
2 cups chopped onion
½ cup diced ham
½ cup sliced mushrooms
⅓ cup sliced celery
⅓ cup chopped green pepper
¼ cup diced pimento
2 cups toasted bread cubes
1½ cups grated Swiss cheese
6 eggs
2 tablespoons flour
1½ cups half-and-half
¼ teaspoon salt
⅛ teaspoon pepper
dash hot pepper sauce
onion rings for garnish

Melt margarine in 12-inch ovenproof skillet. Sauté onion, ham, mushrooms, celery, green pepper and pimento until onion is golden. Layer bread cubes and cheese over onion mixture. Combine eggs, flour, half-and-half and seasonings; beat until blended but not frothy. Pour egg mixture in skillet; top with onion rings. Bake at 350° for 25 minutes or until set and golden. Yield: 6 servings. *Simply delicious!*

BEEF QUICHE

½ pound ground beef
½ cup mayonnaise
½ cup milk
⅓ cup green onion, chopped
2 eggs
1 tablespoon cornstarch
½ pound Cheddar cheese, shredded
salt and pepper to taste
1 (9-inch) deep-dish pie shell, unbaked

Brown beef and drain. Mix mayonnaise, milk, onion, eggs, cornstarch, cheese, salt and pepper in a bowl. Add beef and pour into pie shell. Bake at 350° for 30 minutes. Yield: 6 servings.

BLUE CHEESE QUICHE

2 (3-ounce) packages cream cheese
4 ounces blue cheese
2 tablespoons butter, softened
¼ cup heavy cream
3 large eggs
⅛ teaspoon cayenne
¼ teaspoon salt
⅛ teaspoon white pepper
1 teaspoon chopped dried chives
1 (9-inch) pie shell

Beat cream cheese in a medium bowl until soft; blend in blue cheese. Add butter, cream, eggs and spices. Mix well and pour into unbaked pie shell. Bake at 375° for 45 minutes or until puffy and brown. Cool 5 minutes before serving. Yield: 8 to 10 servings.

CALIFORNIA QUICHE

1 pound yellow squash or zucchini
½ onion, thinly sliced
2 tablespoons fresh parsley
4 eggs
½ cup milk
1½ to 2 cups shredded cheese (Swiss or combination Swiss and Cheddar)
salt and pepper to taste
¼ teaspoon dried oregano
¼ teaspoon dried basil

Steam squash and onion slightly; drain. Combine with remaining ingredients. Pour into 8x8x2-inch greased baking dish. Bake uncovered at 325° for 30 to 40 minutes or until set. Yield: 6 servings.

GOLDEN ONION QUICHE

1 frozen deep-dish pie shell
2 teaspoons Worcestershire sauce
1 cup shredded mozzarella cheese
5 slices bacon, cooked and crumbled
1 (6-ounce) can mushrooms

3 eggs, beaten
1 (8-ounce) carton whipping cream
3 drops hot pepper sauce
1 (3-ounce) can French fried onions
1 tablespoon dried chives

Remove pie shell from foil pan and place in 8-inch deep dish glass pie plate. Microwave on high for 1 minute. Using fingers, press shell firmly into pie plate. Brush inside with Worcestersire sauce. Prick shell. Microwave on high for 4 minutes, rotating plate ½ turn after 2 minutes. Sprinkle cheese, bacon and mushrooms over bottom of pie shell. In small bowl, mix eggs, whipping cream and hot pepper sauce. Pour into pie shell. Sprinkle onion and chives over top. Microwave on medium for 12 to 14 minutes, rotating pie ½ turn after 6 minutes. Allow to stand for 5 minutes to firm before serving. Yield: 6 servings.

VARIATION: Use ¾ cup diced ham instead of bacon.

CHRISTMAS QUICHE

1 (9-inch) pie shell
¾ cup cubed cooked chicken
1 cup shredded Cheddar cheese
¼ cup chopped green pepper
3 tablespoons chopped pimento

6 eggs, beaten
1 cup cream
1 tablespoon minced onion
½ teaspoon seasoned salt
¼ teaspoon white pepper

Bake pie shell at 400° for 5 minutes. Prick bottom with a fork. Bake 5 minutes longer. Cool. Layer chicken, cheese, green pepper and pimento in pie shell. Combine remaining ingredients; pour into pie. Bake at 425° for 35 to 40 minutes or until set. Let stand 10 minutes before serving. Yield: 6 servings.

POTATO QUICHE

5 large eggs, beaten
1 (12-ounce) package frozen hash brown potatoes, thawed
1 cup shredded Swiss or Monterey Jack cheese
1 large green onion, minced
½ cup cottage cheese
¼ teaspoon salt
⅛ teaspoon pepper
dash hot pepper sauce
paprika
6 slices bacon, cooked and crumbled

Combine first 8 ingredients. Mix well. Pour into lightly greased 9-inch pie pan. Sprinkle with paprika. Bake at 350° for 25 minutes. Sprinkle bacon on top; bake 5 minutes. Let stand 5 minutes before serving. Yield: 6 servings.

MUSHROOM QUICHE

1 (9-inch) pie shell
2 tablespoons minced green onions
3 tablespoons butter or margarine
½ pound fresh mushrooms, sliced
½ teaspoon salt
1 teaspoon lemon juice
1 tablespoon all-purpose flour
2 tablespoons port wine
3 eggs
1 cup whipping cream
¼ cup shredded Swiss cheese
snipped chives or parsley

Bake pie shell for 8 minutes at 425°. Cool. Sauté onions in butter until tender. Add mushrooms and cook three minutes. Stir in salt, lemon juice, flour and wine. Simmer five minutes or until liquid has evaporated. Cool. Beat together eggs and cream until mixed but not frothy. Stir in mushroom mixture. Pour into shell and sprinkle with cheese. Bake in preheated 375° oven 25 to 30 minutes or until set. Garnish with chives or parsley. Yield: 6 servings.

SALSA ALLA CARBONARA
(Bacon and Egg Sauce)

12 slices bacon, minced
2 tablespoons olive oil
3 raw eggs
1 teaspoon salt
¼ teaspoon black pepper
¼ cup fresh parsley, minced
⅓ cup freshly grated Parmesan cheese
1 (1-pound) box linguini

Fry minced bacon in oil until crisp and golden brown. Beat eggs with salt, pepper and parsley. Cook pasta. Drain well and place in pre-warmed serving bowl. Pour egg mixture over hot pasta and toss until each strand is coated. Add bacon and pan oil and mix again. Add Parmesan cheese and toss lightly. Yield: 4 to 6 servings. *This is a wonderful recipe for unexpected dinner guests. Enjoy!*

Mama Canale
Emilio's Italian Restaurant

BASIC OMELET

3 eggs
1½ teaspoons water
salt and pepper
3 tablespoons butter
fillings: crumbled bacon, strips of ham, chopped fresh herbs, grated cheese, minced shrimp, sautéed mushrooms

Break eggs into bowl. Add water, salt and pepper; beat well. Place butter in a heavy, cold skillet or omelet pan. Melt butter over medium heat until bubbly. Pour eggs into middle of pan and raise heat slightly. Lift edges of omelet with spatula to allow uncooked egg to run under cooked portion. When omelet is soft and slightly set, lay pre-cooked filling or herbs across center of omelet. Fold ⅓ of omelet over filling. Tip pan and roll out onto warmed plate. Yield: 2 servings.

PERFECT CHEESE SOUFFLÉ

4 tablespoons butter
6 tablespoons all-purpose flour
1 cup evaporated milk
1 cup shredded Cheddar cheese

6 eggs, separated
1 teaspoon salt
pinch of cream of tartar

Preheat oven to 350°. Prepare soufflé pan as follows: wrap a greased aluminum foil collar around edge of lightly greased 2-quart soufflé dish. Collar should extend at least 1½ inches above rim of dish. Secure collar with string. Melt butter in saucepan; slowly stir in flour. Gradually stir in milk. Simmer, stirring constantly, until thickened. Add cheese, well-beaten egg yolks and salt. Cook over low heat until cheese melts and mixture is smooth (stirring with a wire whisk prevents lumps). Remove from heat and allow to cool 30 minutes. Allow egg whites to reach room temperature. Beat egg whites. At foamy stage, add a pinch of cream of tartar. Continue beating until egg whites are stiff. Fold stiffly beaten egg whites into cooled cheese mixture. Pour into soufflé dish. Bake at 350° for 30 minutes. Remove collar; cut portions with a fork, then spoon onto plates. Yield: 8 servings.

BREAKFAST CASSEROLE

8 slices white bread
butter
1 pound sausage, cooked and drained
2 cups shredded Cheddar cheese

5 eggs
2 cups milk or half-and-half
1 teaspoon dry mustard
½ teaspoon pepper

Spread bread with butter. Using a sharp knife, cube each slice. Place cubes in 9x13-inch baking dish; sprinkle with crumbled sausage. Top with shredded cheese. Combine eggs, milk, mustard and pepper and beat well. Pour egg mixture over cheese. Chill at least 8 hours or overnight. Remove from refrigerator 15 minutes before baking and bake at 350° for 40 to 50 minutes. Yield: 6 to 8 servings.

POTATO BREAKFAST CASSEROLE

6 slices bacon	1 cup shredded Swiss cheese
1 (6-ounce) package hash brown potato mix with onions	1 green onion, chopped
	1 teaspoon salt
1 quart hot water	1/8 teaspoon pepper
5 eggs	4 drops hot sauce
1/2 cup cottage cheese	paprika

Cook bacon; drain, crumble and set aside. Cover hash browns with hot water and set aside for 10 minutes. Drain potatoes. Beat eggs; add potatoes and remaining ingredients, except bacon and paprika. Pour mixture into buttered 10-inch pie pan. Sprinkle with bacon and paprika. Cover and refrigerate overnight. Place cold, uncovered pie pan in cold oven. Bake at 350° for 40 minutes or until eggs are set. Yield: 6 servings.

MACARONI AND CHEESE

1 (8-ounce) package elbow macaroni	1/4 teaspoon pepper
	3/4 teaspoon Worcestershire sauce
6 tablespoons butter or margarine, divided	3 cups milk
1/4 cup all-purpose flour	1 teaspoon instant minced onion
1/2 teaspoon dry mustard	3/4 pound sharp cheese, shredded
1 teaspoon salt	3/4 cup breadcrumbs

Cook macaroni according to package directions and drain. Melt 4 tablespoons butter; blend in flour and seasonings. Add milk and onion. Cook until thickened, stirring constantly. Add cheese and stir into macaroni. Pour into 2½-quart casserole dish. Top with crumbs mixed with 2 tablespoons melted butter. Bake at 350° for 40 minutes. Yield: 4 to 6 servings.

NIGHTMARE SANDWICHES

16 slices bread	8 slices sandwich cheese
8 slices sandwich ham	5 eggs
butter	1 teaspoon salt

Remove crust; butter both sides of bread. Place eight bread slices in bottom of 9x13-inch baking dish. Layer each bread slice with ham, cheese, and remaining bread slices. Beat eggs and salt together and pour over sandwiches. Cover with foil and refrigerate overnight. Remove from refrigerator and leave at room temperature for 1 hour. Bake uncovered at 250° for 1½ hours. Yield: 8 servings.

POULTRY AND GAME

STUFFED CHICKEN BREAST WITH BRANDY SAUCE

Chicken:
6 skinless, boneless chicken breasts, pounded thin
6 slices ham
6 slices Swiss cheese
12 boiled jumbo shrimp
½ cup butter

Sauce:
¼ cup butter
¼ cup all-purpose flour
4 cups half-and-half
2 bay leaves
1 tablespoon brandy (sherry may be substituted)
salt and pepper to taste

Place chicken breast out flat. Place piece of ham on each breast. Place 1 slice of cheese on top of the ham. Put 2 shrimp on cheese; roll up jellyroll fashion. Place rolled up chicken in a casserole dish, seam side down. Drizzle with ½ cup melted butter and bake at 350° for 25 to 30 minutes. To make sauce, melt remaining ¼ cup butter in saucepan. Using a whisk, stir in flour and cook 2 minutes over medium heat. Add half-and-half, stirring often until thick. Add bay leaves, salt, pepper and brandy and simmer 2 minutes. Arrange chicken breast on platter and spoon sauce over chicken. Yield: 6 servings.

Bryan's Restaurant
Augusta, Georgia

CHICKEN CORDON BLEU

¼ pound thin sliced ham
½ pound thin sliced Swiss cheese
12 chicken breast halves
½ cup butter
1 cup breadcrumbs
1 teaspoon salt
1 teaspoon pepper
1 teaspoon paprika
Mustard Sauce (See Index)

Place 1 slice of ham and 1 slice of cheese on each chicken breast. Roll up and secure with toothpicks. Melt butter in pie plate. Mix breadcrumbs and seasonings. Roll chicken in butter, then in crumbs. Place in buttered baking dish and refrigerate several hours. Bake uncovered at 400° for 40 minutes. Serve topped with Mustard Sauce (See Index). Yield: 6 to 8 servings.

PETTI DI POLLO ALLA BOLOGNESE

4 chicken breasts, skinned and boned
salt
pepper
1 cup all-purpose flour
1 tablespoon butter
2 tablespoons oil
8 thin ham slices
8 thin slices of imported Bel Paese or fonting cheese
½ cup chicken stock
4 tablespoons grated Parmesan cheese

Preheat oven to 350°. Slice each chicken breast in half horizontally to make eight very thin slices. Place chicken pieces between two pieces of plastic wrap. With the flat side of a cleaver or mallet, flatten chicken as thin as possible. Remove chicken pieces from paper and sprinkle with salt and pepper. Dip into flour; shake off excess. In a large, heavy skillet, melt butter and oil together. Cook chicken slices until golden brown on both sides. Transfer chicken pieces to a buttered baking dish. Place ham and cheese slices on top of the chicken. Sprinkle with chicken stock and Parmesan cheese. Bake uncovered for about 10 minutes or until the cheese is melted and light brown. Serve immediately. Yield: 8 servings.

COQ AU VIN

½ cup all-purpose flour
1 teaspoon salt
½ teaspoon pepper
1 (3 to 3½-pound) fryer, cut up
6 slices bacon
1 clove garlic, minced
1 large onion, chopped
2 (6-ounce) cans sliced mushrooms, drained
½ teaspoon dried thyme
1 bay leaf
1 teaspoon dried parsley
3 carrots, sliced
2 chicken bouillon cubes
1 cup hot water
1 cup dry red wine

Mix flour, salt and pepper. Roll chicken in flour mixture. Fry bacon in large skillet until crisp. Remove bacon; crumble and set aside. Brown chicken in bacon fat; remove chicken. Add garlic and onion and sauté 5 minutes. Add mushrooms, seasoning, carrots, bouillon dissolved in hot water and wine. Return chicken to skillet. Simmer 1 hour or until chicken is tender. Serve in individual bowls with French bread for dunking. Yield: 6 servings.

CHICKEN NORMANDY

Chicken:
4 chicken breast halves, boned and skinned
1 teaspoon salt, divided
4 tablespoons butter or margarine
½ cup chopped onion
½ cup chopped celery

1 cup grated apple
½ cup chopped pecans
1 cup toasted plain bread cubes
¼ teaspoon cinnamon
¼ teaspoon dried leaf thyme
1 teaspoon fresh lemon juice

Sauce:
1 tablespoon cornstarch
⅛ teaspoon salt
¼ teaspoon cinnamon
¼ teaspoon dried leaf thyme

2 cups unfiltered apple juice or apple brandy
2 apples, unpared, cored, cut in wedges

CHICKEN: Place chicken breasts on a work surface, dull side down, and flatten with a mallet. Sprinkle chicken with ½ teaspoon salt; set aside. In a large skillet, melt butter. Add onion and celery; cook 5 minutes or until onion is soft (not brown). Remove from heat and stir in grated apple, nuts, breadcrumbs, ½ teaspoon salt, cinnamon, thyme and lemon juice. Place about ¼ cup stuffing mix on center of each breast. Fold sides in and roll chicken up. Place breasts in baking dish, seam side down.

SAUCE: In a medium saucepan, mix together cornstarch, salt, cinnamon and thyme. Stir in juice and cook over medium heat, stirring constantly, until mixture thickens and comes to a boil. Stir in apples and pour over chicken. Bake uncovered at 375° 45 minutes. Stuffing recipe may be doubled. Extra stuffing may be placed in bottom of baking dish and topped with chicken bundles. Yield: 4 servings.

CREAMY BAKED CHICKEN BREASTS

4 whole chicken breasts, split, skinned and boned
8 slices Swiss cheese
1 (10¾-ounce) can cream of chicken soup
¼ cup dry white wine
1 cup stuffing mix, crushed
¼ cup margarine, melted

Arrange chicken in a lightly greased 13x9x2-inch baking dish. Top with cheese slices. Combine soup and wine; stir well. Spoon sauce evenly over chicken. Sprinkle with stuffing mix. Drizzle margarine over crumbs. Bake at 350° for 45 to 55 minutes. Yield: 8 servings.

EASY CHICKEN CHOP SUEY

1 medium onion, chopped
¼ cup butter
1 chicken bouillon cube
1½ cups hot water
1 cup celery, chopped
1 (14-ounce) can chop suey vegetables
2 cups cubed chicken
2 tablespoons cornstarch
2 tablespoons water
1 teaspoon sugar
2 tablespoons soy sauce

Cook onions in butter 3 minutes. Dissolve bouillon cube in hot water. Combine onions, celery and bouillon. Cook 5 minutes. Add vegetables and bring to a boil. Add chicken. In a small bowl, combine cornstarch, water, sugar, and soy sauce. Add to chicken mixture and heat until mixture thickens. Serve over rice or Chinese noodles. Yield: 4 servings.

APRICOT BRANDY CHICKEN

4 whole chicken breasts, split, boned and skinned
3 tablespoons butter
1 teaspoon salt
¼ teaspoon white pepper
½ cup apricot brandy
1 large clove garlic, minced
2 tablespoons minced onion
1 teaspoon tarragon
1 cup heavy cream
1 tablespoon lemon juice
wild rice

Cook chicken in butter until tender (about 20 minutes). Sprinkle with salt and pepper. Pour ¼ cup brandy over chicken; ignite carefully. When flame dies, remove chicken to heated serving dish. To drippings add garlic, onions, remaining brandy, tarragon, cream and lemon juice. Cook, stirring constantly, until sauce is reduced and slightly thickened. Place chicken breasts on a bed of wild rice and pour sauce over chicken. Yield: 8 servings.

CHICKEN BREASTS WITH CREAM

Chicken:
4 boneless, skinless chicken breasts
juice of 1 lemon
freshly ground pepper
4 tablespoons sweet butter

Sauce:
1 tablespoon sweet butter
¼ cup chopped shallots
¼ cup sliced fresh mushrooms
¼ cup chicken broth
¼ cup dry sherry
1 cup whipping cream
lemon juice to taste
2 tablespoons fresh minced parsley

CHICKEN: Rub chicken breasts with lemon juice and sprinkle with pepper. Heat butter in a large skillet; sauté chicken 6 to 8 minutes (chicken will be springy to the touch). Remove chicken to platter; cover and keep warm while making sauce.

SAUCE: Melt butter in same skillet in which chicken was cooked. Add shallots and mushrooms; sauté 5 minutes. Add broth and sherry; boil quickly until mixture is syrupy. Stir in cream and boil until cream thickens slightly. Remove from heat. Add lemon juice. Pour sauce over chicken, sprinkle with parsley and serve at once. Yield: 4 servings.

CHICKEN BREASTS IN WINE

4 chicken breast halves
¼ teaspoon garlic salt
¼ cup butter, melted
1 tablespoon paprika
1 tablespoon lemon juice
½ cup sherry
½ teaspoon Worcestershire sauce
1 (3-ounce) can mushrooms
¼ cup slivered almonds, toasted
2 tablespoons all-purpose flour
¼ cup sour cream

Sprinkle chicken breasts with garlic salt. Mix butter, paprika and lemon juice. Dip each breast in butter mixture and place in baking dish. Bake at 300° for 30 minutes. Remove from oven and cover with sherry, Worcestershire, mushrooms and almonds. Return to oven and cook for 30 minutes. Remove chicken from baking dish and place on serving platter. Pour drippings into a saucepan. Add flour and blend well. Cook for 3 minutes. Add sour cream and blend. Pour gravy over chicken and serve. Yield: 4 servings.

GRILLED CHICKEN WITH MARINADE

½ cup butter or margarine
1 small onion, chopped
½ cup *fresh* lemon juice (about 3 lemons)
1 tablespoon paprika
1 tablespoon oregano
1 teaspoon chopped garlic
½ teaspoon salt
¼ teaspoon pepper
4 chicken breasts

Melt butter and sauté onion until soft. Add remaining ingredients, except chicken, and mix. Place chicken in glass or plastic dish and top with marinade. Marinate 8 hours or overnight. Remove from refrigerator 1 hour before grilling. Place chicken pieces, bone side down, over medium coals. Turn after 20 to 30 minutes and cook 30 to 40 minutes longer. Brush chicken often with marinade. Yield: 4 servings.

GRILLED GINGER CHICKEN

½ cup oil
¼ cup lemon juice
1 tablespoon soy sauce
½ teaspoon ground ginger
1 medium clove garlic, crushed
1 broiler fryer (2½ to 3 pounds), cut up, or 4 chicken breasts

Mix oil, lemon juice, soy sauce, ginger and garlic. Pour over chicken; marinate in refrigerator at least 2 hours, turning occasionally. Grill 10 minutes, skin side up, 6 inches from heat. Turn, baste and grill 15 to 20 minutes. Baste often with marinade. Chicken is done when tender and juices run clear when pierced with fork. Yield: 4 servings.

MUSTARD CHICKEN

4 chicken breast halves, skinned, boned
4 teaspoons Dijon mustard
1 teaspoon honey

Place chicken breasts between pieces of transparent wrap and pound flat. Mix mustard and honey. Spread both sides of chicken with mixture. Grill chicken 7 minutes on each side. Yield: 4 servings.

MOZZARELLA CHICKEN

1 egg
1 tablespoon water
2 pounds chicken breasts, boned
½ cup Italian breadcrumbs
2 tablespoons shortening
1 (10-ounce can) tomato sauce with herbs and spices
¼ cup water or white wine
¼ cup onions, chopped
½ teaspoon garlic powder
½ teaspoon basil
½ teaspoon crushed oregano leaves
1½ cups shredded mozzarella cheese
1 (8-ounce) box spaghetti

Beat egg and water. Roll chicken in egg mix, then in breadcrumbs. Brown chicken in shortening. Pour off fat. Remove chicken from skillet. To skillet, add tomato sauce, water or wine, onions and seasonings. Stir to blend. Return chicken to skillet; cover and cook over low heat 45 minutes or until done. Sprinkle each chicken breast with mozzarella cheese. Heat until cheese melts. Prepare spaghetti according to package directions. Use spaghetti as side dish covered with sauce. Yield: 4 to 6 servings.

FRIED CHICKEN

1 (2½ to 3-pound) chicken, cut up
1 cup buttermilk
1 tablespoon monosodium glutamate
1 teaspoon garlic powder
1 egg
1 cup all-purpose flour
1 tablespoon pepper
vegetable oil

Wash chicken pieces and pat dry. Beat together buttermilk, monosodium glutamate, garlic powder and egg. Combine flour and pepper. Dip each piece of chicken into milk and egg mixture; then roll pieces in flour. Dip chicken in egg mixture again, then in flour a second time. Pour enough vegetable oil in a heavy skillet to fill the skillet half full. Fry chicken in hot oil, skin side up, 10 to 15 minutes. Turn chicken only once and fry for 10 minutes longer. Drain on paper towels. Yield: 4 to 6 servings.

HERBED CHICKEN

4 chicken breast halves, skinned
juice of 1 lemon
½ teaspoon black pepper
1 teaspoon garlic powder
2 tablespoons Worcestershire
2 tablespoons soy sauce

1 teaspoon each: dried oregano leaves, basil leaves, parsley, dried thyme
2 chicken bouillon cubes dissolved in 1 cup hot water

Sprinkle chicken with lemon juice, pepper and garlic powder. Place chicken in shallow baking dish. Combine remaining ingredients and pour over chicken. Bake uncovered 1 hour at 325°. Baste occasionally. Yield: 4 servings.

SWEET AND SOUR CHICKEN

salt
pepper
flour
2 pounds chicken, cut into serving pieces
4 tablespoons vegetable oil
2 (1-pound 4-ounce) cans chunk pineapple
2 cups sugar
4 tablespoons cornstarch
1½ cups cider vinegar
2 tablespoons soy sauce
½ teaspoon ginger
2 chicken bouillon cubes
1 large green pepper, sliced
2 carrots, sliced
1 medium onion, cut lengthwise
cooked rice

Salt, pepper and flour chicken pieces. Brown in hot oil. Arrange chicken in 13x9-inch baking dish. Drain pineapple, reserving syrup. Add enough water to syrup to make 1¼ cups. In large saucepan, combine sugar, cornstarch, cider vinegar, soy sauce, ginger, bouillon cubes and pineapple syrup. Bring to a boil, stirring constantly. Boil 2 minutes. Pour over chicken. Sprinkle peppers and carrots on top and bake uncovered for 30 minutes at 350°. Add pineapple and onions; bake 30 minutes longer or until chicken is tender. Serve with fluffy white rice. Yield: 4 to 6 servings.

EASY SWEET AND SOUR CHICKEN

6 to 8 chicken pieces
1 envelope onion soup mix
1 (1-pound) jar apricot preserves
1 (8-ounce) bottle Russian dressing

Place chicken in baking dish. Sprinkle with soup mix. Spread with preserves; then, top with dressing. Bake uncovered 1 hour at 350°. Yield: 6 to 8 servings.

ORANGE CHICKEN

2 cups chopped celery
1 cup chopped onion
1 cup butter or margarine
8 cups crumbled whole wheat bread
1½ cups chicken broth
8 chicken breast halves, boned

Orange Sauce:
1 tablespoon butter or margarine
6 tablespoons flour
½ cup sugar
3 cups orange juice
½ cup white wine

Sauté celery and onions in margarine. In a large bowl, combine bread, celery, onions and broth. In a 9x13-inch baking dish, place dressing in 8 mounds. Place one uncooked chicken breast on each mound.

FOR ORANGE SAUCE: Melt butter or margarine in saucepan; add flour; blend well. Add sugar, orange juice and wine. Cook, stirring constantly, until thickened. Pour Orange Sauce over chicken and bake at 350° for 1½ hours. Yield: 8 servings.

PENTHOUSE CHICKEN

2 pounds chicken pieces
¼ cup all-purpose flour seasoned with salt and pepper
2 tablespoons shortening
½ medium green pepper, cut into strips
1 medium onion, sliced
⅛ teaspoon crushed thyme leaves
1 (10¾-ounce) can tomato soup
¼ cup water
1 teaspoon vinegar

Dust chicken with seasoned flour. Brown in heated shortening. Cover and cook over low heat until done (30 to 40 minutes). Remove cover and cook for 10 minutes to crisp chicken. Remove chicken and place on serving platter. Pour off all but 2 tablespoons of drippings. Cook peppers, onions and thyme in drippings until tender. Add remaining ingredients. Heat thoroughly, stirring to loosen browned bits of chicken. Spoon sauce over chicken. Yield: 4 to 6 servings.

SPICY BAKED CHICKEN

½ cup fine dry breadcrumbs
1 teaspoon brown sugar
1 teaspoon chili powder
½ teaspoon garlic powder
¼ teaspoon dry mustard
¼ teaspoon celery seed
⅛ teaspoon cayenne pepper
1 (2½ to 3 pound) broiler fryer chicken, cut into serving pieces
salt and pepper
¼ cup butter or margarine, melted

Combine breadcrumbs, brown sugar, chili powder, garlic powder, dry mustard, celery seed and cayenne. Season chicken with salt and pepper. Brush each chicken piece with melted butter. Roll in crumb mixture to coat. In a shallow baking dish, arrange chicken pieces skin side up. Do not let pieces touch. Sprinkle with remaining crumb mixture. Bake uncovered at 375° about 50 minutes or until tender. Do not turn. Yield: 6 servings.

CRESCENT CHICKEN SQUARES

1 (3-ounce) package cream cheese, softened
2 tablespoons margarine, softened
2 cups chicken, cooked and cubed
¼ teaspoon salt
⅛ teaspoon pepper
2 tablespoons milk
1 small onion, chopped
¼ green pepper, chopped
1 stalk celery, chopped
1 tablespoon pimento, chopped
1 (8-ounce) can crescent rolls
¼ cup margarine, melted
sesame seeds, optional

Blend cream cheese and 2 tablespoons margarine until smooth. Add chicken, salt, pepper, milk, onion, green pepper, celery and pimento. Blend ingredients together. Separate crescent rolls into 4 rectangles and seal perforations. Spoon ¼ of mixture into center of each. Pull 4 corners of dough to center of each to seal. Brush tops with melted margarine and sprinkle with sesame seeds. Bake on ungreased cookie sheet at 350° for 20 to 25 minutes. Yield: 4 servings.

CHICKEN WITH MUSHROOMS

6 chicken breasts, skinned
salt and pepper to taste
4 tablespoons butter
¼ cup cream
1 (10¾-ounce) can cream of mushroom soup
1 (6-ounce) can mushroom bits and pieces

Salt and pepper chicken. Cook chicken in butter 5 minutes on each side. Arrange pieces in 9x12-inch baking dish. Combine cream, soup and mushrooms; pour over chicken. Cover and bake for 1 hour at 325°. Serve chicken and gravy over rice. Yield: 6 servings.

CHEESY CHICKEN

3½ cups diced cooked chicken
1½ cups cooked medium egg noodles
1 cup shredded sharp Cheddar cheese
¼ cup Parmesan cheese
½ cup chicken broth
¼ cup dry white wine
½ cup mayonnaise
1 (2-ounce) jar diced pimento
1 tablespoon minced onion
1 tablespoon parsley flakes
1 tablespoon celery flakes
½ teaspoon salt
½ teaspoon coarsely ground pepper

Combine all ingredients; spoon into a greased 8-inch baking dish. Cover and bake at 350° for 30 minutes or until casserole is heated through. Yield: 4 to 6 servings.

CHICKEN TETRAZZINI

1 (8-ounce) package thin spaghetti
1¾ cups shredded Cheddar cheese, divided
4 tablespoons Parmesan cheese, divided
2 cups diced cooked chicken or turkey
1 (2-ounce) jar diced pimentos
¼ cup chopped green pepper
½ cup chopped onion
1 (10½-ounce) can cream of mushroom soup
½ cup chicken broth
¼ cup vermouth or white wine
salt and pepper to taste

Cook spaghetti according to package directions. Combine 1 cup Cheddar cheese, 2 tablespoons Parmesan cheese and remaining ingredients. Toss with spaghetti. Pour into greased 9x13-inch baking dish. Top with remaining cheese. Bake, uncovered, for 35 to 45 minutes at 350°. Yield: 8 to 10 servings.

CHICKEN GUMBO

1 (3-pound) fryer
water
2 whole cloves
1 carrot, sliced
1 bay leaf
1 large onion, sliced
1 rib celery
½ cup white wine
1 teaspoon salt
1 teaspoon black pepper
¼ cup oil
1 tablespoon all-purpose flour

2 large onions, chopped
¼ cup chopped celery
½ cup chopped green pepper
1 cup chopped, peeled tomatoes
1 teaspoon dried parsley
3 cloves garlic, minced
4 tablespoons Worcestershire sauce
4 bay leaves
1 cup sliced okra
cooked white rice

Place fryer in large soup pot. Cover with water. Add next 8 ingredients. Cook over medium heat until done. Remove meat from bone, chop and set aside. Strain stock and reserve. Make a dark roux with oil and flour. Add 1½ cups reserved stock. Stir to blend. Add remaining ingredients except okra, rice and chicken. Simmer 30 minutes. Add okra and chicken; simmer 2 hours, stirring occasionally. To serve, place one mound of rice in each serving bowl and top with gumbo. Freezes well. Yield: 10 to 12 servings.

CHICKEN AND SAUSAGE JAMBALAYA

1 (3 to 4-pound) chicken
water
1 pound bulk sausage, cooked
1 tablespoon corn oil
1 small onion, chopped
1 green pepper, chopped
1 cup raw rice

¼ teaspoon minced garlic
⅛ teaspoon paprika
¼ teaspoon chili powder
1 tablespoon Worcestershire sauce
dash of hot pepper sauce
salt and pepper to taste

Boil chicken in enough water to cover. Remove from liquid, reserving broth and cool. Take chicken off the bone; chop and set aside. Heat oil in a large skillet and cook onion and green pepper until tender. Add rice, 2 cups chicken broth and remaining seasonings. Cook over medium low heat for 10 minutes; add chicken and sausage. Cook 20 minutes longer or until rice is done. Yield: 8 servings.

AMARETTO CHICKEN SALAD

Salad:
2 cups cubed, cooked chicken
¼ cup mayonnaise
1 (8¼-ounce) can crushed
    pineapple, drained
1 tablespoon amaretto
1 teaspoon salt
2 tablespoons toasted slivered
    almonds
½ cup chopped celery

Dressing:
2 tablespoons amaretto
½ cup mayonnaise

SALAD: Combine all ingredients. Chill overnight.

DRESSING: Combine ingredients; cover and chill overnight. To serve, place salad on a bed of lettuce leaves or in hollowed out pineapple boats. Top with dressing and garnish with additional almond slices. Yield: 4 to 6 servings.

HOT CHICKEN SALAD

2 cups cubed cooked chicken
½ cup slivered almonds
1 cup sliced water chestnuts
½ cup diced pimento
¼ teaspoon celery salt
⅛ teaspoon pepper
2 tablespoons lemon juice
¾ cup mayonnaise
½ cup crumbled French fried
    onion rings
¾ cup shredded Cheddar cheese

Mix chicken, almonds, chestnuts, pimento, celery salt, pepper, lemon juice and mayonnaise. Pour into 1½ quart casserole. Mix onions and cheese. Sprinkle over top of chicken. Bake in a preheated 350° oven for 30 minutes. Yield: 6 to 8 servings.

CHICKEN CURRY SALAD

1 (3 to 4-pound) whole chicken
water
salt to taste
½ cup plain yogurt
¼ cup mayonnaise
1 tablespoon curry powder
¼ cup diced green pepper
¼ cup diced onion
¼ cup diced celery
salt and pepper to taste
spinach leaves

Cook chicken in boiling, salted water. Drain chicken; cool, bone and chop. Add remaining ingredients. Serve on bed of spinach leaves. Yield: 4 to 6 servings.

TURKEY BREAST IN A BAG

1 (4-pound) frozen turkey breast
½ cup margarine, melted
1 package dry Italian dressing mix
1 package dry onion soup mix
1 cooking bag

Thaw frozen turkey breast in original wrapper in refrigerator (allow 24 hours for 4 pound breast). Mix margarine and dry mixes. Place turkey in cooking bag and pour butter mixture over turkey. Fasten with closure. Make slits in bag. Bake according to bag directions. To microwave, melt butter in microwave and add dry mixes. Stir well and pour over turkey in bag. Using temperature probe, cook on high to 190°. Yield: 6 to 8 servings.

CORNISH HENS

8 Cornish game hens
salt and pepper
8 medium onions, peeled
¾ cup butter or margarine
¼ cup liquid browning sauce
1 (8-ounce) jar orange marmalade

Clean and dry hens. Season inside and out with salt and pepper; refrigerate overnight. When ready to bake, insert one whole onion in each cavity and place in open roasting pan. Do not let sides of hens touch. In a small saucepan place butter, browning sauce and orange marmalade. Heat together until butter melts and mixture is blended. Spoon mixture over the hens and bake at 350° until hens are tender, about 1 to 1½ hours, basting often. If sauce cooks down before hens are done, add a little hot water to the pan to assure having enough sauce. Yield: 8 servings.

DRUNKEN DOVES

6 doves
½ cup butter
1 cup white wine
¼ cup minced onion
2 tablespoons minced celery leaves
salt and pepper to taste
½ teaspoon tarragon

Split doves. Cook in butter until lightly browned, about 5 minutes. Add wine, onion, celery leaves, salt and pepper. Cover and simmer over low heat 20 to 30 minutes. Add tarragon; simmer, uncovered, 15 minutes. Yield: 3 to 4 servings.

BAKED DOVE

8 to 10 dove breasts
celery salt and pepper
½ cup butter
1 (10¾-ounce) can cream of
　mushroom soup
½ cup cooking sherry

Season birds with celery salt and pepper. Brown in butter. Make sauce with cream of mushroom soup and sherry. Place birds in baking dish and pour sauce over birds. Bake at 350° 30 to 45 minutes or until tender, basting frequently. Yield: 3 to 4 servings.

PHEASANT

2 pheasants
salt and pepper
seasoned salt
flour to dredge
1 (10-ounce) can beef consommé
½ cup sherry
1 (10-ounce) can beef gravy
4 large green onions, chopped
½ bunch parsley
1 (6-ounce) can mushrooms

Half each pheasant; dry thoroughly with cloth. Season to taste with salt, pepper and seasoned salt. Dredge with flour. Brown on both sides under broiler or in Dutch oven with a small amount of oil. Remove to roasting pan and add consommé, sherry and gravy. Reserve some of the gravy mixture for basting during cooking. Bake at 300° 45 minutes or 1 hour. Remove from pan and add green onions and parsley. Simmer until onions are tender. Add mushrooms and more consommé if additional gravy is needed. Yield: 4 servings.

FRIED QUAIL

12 quail
flour seasoned with salt and
　pepper
1 cup butter
½ cup hot water
1 (6-ounce) can sliced
　mushrooms

Dust quail with seasoned flour. Melt butter in frying pan. Brown birds; add hot water and cover pan. Simmer until tender, about 30 minutes. Add mushrooms; stir and serve. Yield: 6 to 8 servings.

VENISON ROAST

1 (8 to 10-pound) venison roast
2 cups peach brandy
1 package oil and vinegar dressing mix
½ cup brown sugar
½ cup syrup
1 (16-ounce) can crushed pineapple
½ cup Worcestershire sauce
1 tablespoon garlic powder
salt and pepper

Using fillet knife, remove thin layer of membrane from roast. Place roast in large plastic bag and add all ingredients. Place in large roasting pan and refrigerate for 24 hours, turning bag frequently to cover meat thoroughly. Remove from marinade and cook over medium heat on outdoor grill for 2 hours, basting each side frequently with marinade. Yield: 6 to 8 servings.

VENISON STEW

2 slices bacon
6½ pounds venison, cut into cubes
1 clove garlic, minced
1 (12-ounce) package fresh mushrooms
1 (16-ounce) package frozen small whole onions
1 (10½-ounce) can condensed beef broth, undiluted
3 cups water
1 cup dry red wine
1 teaspoon salt, optional
1 teaspoon thyme leaves
1 bay leaf
2 pounds small red potatoes, pared around center
⅓ cup unsifted all-purpose flour

In 8 to 10-quart Dutch oven or kettle, fry bacon until crisp. Remove, drain and crumble. Set aside. In drippings, cook venison, a third or half at a time, in a single layer, until browned on all sides. Remove meat to large bowl. Add garlic and mushrooms to pan; cook until mushrooms are lightly browned. Remove to medium-sized bowl. Add frozen onions to pan. Cook 1 minute and remove to bowl with mushrooms. Discard all drippings from pan. Add beef broth, 2 cups water, wine, salt, thyme, and bay leaf. Return meat to pan. Heat to boiling; cover and simmer 1½ hours or just until meat is fork tender. Discard bay leaf. Add potatoes and mushroom-onion mixture. Cook about 20 minutes or until potatoes are tender. In small bowl, combine flour and 1 cup water; stir until smooth. Move meat and potatoes to one side of pan; stir flour mixture into sauce. Cook until thickened, stirring carefully. Skim off any fat from surface of sauce. Sprinkle with crumbled bacon before serving. Yield: 8 servings. *Beef shortribs may be used in place of venison.*

SIX LAYER VENISON DISH

2 teaspoons salt
½ teaspoon pepper
1 teaspoon dried thyme
1 teaspoon garlic powder
2 cups sliced raw potatoes
2 cups thinly sliced celery
2 cups ground venison or thin slices of a tender cut
1 cup thinly sliced onions
1 cup chopped green pepper
2 cups canned tomatoes
1 or 2 cups grated sharp Cheddar cheese

Combine salt, pepper, garlic powder and thyme. Butter a 2-quart baking dish and layer potatoes, celery, venison, onions, green pepper and tomatoes. Sprinkle each layer with seasoning mixture. Cover baking dish and bake at 350° for 2 hours. Remove cover during last 15 minutes of baking and sprinkle with cheese. Yield: 4 to 6 servings.

FISH AND SEAFOOD

BAKED STUFFED FLOUNDER FILLETS

3 tablespoons lemon juice
6 flounder fillets
Seafood Dressing (below)

6 tablespoons fine breadcrumbs
6 tablespoons butter, melted

Seafood Dressing:
6 tablespoons butter
¼ cup finely chopped celery
½ cup finely chopped onion
½ pound shrimp, cooked, peeled and diced
1 teaspoon fresh parsley, chopped (½ teaspoon dried)

1 teaspoon finely chopped pimento
1 teaspoon Worcestershire sauce
salt and pepper to taste
¼ cup dry sherry
1½ cups breadcrumbs

SEAFOOD DRESSING: Melt butter; add vegetables; sauté until tender. Add remaining ingredients, except breadcrumbs; cook for 10 minutes on low heat. Remove from heat; add breadcrumbs. Mix thoroughly.

TO ASSEMBLE: Sprinkle lemon juice over fillets. Place 4 to 6 tablespoons dressing on each fillet. Roll up fillet and place seam side down in greased shallow baking dish. Sprinkle breadcrumbs over fish; pour butter over fish. Bake at 375° for 25 to 30 minutes or until fish flakes easily. Yield: 6 servings.

FLOUNDER À LA MOUTARDE

1 pound fresh flounder fillets
salt and pepper to taste
1 tablespoon vegetable oil
2 tablespoons mayonnaise

1 tablespoon Dijon-style mustard
2 teaspoons chopped parsley
4 lemon or lime wedges

Preheat broiler. Place fillets on broiling pan; sprinkle with salt and pepper and brush with oil. Blend mayonnaise, mustard and parsley. Spread evenly over fillets. Broil fillets under broiler 3 to 4 inches from heat. Broil about 2 minutes or until golden brown and fish is just cooked through. Serve with lemon or lime wedges. Yield: 4 servings.

STUFFED DOVER SOLE

12 shrimp, cooked, peeled and chopped
4 green onions, chopped
4 fillet of sole
2 tablespoons butter
2 tablespoons all-purpose flour
⅓ cup sherry
chopped fresh parsley

Combine shrimp and onions. Place ¼ of shrimp mixture crosswise on each fillet. Roll up fillet and place, seam side down, in greased 8-inch baking dish. Melt butter in saucepan; add flour. Cook 2 minutes. Add sherry, stirring constantly. Pour over fillets. Cover and bake 30 minutes at 350°. Top with parsley just before serving. Yield: 4 servings. *Allow ⅓ pound fish fillets per serving; allow ½ pound per serving if fish is whole.*

SAUTÉED SCROD

4 scrod fillets (¼ to ½ pound each)
½ teaspoon each ground ginger, basil and thyme
1 tablespoon soy sauce
1 tablespoon corn oil
2 large cloves garlic
4 large mushrooms, coarsely chopped
1 green onion, sliced
1 small rib celery, minced
½ cup dry vermouth
lemon wedges

Wash fish and pat dry. Mix ginger, basil, thyme and soy sauce. Sprinkle both sides of fish with mixture. Heat oil in non-stick skillet until hot. Add garlic, mushrooms, onion and celery. Sauté for 1 minute. Spread vegetable mixture evenly over bottom of skillet. Lay fillets on top of mixture; sauté over medium high heat for 5 minutes. Turn; sauté for 2 minutes. Add vermouth; cook for 3 minutes, continually spooning sauce over fish. Arrange fish on serving dish and spoon sauce on top. Garnish with lemon wedges. Yield: 4 servings.

STRIPED BASS IN BUTTER SAUCE

4 pounds skinless, boneless, striped bass fillets
2 small carrots
2 cups butter, divided
1 cup minced onions
1 cup minced celery
½ cup minced mushrooms
1 cup dry white wine, divided
salt and pepper to taste
juice of 1 lemon
1 cup heavy cream

Cut fillets into 8 servings. Cover; refrigerate. Scrape carrots; cut into thin rounds. Heat 1 cup butter in a heavy saucepan. Add carrots, onions, celery and mushrooms. Add ⅓ cup wine. Cook until wine is reduced, about 10 minutes. Add another ⅓ cup wine and reduce liquid 10 minutes. Add last ⅓ cup wine and reduce liquid 10 minutes. Add cream to saucepan and bring to a boil. Add remaining butter to sauce, 2 tablespoons at a time. Sprinkle fish with salt, pepper and lemon juice. Lay in a single layer in a buttered baking dish. Pour sauce over fish. Bake 20 minutes at 350° or until fish flakes easily. Yield: 8 servings.

SALMON CUTLETS WITH BROWNED BUTTER

1½ pounds salmon fillets
1½ cups fine breadcrumbs, divided
1 cup heavy cream, divided
salt and pepper to taste
pinch cayenne pepper
⅛ teaspoon dried dill
4 tablespoons vegetable oil
8 tablespoons butter, divided

Using a sharp knife, chop salmon very fine. A blender or food processor will cut fish too fine. In a mixing bowl, combine salmon, ½ cup breadcrumbs, ⅓ cup cream, salt, pepper, cayenne and dill. Stir briskly. On a piece of waxed paper, divide the mixture into 6 portions. Shape each portion into round patties. Patties may be refrigerated until ready to use. Dip patties in remaining crumbs. Heat oil and 4 tablespoons butter. Cook salmon 4 minutes on each side. Remove to warm platter. Wipe skillet clean with paper towel. Add remaining butter and cook, shaking the skillet until the butter starts to brown. Do not let the butter burn. Pour hot butter over salmon. Yield: 6 servings.

SALMON TIMBALES

1 (16-ounce) can red salmon
½ cup whipping cream
½ teaspoon salt
⅛ teaspoon white pepper
¼ cup chopped onion

1 tablespoon parsley
1 teaspoon lemon juice
4 eggs, separated
Lemon Dill Horseradish Sauce
 (See Index)

Preheat oven to 400°. Drain salmon, remove bones and skin. Flake and mash with fork. Add cream, salt, pepper, onions, parsley and lemon juice. Beat egg yolks; add to salmon mixture. Beat egg whites until soft peaks form; fold into salmon mixture. Grease 6 (4-ounce) ramekins or timbales and spoon in salmon mixture. Place ramekins in baking dish with 2-inch sides. Pour boiling water into baking dish to 1-inch depth. Bake 20 minutes. Unmold ramekins onto serving dishes and top with Lemon Dill Horseradish Sauce (See Index). Yield: 6 servings. *This makes a nice luncheon dish. Serve with steamed asparagus and Cucumber Salad (See Index).*

BAKED SALMON STEAKS

4 (8-ounce) salmon steaks,
 1-inch thick
⅓ cup mayonnaise
2 lemons, cut into ¼-inch slices
4 slices bacon, cut in half
 crosswise

1 medium onion, cut into ¼-inch
 slices
1 (16-ounce) can whole
 tomatoes, undrained and
 chopped

Place salmon steaks in a lightly greased 13x9x2-inch baking dish. Spread mayonnaise over top of steaks; top with lemon slices. Place 2 pieces of bacon over each steak; top with onion slices. Pour tomatoes over onion and around steaks. Cover and bake at 350° for 45 minutes or until fish flakes easily when tested with a fork. Yield: 4 servings.

GRILLED SALMON

4 salmon steaks (¾-inch thick)   mayonnaise

Brush salmon steaks on each side with mayonnaise. Place on grill over medium coals. Cook 5 to 7 minutes on each side. Yield: 4 servings. *Delicious dipped in melted butter and lemon juice.*

CATFISH STEW

3 pounds catfish, cooked and boned
4 slices fat back
3 pounds potatoes, peeled and thinly sliced
3 pounds onions, thinly sliced
2 tablespoons salt
2 tablespoons pepper
hot pepper sauce

Boil catfish, reserving broth, bone and set aside. Over high heat, in large Dutch oven, brown fat back. Lower heat; discard fat back, leaving drippings in pan. Add one layer of potatoes and one layer of onions. Top with all of fish. Repeat layers of potatoes and onions. Pour about half of the broth over top. Add several dashes hot pepper sauce and salt and pepper. Do Not Stir! Cover and let simmer for approximately 2 hours. Just before serving, stir well. Yield: 6 to 8 servings.

BAKED RED SNAPPER

1 tablespoon margarine
1 large onion, sliced thin
1 green pepper, coarsley chopped
1 (14½-ounce) can tomato wedges, drained
dash garlic powder
ground black pepper
1½ pounds red snapper fillets
grated Parmesan cheese

Melt margarine in sauté pan. Add onions and green peppers. Cook until tender. Add tomato wedges, garlic powder and pepper; cook until tomatoes are heated through. Place snapper fillets in a greased 13x9-inch baking dish. Top with vegetables. Bake at 350° for 15 minutes. Sprinkle with grated Parmesan cheese just before serving. Yield: 4 servings.

TROUT BAKED WITH SHRIMP

5 pounds trout or pompano fillets
1½ teaspoons salt
½ teaspoon pepper
⅔ cup butter, melted, divided
5 pounds shrimp, cooked, peeled, deveined
⅓ cup pitted black olives, halved
5 (10½-ounce) cans cream of shrimp soup
6 drops hot pepper sauce
⅛ teaspoon cayenne pepper
2 tablespoons Worcestershire sauce
3 tablespoons lemon juice
1 teaspoon powdered thyme
2 tablespoons chopped parsley
1 teaspoon seasoned salt
⅓ cup sherry
½ cup sliced almonds
1 cup grated Parmesan cheese

Wash fish fillets and dry on paper towels. Sprinkle fillets with salt and pepper. Grease bottoms of 3 (7½x11¾-inch) casseroles with ⅓ cup butter. Lay fillets, skin side down in casseroles. Distribute shrimp equally over fish; then sprinkle with olives. In a mixing bowl, combine soup, hot pepper sauce, cayenne, Worcestershire, lemon, thyme, parsley, salt and sherry. Pour over fish. Top sauce with almonds; drizzle remaining butter over top. Sprinkle casseroles with cheese. Bake at 350° for 25 minutes. Yield: 20 servings.

BROILED TROUT FILLETS

½ cup butter, melted
1 small onion, chopped
1 cup dry white wine
¼ teaspoon garlic powder
salt and pepper
2 to 3 pounds fresh speckled trout fillets
juice of 1 lemon
1 teaspoon chopped parsley
paprika
lemon or lime slices for garnish

Melt butter in saucepan; sauté onions until transparent. Add wine and garlic powder. Bring to a boil, then remove from heat. Salt and pepper fillets; place in baking dish, skin side down. Sprinkle with lemon juice and parsley. Pour sauce over fillets. Broil fish 6 to 8 inches from heat at 450° until fish turns white and flakes easily (15 to 20 minutes). Do not overcook. To serve, sprinkle paprika over fish and garnish with fresh lemon or lime slices. Yield: 4 servings.

CREOLE FISH

1¾ pounds skinless, boneless white fish fillets
6 tablespoons butter, divided
1 cup chopped onion
1 clove garlic, chopped
1 cup chopped bell pepper
salt and pepper to taste
1 (17-ounce) can imported tomatoes
2 tablespoons tomato paste
½ teaspoon dried basil
¼ teaspoon liquid pepper sauce
1 tablespoon dried parsley flakes

Preheat oven to 450°. Cut fish into 6 serving pieces and set aside. Melt 4 tablespoons butter in saucepan; add onion, garlic and green peppers; sauté until vegetables are wilted. Add salt, pepper, tomatoes, tomato paste, basil and pepper sauce. Cover and simmer 15 minutes. Place fish in buttered baking dish. Sprinkle fish with salt and pepper. Dot fish with 2 tablespoons of butter. Spoon sauce over fish; sprinkle parsley over fish and bake for 15 minutes. Yield: 6 servings.

QUICK AND EASY FISH

1 pound snapper, butterfish or similar fish
diet margarine
salt
pepper
Parmesan cheese

Pan fry fish fillets in diet margarine until opaque in color. Season with salt and pepper. Sprinkle with Parmesan cheese on both sides and fry one minute longer. Yield: 4 to 6 servings.

CURRIED FISH FILLETS

½ cup all-purpose flour
1 teaspoon curry powder
¼ teaspoon salt
1 pound fish fillets, fresh or frozen
½ cup butter or margarine
⅓ cup slivered almonds
chutney filled lemons

Combine flour, curry powder and salt. Roll fillets in seasoned flour to coat thoroughly. Heat butter in large skillet. Add floured fillets and cook over moderate heat until browned, about 3 minutes on each side. Remove fish to heated platter. Add almonds to remaining butter in skillet. Sauté almonds until browned. Pour over fish. Garnish with chutney filled lemons (remove pulp from lemons and fill with chutney). Yield: 4 servings.

GRILLED SWORDFISH WITH HORSERADISH SAUCE

4 tablespoons butter or
   margarine, melted
juice of 1 lemon

2 teaspoons soy sauce
4 swordfish steaks (½ pound
   each)

Combine butter or margarine, lemon juice and soy sauce. Brush on swordfish. Place swordfish in wire basket and grill over medium coals for 6 to 8 minutes per side. Brush steaks with butter sauce while grilling. Serve with Lemon Dill Horseradish Sauce (See Index).

FISH AND CHIPS

4 large Idaho potatoes
oil for deep frying, about 8 cups
½ cup all-purpose flour
salt and pepper to taste
8 small, skinless, boneless
   flounder fillets (or other white
   fish)

Batter
malt vinegar

Batter:
1 cup cold water
½ teaspoon yellow food coloring
2 tablespoons corn oil

1 teaspoon salt
1 cup all-purpose flour
1 teaspoon baking powder

BATTER: Combine cold water, food coloring, oil and salt. Gradually add flour, stirring with wire whisk. Just before using, stir in baking powder and blend evenly. Peel potatoes; cut in ½-inch slices, then ½-inch strips. Heat 6 cups oil in deep fryer. Fry potatoes 2 minutes. Drain on paper towels. Blend flour, salt and pepper. Dredge fillets in flour. Dip fillets, one at a time, in batter. Fry in 350° oil for 1½ to 2 minutes. Do not crowd fillets. Remove fillets. Add 2 cups oil to fryer and allow grease to reach 400°. Return potatoes, in small batches, and cook 2 minutes or until crisp. Drain. Serve fish and potatoes with malt vinegar. Yield: 4 servings.

SAVORY BAKED FISH

½ cup chopped celery
1½ pounds flounder or sole fillets, fresh or frozen
½ teaspoon salt
¼ teaspoon crumbled rosemary
¼ teaspoon white pepper
¼ teaspoon paprika
1 large tomato, sliced
½ cup chopped green onion
¼ cup dry white wine

Sprinkle celery in bottom of shallow baking dish. Place fish on top of celery, overlapping fillets slightly. Sprinkle fish with salt, rosemary, pepper and paprika. Top with tomato slices and green onions. Add wine. Bake at 350° for 25 minutes, or until fish is fork tender. Yield: 4 servings.

FRENCH FRIED FISH

2 pounds pan-dressed fish
salt
pepper
plain corn meal
peanut oil

Sprinkle both sides of each fish with salt and pepper. Place corn meal in large grocery bag. Add fish to bag and shake vigorously to coat fish well with meal. Add fish to deep kettle, half-full of peanut oil heated to 400°. Maintain constant temperature during frying. Do not place too many fish in kettle at one time. Fish will come to top of oil when done. Drain well. Serve immediately with hush-puppies and cole slaw. Yield: 4 to 6 servings.

TUNA CHEESE BURGER

1 (6-ounce) can tuna, drained
1 tablespoon chopped onion
1 cup shredded Cheddar cheese
2 tablespoons chopped green olives
2 tablespoons mayonnaise
4 hamburger buns
prepared mustard

Combine first 5 ingredients. Spread both halves of hamburger buns with mustard. Spoon tuna mixture onto 4 buns and top with remaining buns. Wrap in foil and bake at 350° for 20 minutes. Yield: 4 servings.

CLAMS CASINO

4 cloves garlic, minced
1 teaspoon oregano
¼ cup breadcrumbs
2 tablespoons olive oil
1 (7½-ounce) can minced clams, undrained
⅛ teaspoon salt
1 teaspoon parsley
Parmesan cheese

Sauté garlic, oregano and breadcrumbs in olive oil. Watch carefully to prevent burning. When mixture is brown, add clams and salt. Spoon into individual baking "shells" and sprinkle with parsley and Parmesan cheese. Bake at 375° for 20 minutes. Yield: 2 servings. *Recipe may be doubled. May be prepared ahead; sprinkle with crumbs and cheese just before baking.*

BAKED CRAB CASSEROLE

½ cup butter
4 tablespoons all-purpose flour
½ cup milk
1 pound crab meat
½ teaspoon salt
½ teaspoon pepper
2 (3-ounce) cans sliced mushrooms, drained
2 cups half-and-half
1 (3-ounce) jar pimentos
3 to 4 tablespoons sherry
breadcrumbs

Make basic white sauce using first three ingredients. While sauce is hot, add remaining ingredients, except breadcrumbs. Pour into casserole and top with breadcrumbs. Heat in 350° oven for 20 minutes. Serve over rice, toast points, or in patty shells. Yield: 6 to 8 servings. *Chopped shrimp, flaked white fish, lobster, or scallops may be substituted for crab.*

CRAB AND SHRIMP CASSEROLE

1½ cups hot cooked rice
1 cup mayonnaise
1 cup crab meat
1 (4-ounce) can mushrooms
2 cups cut up shrimp
1 small onion, chopped
3 tablespoons Worcestershire sauce
⅛ teaspoon pepper
½ teaspoon salt
1 medium bell pepper, chopped
1 cup breadcrumbs

Stir mayonnaise into hot rice. Add remaining ingredients, except breadcrumbs, and turn into greased 2-quart casserole. Top with breadcrumbs. Bake at 325° for 30 minutes. Yield: 8 servings.

SHRIMP IN PATTY SHELLS

1½ cups milk
3 tablespoons coarsely chopped onion
4 sprigs parsley
1 clove garlic, crushed
1 bay leaf
3 tablespoons butter or margarine
3 tablespoons all-purpose flour
½ teaspoon salt
⅛ teaspoon pepper
1 cup cooked green peas
1 cup cooked and peeled shrimp
2 egg yolks, slightly beaten
2 teaspoons lemon juice
4 baked patty shells

Combine milk, onion, parsley, garlic and bay leaf in saucepan. Heat to scalding; strain. Melt butter in skillet. Blend in flour, salt and pepper. Cook over low heat, stirring until mixture is smooth and bubbly. Remove from heat and stir in hot milk. Heat to boiling, stirring constantly. Boil 1 minute. Add peas and shrimp; heat through. Stir a little hot mixture into egg yolks; then add egg yolks to remaining hot mixture. Stir in lemon juice and cook one minute longer. Serve hot in patty shells. Yield: 4 servings.

SHRIMP CREOLE

1 pound shrimp, boiled and cleaned
4 tablespoons butter
1 stalk celery, chopped
1 medium onion, chopped
1 green pepper, chopped
½ pound fresh mushrooms, sliced or 1 (4-ounce) can sliced mushrooms
1 clove garlic, crushed
6 peeled fresh tomatoes or 1 (32-ounce) can tomatoes
1 bay leaf, crushed
1 teaspoon salt
dash red pepper
2 heaping tablespoons tomato paste
1 teaspoon Worcestershire sauce
⅛ teaspoon basil

In a heavy skillet, sauté shrimp in butter for 3 minutes. Remove shrimp. Add to skillet, celery, onion, green peppers, mushrooms and garlic. Sauté until slightly browned. Add tomatoes, bay leaf, salt, red pepper, tomato paste, Worcestershire sauce and basil. Simmer 20 minutes or until thickened. Add shrimp; reheat briefly and serve over rice. Yield: 6 servings.

SHRIMP CASSEROLE

1 (10¾-ounce) can cream of mushroom soup
2 tablespoons chopped green bell pepper
2 tablespoons chopped onions
1 tablespoon lemon juice
2 cups cooked wild rice
½ teaspoon Worcestershire sauce
½ teaspoon dry mustard
½ teaspoon black pepper
¼ cup cubed Cheddar cheese
1½ pounds peeled raw shrimp

Mix all ingredients and pour into a 1½-quart buttered casserole. Bake at 375° for 30 to 35 minutes. Yield: 4 servings.

SHRIMP REMOULADE

½ cup chopped onions
½ cup oil
¼ cup tarragon vinegar
½ cup creole mustard
1 teaspoon paprika
¼ teaspoon cayenne pepper
2 teaspoons salt
1 clove garlic, minced
½ cup chopped green onions
1 head lettuce, shredded
2 pounds shrimp, boiled and peeled

Blend first 8 ingredients in blender for 6 seconds. Stir and blend 6 more seconds. Add onions. Blend 2 seconds. Chill sauce overnight. To serve, arrange shredded lettuce on salad plates; top with shrimp and cover with chilled sauce. Yield: 4 to 6 servings.

BATTER FOR FRIED SHRIMP

1 cup all-purpose flour
½ teaspoon salt
1 egg
1 cup ice water
2 tablespoons oil

Mix ingredients together until well blended. Dip dry, cleaned, deveined shrimp into batter. Fry until golden brown. Yield: 1½ cups.

CRAB STUFFED EGGPLANT

2 large eggplants
olive oil
6 tablespoons butter
1 cup chopped onion
4 tablespoons dried parsley
salt and pepper to taste
1 pound lump crab meat
breadcrumbs
grated Parmesan cheese

Cut eggplants in half lengthwise; rub cut surface with olive oil; place cut side down in roasting pan. Bake 30 minutes at 350°. Carefully remove pulp from shells, leaving skin intact. Melt butter in heavy saucepan and sauté onion. Add parsley, salt, pepper and eggplant pulp. Simmer 5 minutes. Add crab meat and mix well. Stuff eggplant shells with mixture; sprinkle with breadcrumbs and cheese. Bake at 350° for 30 minutes. Yield: 4 servings.

HAWAIIAN SHRIMP CURRY

Coconut Milk:
2 cups hot milk
1 cup flaked coconut

Shrimp:
¾ cup minced onion
1 clove garlic, crushed
2 tablespoons butter, melted
2 tablespoons cornstarch
1 tablespoon curry powder
1 teaspoon salt
1½ cups diluted evaporated milk
2 cups coconut milk
2 pounds shrimp, cooked and shelled
½ teaspoon monosodium glutamate
2 tablespoons sherry
condiments: raisins, toasted coconut, mandarin orange slices, chutney, crumbled bacon, chopped scallions, banana slices

COCONUT MILK: Pour hot milk over coconut. Let stand 1 hour. Squeeze all liquid from coconut. Discard coconut. Use liquid as directed.

SHRIMP: Sauté onion and garlic in butter. Blend in cornstarch, curry powder and salt. Stir in milk and coconut milk, stirring constantly until thickened. Add shrimp and heat through. Just before serving, stir in monosodium glutamate and sherry. Serve over rice and top with condiments. Yield: 6 to 8 servings.

SHRIMP SEA ISLAND

Shrimp:
5 pounds shrimp, boiled and cleaned
10 mild small onions, sliced into rings

Dressing:
1 pint olive oil
¾ pint cider vinegar
1 (3 to 4-ounce) bottle of capers with juice
dash salt
1 tablespoon sugar
2 dashes liquid pepper sauce
2 teaspoons Worcestershire sauce

In a deep bowl layer shrimp and onions. Combine all dressing ingredients and pour over the shrimp. Refrigerate 12 hours. Serve and enjoy. Yield: 10 servings.

COQUILLES ST. JACQUES

1½ pounds scallops
1 tablespoon chopped shallots
¼ teaspoon salt
dash white pepper
½ cup dry white wine
1 cup cream
4 tablespoons butter
1 tablespoon all-purpose flour
Parmesan cheese

Combine scallops, shallots, salt, pepper and wine in a saucepan. Bring to a boil; lower heat and simmer 2 minutes. Spoon scallops into 4 individual baking dishes. Boil liquid to reduce by half; add cream and boil sauces until thick and syrupy. In a separate saucepan, melt butter; add flour and cook until golden. Add cream sauce to flour-butter mixture. Pour sauce over scallops; sprinkle with Parmesan cheese. Brown under broiler. Yield: 4 servings.

SCALLOPS IN WINE SAUCE

1 pound scallops (quartered if large)
1 cup dry white wine
1 tablespoon lemon juice
¼ pound fresh mushrooms, sliced or 1 (3-ounce) can, drained
4 green onions, chopped
1 tablespoon chopped parsley
3 tablespoons butter
1 tablespoon all-purpose flour
2 tablespoons milk
salt and pepper to taste
2 tablespoons breadcrumbs
butter

Place scallops, wine and lemon juice in a shallow pan. Cover and simmer 5 minutes. Drain, reserving liquid. Sauté mushrooms, onions and parsley in butter until onions are tender. Stir in flour; blend in reserved liquid and milk. Bring to a boil, stirring constantly. Season to taste with salt and pepper. Add scallops to sauce; pour into greased shallow baking dishes, ramekins or shells. Sprinkle with breadcrumbs and dot with butter. Place in preheated 350° oven for 15 minutes. Yield: 4 servings. *Recipe may be doubled.*

SCALLOPS FLORENTINE

1 (10-ounce) box frozen spinach
1 pound scallops
2 tablespoons chopped green onions
3 tablespoons butter, divided
salt and pepper to taste
¼ cup white wine
2 tablespoons all-purpose flour
1 cup milk
½ cup heavy cream
2 tablespoons grated Parmesan cheese

Preheat oven to 450°. Boil spinach 5 minutes; drain well, chop and set aside. Combine scallops, onions, 1 tablespoon butter, salt, pepper and wine. Bring just to a boil, then remove from heat immediately. Drain scallops, reserving liquid. Melt 2 tablespoons butter in a saucepan; add flour, stirring with a wire whisk. Add milk; stir rapidly until smooth and thick. Add cream and simmer 5 minutes. Spoon spinach into buttered oval au gratin dish or 1½-quart baking dish. Spread scallops over spinach; spoon sauce over scallops; sprinkle with Parmesan. Bake at 450° for 5 minutes. Yield: 4 to 6 servings.

MEATS

INDIVIDUAL BEEF WELLINGTONS

Steaks:
6 (4 to 5-ounce) filets mignon
1 teaspoon salt
¼ teaspoon pepper
½ cup chopped onion
½ cup chopped carrots
½ cup chopped celery

¾ cup vegetable oil
1 cup red wine
2 tablespoons brandy
½ teaspoon fine herbs
1 tablespoon butter

Mushroom Filling:
2 pounds fresh mushrooms, finely chopped
¼ cup minced green onions

2 tablespoons butter
½ cup Madeira
salt and pepper to taste

Pastry:
3 cups all-purpose flour
1½ teaspoons salt
¾ cup plus 2 tablespoons butter or margarine, chilled and cubed

¼ cup shortening, chilled
⅓ to ½ cup ice water
2 egg yolks plus 2 teaspoons water

Sauce:
2 cups beef broth
1 tablespoon tomato paste

2 tablespoons cornstarch
¼ cup Madeira

Garnish:
Sliced mushrooms, carrot curls, celery fans, parsley sprigs

FILETS: Sprinkle filets with salt and pepper and place in a shallow dish. Sauté onion, carrots, and celery in oil until tender. Add wine, brandy, and herbs. Pour mixture over filets, cover, and marinate in refrigerator overnight. Drain steaks, reserving liquid. In a skillet, sauté filets in 1 tablespoon butter until lightly browned on both sides. Place filets in a pan; cover and freeze 10 minutes. Remove from freezer and refrigerate 2 hours.

MUSHROOM FILLING: Place mushrooms in a clean towel or cheesecloth and squeeze until barely moist, reserving juice. Sauté mushrooms and onions in butter. Add Madeira and cook until liquid evaporates. Add salt and pepper. Chill at least 2 hours.

PASTRY: In a large bowl combine flour and salt. Cut in chilled butter and shortening with pastry blender or fork until mixture resembles coarse meal. Sprinkle ice water evenly over surface. Stir with a fork until all dry ingredients are moistened. Shape dough into a ball; chill 2 hours.

TO ASSEMBLE: On a lightly floured surface, roll dough into an 18-inch square. Cut into six 9x6-inch rectangles. Spread each rectangle with ⅓ cup mushroom filling. Top filling with one filet. Combine 2 egg yolks and 2 teaspoons water. Brush edges of pastry with egg mixture to seal. Trim away any excess pastry. Place Wellingtons, seam side down, on a lightly greased baking sheet. Brush with egg mixture; wait one minute and brush again. Roll out pastry trimmings and cut in decorative shapes. Arrange pieces on top. Bake at 400° for 25 minutes or until golden brown.

TO PREPARE SAUCE: Combine reserved marinade, reserved mushroom juice, beef broth, and tomato paste in a saucepan; simmer one hour. Dissolve cornstarch in Madeira; stir into broth mixture and cook until thickened, stirring constantly. Spoon sauce over Wellingtons and garnish. Yield: 6 servings.

BEEF CARBONNADE

3 pounds lean beef (chuck, rump, or round)
4 tablespoons butter
6 cups thickly sliced onions
1 teaspoon salt
freshly ground pepper
1 (10-ounce) can beef bouillon
2 (10-ounce) cans beer
2 tablespoons brown sugar
1 tablespoon dried thyme
1 bay leaf
buttered noodles
2 tablespoons chopped parsley

Preheat oven to 325°. Cut beef into ½-inch cubes. Melt butter in heavy skillet. Add beef and brown quickly. Remove beef to 4-quart ovenproof casserole. Brown onions in same skillet used to brown beef (about 10 minutes). Remove from heat, season with salt and pepper, and add to beef. Heat bouillon in skillet, scraping bits from bottom. Pour bouillon over beef and onions. Add enough beer to barely cover beef. Stir in brown sugar, thyme, and bay leaf. Bring casserole to simmer on top of stove. Cover casserole and place in oven for 2½ hours. Spoon beef and onions over buttered noodles and sprinkle with parsley. Yield: 8 servings.

NEW ORLEANS STEAK DIANE

4 tablespoons butter
4 small (1¼-inch thick) tournedos or filets
3 cloves garlic, minced
1 small onion, minced
2 stalks celery, minced
1 teaspoon dried parsley
1½ teaspoons salt
¾ teaspoon black pepper
¾ cup Worcestershire sauce
juice of ½ lemon
3 dashes liquid pepper sauce

Melt butter in skillet. Simmer meat in melted butter 5 minutes on each side. Remove meat to platter and keep warm. To skillet add vegetables, parsley, salt and pepper. Simmer 5 minutes. Add Worcestershire, lemon juice, and pepper sauce. Cook until sauce is slightly thickened. Return steaks to skillet and cook for one minute on each side. Serve steaks with sauce spooned on top. Yield: 4 servings.

STEAK AND VEGETABLE KABOBS

½ cup red wine vinegar
4 tablespoons vegetable oil
4 tablespoons soy sauce
4 tablespoons ketchup
½ teaspoon onion salt
½ teaspoon garlic powder
¼ teaspoon black pepper
2 pounds (1½-inch thick) boneless sirloin steak, cut into 1-inch cubes
½ pound fresh mushrooms
2 large green peppers, cut into 1½-inch pieces
1 pint cherry tomatoes

Combine first seven ingredients. Place meat in non-aluminum container. Pour marinade over meat and marinate for 4 to 6 hours. Drain, reserving marinade. Alternate meat and vegetables on skewers. Grill over medium coals 10 to 15 minutes or to desired degree of doneness. Baste often with marinade. Yield: 4 to 5 servings.

SKIRT STEAK ORIENTAL

2 tablespoons brown sugar
1 teaspoon dry mustard
½ cup vinegar
½ cup salad oil
3 tablespoons sherry

2 tablespoons minced onion
¼ cup orange juice
6 beef skirt steak rolls, ¾-inch thick

Combine brown sugar and mustard; add vinegar, oil, sherry, onion, and juice. Stir to dissolve sugar. Place steaks in glass dish and pour marinade over them. Cover and refrigerate steaks 4 hours or overnight, turning several times. Grill steaks 3 to 4 inches from heat. Turn after 5 or 6 minutes and grill 5 to 7 minutes on second side. Brush steaks often with marinade. Yield: 6 servings. *Good served with rice pilaf and mandarin orange salad.*

BEEF BURGUNDY

1 carrot, peeled and quartered
1 sprig parsley
1 bay leaf
½ teaspoon thyme
¼ pound bacon, diced
2 tablespoons all-purpose flour
1½ teaspoons salt
¼ teaspoon pepper
2 pounds lean beef cut into 2-inch cubes

1½ cups dry red wine
1½ cups water
1 clove garlic, pressed
1 pound (or one 16-ounce can) small whole onions
½ pound (or one 8-ounce can) sliced mushrooms
minced parsley

Preheat oven to 350°. Place carrot, parsley, bay leaf, and thyme on a piece of cheesecloth; tie securely and set aside. Fry bacon until crisp; drain on an absorbent paper and set aside. Reserve bacon drippings. Brown beef cubes in 2 tablespoons bacon drippings. Combine flour, salt, and pepper; add beef and toss to coat well. Combine beef and bacon in a 2½-quart casserole; set aside. Combine wine, water, garlic, and cheesecloth bag in a saucepan. Bring to a boil. Pour over meat mixture. Bake for 2 hours. Sauté onions and mushrooms in 1½ teaspoons bacon drippings. Add to meat mixture during last 30 minutes of baking. Remove cheesecloth bag and discard. Garnish with parsley. Yield: 4 to 6 servings. *Good!*

BROILED SIRLOIN STEAK WITH GARLIC SAUCE

3 tablespoons butter
1 teaspoon garlic powder
3 tablespoons Worcestershire sauce
½ cup steak sauce
2½ pounds choice sirloin steak

Melt butter in saucepan over low heat. Add garlic powder, Worcestershire sauce, and steak sauce; mix well. Bring to a boil; remove from heat. Place steak on broiler pan. Brush top of steak with sauce, covering well. Place 3 inches from source of heat. Broil for 5 minutes. Turn; brush generously with sauce. Broil 5 minutes longer or to desired doneness. Yield: 4 servings.

SWEET 'N' SOUR FLANK STEAK

1½ pounds flank steak
5 green onions, chopped
¾ cup vegetable oil
½ cup soy sauce
1½ teaspoons ginger
1½ teaspoons garlic powder
3 tablespoons honey
2 tablespoons vinegar

Place steak in a large, shallow dish (glass or plastic). Combine remaining ingredients, mixing well. Pour over steak. Cover and marinate in refrigerator 8 hours, turning occasionally. Drain steak, reserving marinade. Grill over hot coals 5 to 10 minutes on each side or until desired degree of doneness. Baste with marinade while grilling. To serve, slice steak across grain into thin slices. Steak should be very rare. Yield: 6 servings.

GRILLED ROUND STEAK

4 pounds round steak
¼ cup vegetable oil
½ cup water
2 tablespoons vinegar
2 cloves garlic, minced
2 tablespoons Worcestershire sauce
dash hot pepper sauce
½ teaspoon beef bouillon granules
½ teaspoon dry mustard
¼ teaspoon chili powder
¼ teaspoon salt

Trim excess fat from steak. Combine remaining ingredients; cover meat with mixture and marinate meat in non-aluminum container for 3 to 4 hours. Grill over medium hot coals for 15 to 20 minutes, turning several times. Yield: 8 servings.

CURRIED BEEF AND PEPPERS

½ to ¾ pound beef round steak
2 teaspoons salad oil
1 beef bouillon cube
1½ cups water
1 teaspoon curry powder
scant teaspoon sugar
½ teaspoon salt

1 small green pepper cut into 1-inch strips
1 medium onion, wedged
2 tablespoons cornstarch
2 tablespoons water
1 tomato, peeled and wedged
rice

Cut meat into ¾-inch strips. Heat oil and brown meat 10 minutes; drain. Add bouillon cube, water, curry powder, sugar, and salt. Heat to boiling, stirring occasionally. Reduce heat. Cover and simmer for 1 hour. Add green pepper and onion; cover and simmer until vegetables are tender, about 5 minutes. Mix cornstarch and water and add to beef. Cook and stir until thickened. Add tomato wedges and cook about 3 minutes. Serve over rice. Yield: 4 servings.

PEPPER STEAK

1 pound flank or round steak
2 large green peppers
⅛ pound margarine
1 teaspoon salt
4 teaspoons cornstarch

2 teaspoons sugar
2 teaspoons monosodium glutamate
2 cups soup stock or water
1 teaspoon soy sauce

Cut beef into small slices. Cut each green pepper into eight pieces. Sauté beef in hot skillet (about 150°) with margarine and salt for 4 minutes. Add green peppers and cook 2 minutes. Combine cornstarch, sugar, monosodium glutamate, water and soy sauce in small bowl. Pour into beef mixture and stir well. Cover and bring to a boil. Serve immediately. For variety add 1 small onion, sliced, and 1 fresh tomato, cut in wedges, at the same time peppers are added.

Madison Woo's Chinese Restaurant
Augusta, Georgia

ORIENTAL BEEF

1 (6-ounce) package frozen Chinese pea pods
1½ pounds boneless sirloin steak
2 tablespoons soy sauce
2 cloves garlic, crushed
1 teaspoon sugar
½ teaspoon ground ginger
3 tablespoons vegetable oil
1 cup sliced fresh mushrooms
3 green onions with tops, cut in 1-inch pieces
1 (8-ounce) can sliced water chestnuts, drained
1 teaspoon beef flavored bouillon granules
2 tablespoons cornstarch
½ teaspoon salt
1 cup warm water
hot cooked rice

Thaw and drain pea pods; set aside. Trim excess fat from steak. Partially freeze steak; slice diagonally across grain into 2x¼-inch strips. Set aside. Combine soy sauce, garlic, sugar, and ginger; add steak, tossing to coat. Cover and refrigerate 1 hour. Coat wok or skillet with oil. Heat to medium heat (325°) for 2 minutes. Add steak and stir-fry 1 minute. Add pea pods and stir-fry 1 minute. Add next 3 ingredients and stir-fry 2 minutes. Dissolve bouillon granules, cornstarch, and salt in water; stir into steak mixture. Cook until thickened. Serve over rice. Yield: 6 servings.

TERIYAKI FONDUE

1 pound sirloin
⅔ cup soy sauce
¼ cup white wine
2 tablespoons sugar
½ tablespoon ground ginger
1 clove garlic, minced
2 to 4 cups vegetable oil
Fondue Sauces (See Index)

Cut steak into ¾-inch cubes. Combine soy sauce, wine, sugar, ginger, garlic and meat in covered container. Marinate meat at least 1 hour (do not use aluminum container). Drain meat and arrange on platter. Heat oil on stove top to 400°. Pour into fondue pot to a depth of 2 inches. Spear meat and cook 1 to 2 minutes. Serve with Fondue Sauces (See Index). Yield: 4 servings.

VARIATIONS: For chicken fondue, substitute 3 boned and skinned chicken breast halves for beef. For shrimp fondue, substitute 2 pounds medium shrimp shelled and deveined.

BEEF STROGANOFF

4 pounds beef sirloin tip or top round
½ cup all-purpose flour
2 teaspoons salt
dash paprika
onion salt to taste

4 tablespoons vegetable oil
1 cup beef bouillon
1 cup canned mushrooms
1 pint sour cream
hot rice or noodles

Cut beef into ½-inch thick strips. Combine flour, salt, paprika, and onion salt. Roll beef in seasoned flour. Brown beef in oil. Add bouillon (more if needed); cover and let steam 5 to 10 minutes. Add mushrooms and steam 5 minutes longer. Stir in sour cream and heat through. *Do not boil.* Serve over hot rice or noodles. Yield: 8 to 10 servings.

SWISS STEAK

1½ pounds beef round steak, cut ¾-inch thick
3 tablespoons all-purpose flour
1 teaspoon salt
2 tablespoons shortening
1 (16-ounce) can tomatoes, cut up

1 small onion, sliced
1 stalk celery, sliced
1 medium carrot, thinly diced
½ teaspoon Worcestershire sauce
¼ cup cold water
hot cooked rice or noodles

Cut meat into 6 serving pieces. Combine flour and salt; pound 2 tablespoons of flour mixture into meat. Brown meat on both sides in hot shortening. Pour off excess fat. Add undrained tomatoes, onion, celery, carrot, and Worcestershire. Cover and cook over low heat about 1¼ hours or until meat is tender. Remove meat to a serving platter; keep warm. Skim off excess fat from tomato mixture. Combine ¼ cup cold water and remaining flour; stir into tomato mixture. Cook and stir until thickened. Serve meat and sauce over hot cooked rice or noodles. Yield: 6 servings.

BEEF PASTY

Pie Crust (See Index)
4 ounces beef, cubed
¾ cup diced potatoes
1 tablespoon ground onion
¼ cup peas and carrots
salt and pepper to taste
1 egg white
1 tablespoon water

Prepare pie crust and roll on floured surface ⅛-inch thick. Cut into 6 or 8-inch circle. Mix beef, potatoes, onion, peas, carrots, salt and pepper. Place on center of dough; dot with butter. Pull up the crust around mixture and seal on top. Combine egg white and water and brush on top. Bake at 350° for 45 minutes. Serve with gravy or ketchup. Yield: 1 serving.

Jean's Pasties and Pastries
Augusta, Georgia

BARBECUE BEEF SANDWICHES

4 pounds beef chuck
3 medium onions, chopped
1 tablespoon butter
½ cup white vinegar
½ cup water
4 cups canned tomatoes, chopped
½ cup Worcestershire sauce
1 teaspoon salt
1 clove garlic, minced
pepper to taste

Cut beef into 3 or 4 large pieces. Combine all ingredients in Dutch oven. Cook over low heat 3 to 4 hours or until thick. Tear meat into small pieces with fork. Serve on hamburger buns. Yield: 12 servings. *Good dish for a large crowd.*

MOUSSAKA

Potatoes:
½ cup vegetable oil
4 cups thin sliced potatoes

Meat Sauce:
2 pounds ground beef
1 cup chopped onion
1 (6-ounce) can tomato paste
½ cup water
2 teaspoons salt
½ teaspoon cinnamon
⅛ teaspoon pepper

Béchamel Sauce:
2 tablespoons butter
3 tablespoons all-purpose flour
⅛ teaspoon nutmeg
1 teaspoon salt
2 cups milk
2 eggs, slightly beaten
½ to ¾ cup grated Parmesan cheese

POTATOES: In a large skillet, heat oil and brown potatoes. Drain potatoes on paper towels while preparing meat sauce.

MEAT SAUCE: Brown beef in large skillet. Add onion and cook until onion is tender. Add tomato paste, water, salt, cinnamon, and pepper. Stir well and cook until thick, about 10 minutes.

SAUCE: Melt butter in a saucepan. Blend in flour, nutmeg, and salt. When roux has browned, add milk and cook stirring constantly until thick. Add a small amount of hot mixture to eggs, stirring constantly. Add egg mixture to saucepan and cook 1 to 2 minutes longer.

TO ASSEMBLE: Spread ½ of the potatoes in the bottom of a greased 2-quart casserole dish. Top potatoes with meat mixture and ½ of the cheese. Top with remaining potatoes. Pour sauce on top and sprinkle with remaining cheese. Bake at 350° for 35 to 40 minutes. Let stand 10 minutes before serving. Serve with Greek Salad (See Index) and crispy bread. Yield: 6 to 8 servings.

BAKED SPAGHETTI

1 (7-ounce) package spaghetti noodles
1½ pounds lean ground beef
2 large onions, sliced
1 clove garlic, minced
2 green peppers, diced
2 (8-ounce) cans tomato sauce
1 (4-ounce) can sliced mushrooms, drained
½ teaspoon salt
¼ teaspoon pepper
1 tablespoon Worcestershire sauce
½ pound sharp Cheddar cheese, shredded
½ cup slivered almonds

Break noodles into 2-inch pieces and cook according to directions; drain. Brown ground beef. Add onions, garlic, and peppers and cook until tender. Add tomato sauce, mushrooms, salt, pepper and Worcestershire sauce. Reduce heat and cook slowly for 30 minutes, stirring often. If sauce becomes too thick while cooking, add a little water or tomato sauce to thin. Add cooked spaghetti and toss. Spoon into two ungreased 1½-quart casseroles. Sprinkle with cheese and almonds. Bake one casserole at 350° for 30 minutes. Freeze the other. (Bake frozen casserole at 350° for 45 to 50 minutes.) Yield: 4 to 6 servings per casserole.

STUFFED PEPPERS

6 bell peppers
1 pound ground beef
1 cup cracker crumbs
1 small onion, chopped
1 egg, beaten
1 cup tomato juice
salt and pepper to taste

Wash peppers; remove tops and seeds. Boil peppers for 2 minutes. Drain; salt peppers lightly. Mix remaining ingredients. Stuff peppers with mixture. Place in baking dish in ½ inch water. Bake at 375° for 1 hour. Yield: 6 servings.

BAKED ZITI

1 egg
1 pound ricotta cheese
8 ounces mozzarella cheese, shredded
1 small onion, diced
½ pound hamburger meat
1 (32-ounce) bottle meat flavored spaghetti sauce
2 cups large ziti noodles (or elbow noodles)
water

Beat egg and cheeses together; set aside. Sauté onion and brown meat; drain and mix with spaghetti sauce. Boil noodles 10 to 12 minutes and drain. Layer in a deep 3-quart casserole dish with ⅓ sauce, noodles, and cheese mixture. Repeat layers three times. Bake at 350° until heated through, approximately 30 to 45 minutes. Yield: 8 servings. *Excellent for preparing ahead and freezing until needed; however, do not bake before freezing.*

MARVELOUS MEATLOAF

1½ to 2 pounds of lean ground beef
1 egg
1 cup rolled oats
⅓ cup finely chopped onions
1½ teaspoons salt
¼ teaspoon pepper
¼ cup ketchup
¼ teaspoon allspice, optional

Topping:
½ cup ketchup
6 tablespoons brown sugar
1 teaspoon dry mustard
¼ teaspoon nutmeg

Mix all meatloaf ingredients. Press into a 9x5-inch loaf pan. Bake at 350° for 40 minutes. Combine topping ingredients. Spread on meatloaf and bake 20 mintues longer. Meatloaf may be baked for 1 hour and topping served on the side. If served in this manner, topping should be heated for approximately 5 minutes or just long enough for ingredients to blend. Yield: 6 to 8 servings.

ZUCCHINI-BEEF CASSEROLE

2 pounds zucchini, sliced
water
1 pound lean ground beef
1 teaspoon salt
¼ teaspoon garlic powder
¼ teaspoon pepper
1 cup finely chopped onion

3 cups cooked rice
2 eggs, beaten
1½ cups cottage cheese
2 tablespoons grated Parmesan cheese
2 cups shredded Cheddar cheese

Cook zucchini in water for 5 minutes; drain and set aside. Cook meat, seasonings, and onions together until meat is brown and onions are tender. Add rice and zucchini to meat mixture. In a separate bowl, combine eggs, cottage cheese, and Parmesan cheese; stir into meat mixture. Divide mixture into two greased, shallow 2-quart casseroles. Top each casserole with 1 cup of Cheddar cheese. Bake at 350° for 30 minutes. Yield: 12 servings. *Freezes well.*

HAMBURGER CASSEROLE

2 pounds hamburger meat
2 tablespoons butter
2 teaspoons salt
dash pepper
1 teaspoon sugar
3 (8-ounce) cans tomato sauce
1 (3-ounce) package cream cheese

1 cup sour cream
1 small onion, grated
1 (8-ounce) package noodles, cooked
1 cup shredded Cheddar cheese

Sauté meat in butter; add salt, pepper, sugar, and tomato sauce. Cook 5 minutes. Mix cream cheese, sour cream, and onion. Layer half of the noodles, hamburger mixture, and cheese mixture in a greased 2-quart casserole dish. Repeat layers. Top with shredded cheese. Bake at 350° until heated through, approximately 30 to 45 minutes. Yield: 8 servings. *A good "new-neighbor" dish.*

CHILI

1 small green bell pepper, chopped
1 small onion, chopped
1 tablespoon butter
1 pound ground beef
1 (29-ounce) can tomato sauce
1 cup tomato paste
1 (15½-ounce) can light red kidney beans, drained
2½ teaspoons chili powder
1 teaspoon sugar
½ teaspoon salt
½ teaspoon oregano leaves
¼ teaspoon black pepper
⅛ teaspoon garlic powder
shredded Cheddar cheese, optional

Sauté pepper and onion in butter. Add ground beef and brown; drain. Add tomato sauce, tomato paste, beans, chili powder, sugar, salt, oregano leaves, pepper and garlic. Bring to a boil. Cover and simmer on low heat for 1 hour. Top with shredded cheese before serving, if desired. Yield: 4 to 6 servings. *Also good topped with corn chips.*

CHILI CASSEROLE

1 pound ground beef
½ cup chopped onion
½ teaspoon salt
½ teaspoon pepper
1 (16-ounce) can kidney beans
1 (16-ounce) can tomato sauce
½ teaspoon chili powder
1 cup cooked macaroni
1 cup shredded Cheddar cheese

Brown ground beef and onions; add salt and pepper to taste. Add kidney beans, tomato sauce, chili powder, and macaroni. Put into 9-inch greased casserole dish and top with shredded cheese. Cook at 350° for 20 to 30 minutes or until bubbly. Yield: 6 servings.

TACO DINNER

2 pounds ground beef
½ pound sausage
3 large onions, chopped
1 clove garlic
2 (15-ounce) cans kidney beans
1 cup ketchup
2 tablespoons sugar
1 tablespoon prepared mustard
2 tablespoons chili powder
½ cup white vinegar
2 tablespoons Worcestershire sauce
½ teaspoon red pepper
salt and pepper to taste
corn chips
1 head lettuce, shredded
1 onion, chopped
3 tomatoes, chopped
2 cups shredded sharp Cheddar cheese

Brown meat, sausage, onions, and garlic. Drain. Add next ten ingredients. Bake at 200° 8 to 9 hours or in crock pot on low for 8 to 9 hours. Serve sauce over regular size corn chips. Top with lettuce, onion, tomatoes, and Cheddar cheese. Yield: 10 to 12 servings. *Excellent for casual gatherings.*

PERFECT PIZZA

Crust:
¾ cup warm water
1 (¼-ounce) package dry yeast
2½ cups biscuit mix

Filling:
2 (6-ounce) packages sliced mozzarella cheese
¾ cup chopped onion
1 clove garlic
2 cups tomato sauce
1 cup chopped salami; or 1 pound cooked ground beef; or, 1 cup cooked Italian sausage
2 (3-ounce) cans sliced mushrooms, drained
salt and pepper to taste
⅓ cup grated Parmesan cheese
oregano to taste

Pour water into large warm bowl. Sprinkle in yeast; stir until dissolved. Add biscuit mix; beat vigorously. Turn dough out onto surface dusted with biscuit mix. Knead until smooth, about 20 times. Divide dough into 4 balls. Roll each ball into a 10-inch circle. Place on 4 greased baking sheets. Place mozzarella slices on crusts. Mix onion, garlic, and tomato sauce and spoon on top of cheese. Add cooked meat, mushrooms, salt, pepper, Parmesan cheese, and oregano. Bake at 425° for 15 minutes. Yield: four 10-inch pies.

MARINATED GRILL BURGERS

2 pounds ground beef
1 tablespoon dry mustard
1 tablespoon Worcestershire sauce
½ cup butter, melted
juice of 2 lemons

Shape beef into 8 patties and put in glass baking dish. Combine remaining ingredients and pour over beef patties. Marinate 2 to 4 hours. Grill over medium coals to desired doneness. Yield: 8 servings.

REUBEN CASSEROLE

1 (32-ounce) jar sauerkraut, drained
½ cup onion, chopped
½ cup parsley
2 teaspoons caraway seeds
4 cups shredded Swiss cheese, divided
1⅓ cups bottled Thousand Island dressing, divided
1 pound corned beef, thinly sliced
6 slices rye bread, cut into 1½-inch cubes
½ cup margarine, melted

Combine sauerkraut, onion, parsley, and caraway seeds. Mix well and place in bottom of 13x9x2-inch pan. Top with 2 cups cheese, ⅔ cup dressing, and beef. Top beef with remaining dressing and cheese. Toss bread cubes with margarine. Mix well. Sprinkle over top of casserole. Bake at 375° for 35 minutes. Serve hot. Yield: 6 to 8 servings.

VEAL MARSALA

8 veal medallions
¼ cup butter
1 (4-ounce) can sliced mushrooms, drained
1 medium onion, sliced
1 green pepper, sliced into thin strips
1 stalk celery, sliced
¼ teaspoon marjoram
½ cup Marsala wine

Sauté veal in butter. Remove veal to warm plate. Add vegetables to pan drippings and cook until vegetables are tender. Return veal to pan with vegetables. Add seasoning and wine. Simmer for 5 minutes. Yield: 4 servings.

VEAL GRILLADES

2 pounds veal, sliced thin
¼ cup all-purpose flour
½ cup vegetable oil, divided
½ cup chopped green pepper
½ cup sliced celery
½ cup chopped onion
2 cloves garlic, minced
1 (1-pound 12-ounce) can tomatoes
½ cup dry white wine
½ teaspoon thyme
½ teaspoon hot pepper sauce
1 teaspoon Worcestershire sauce
2 teaspoons chopped fresh parsley, optional

Dust veal on both sides with flour. In a large skillet brown veal on both sides in ¼ cup oil. Remove veal from pan and set aside. Add remaining ¼ cup oil to pan. Cook green pepper, celery, onion, and garlic until tender. Stir in tomatoes, wine, thyme, pepper sauce, and Worcestershire sauce. Return veal to skillet. Bring to a boil; reduce heat and cover. Simmer for 1 hour. Serve over grits or rice. Garnish with chopped parsley. Yield: 6 to 8 servings. *May be prepared up to 2 days before serving.*

SWEET VEAL LOAF

2 pounds lean ground veal
6 tablespoons breadcrumbs
1 apple, peeled, cored, and coarsely chopped
1½ tablespoons corn oil
1 medium onion, minced
2 cloves garlic, minced
¼ cup minced green pepper
¼ cup chopped mushrooms
½ teaspoon each allspice, ginger, and dried tarragon leaves
½ teaspoon ground cinnamon
½ cup unsweetened apple juice, divided

Combine veal, breadcrumbs, and apple; mix well. Heat oil and cook onion, garlic, green pepper, and mushrooms until lightly browned. Sprinkle vegetables with allspice, ginger, and tarragon. Stir to blend. Add vegetable mixture to meat and mix well. Press mixture into 8x4-inch loaf pan. Sprinkle loaf with cinnamon. Bake at 400° for 15 minutes. Pour off fat. Pour ¼ cup apple juice over loaf and return to oven for 10 minutes. Add ¼ cup of juice to loaf and bake 15 additional minutes. Yield: 6 servings.

STUFFED VEAL CHOP CRABES

6 (10-ounce) veal rib chops
12 ounces fresh lump crab meat
6 teaspoons lemon juice
¾ pound unsalted butter, softened
1 tablespoon paprika
2½ teaspoons salt
¾ teaspoon white pepper
¾ teaspoon black pepper
1 teaspoon ground cayenne pepper
1 teaspoon dry, granulated garlic
1 teaspoon onion powder
½ teaspoon ground oregano
½ teaspoon thyme leaves

Cut ½-inch slot to make pocket in each veal chop. Combine crab meat, lemon juice and 3 tablespoons melted butter and stuff each chop. Coat each chop with softened butter. Mix next 9 ingredients together and coat each chop generously with seasoning mixture. Heat cast iron skillet for 5 minutes over high heat. Add 2 tablespoons butter. (Butter will flame so be careful!) Carefully place veal chop in skillet for 2 minutes per side. Veal chops will be cooked to medium rare. Yield: 6 servings.

Le Cafe Restaurant
Augusta, Georgia

VEAL SCALLOPINI

1 chicken bouillon cube
½ cup hot water
2 pounds veal, sliced thin or pounded thin
½ cup butter, melted
dash of paprika
2 tablespoons all-purpose flour
½ cup whole milk
6 tablespoons sherry
1 (3-ounce) can sliced mushrooms, drained
dash of nutmeg
½ pound Swiss cheese, sliced

Dissolve bouillon cube in hot water and set aside. In a large skillet, brown veal in melted butter. Place browned veal in a single layer in a 13x9-inch baking dish. Sprinkle veal with paprika. Brown flour in pan drippings and add milk and bouillon. Cook and stir until thick. Add sherry, mushrooms, and nutmeg to sauce. Pour sauce over meat. Top meat with cheese. Bake uncovered at 425° for 20 minutes. May be prepared ahead and baked just before serving. Yield: 4 to 6 servings.

APPLE BRANDY PORK CHOPS

4 tablespoons vegetable oil
4 loin chops, 1-inch thick
¼ teaspoon pepper
¼ teaspoon ground cinnamon
1 pound fresh mushrooms, sliced
4 medium onions, quartered
½ cup apple brandy or unfiltered apple juice
½ cup cream
minced parsley

In a heavy skillet, heat oil over medium heat; add chops and brown both sides. Add pepper, cinnamon, mushrooms, and onions. Cook 15 minutes, turning chops occasionally. Remove chops, onions, and mushrooms to platter; keep warm. Add brandy (or juice) to skillet; scrape meat bits from bottom. Gradually add cream to pan; cook until slightly thickened. Pour sauce over pork and vegetables. Sprinkle with parsley. Yield: 4 servings.

BAKED PORK CHOPS

1 (10¾-ounce) can cream of mushroom soup
½ can water
1 cup red or white wine
1 cup white rice
6 pork chops
1 package dry onion soup mix
½ cup slivered almonds

In bowl, combine mushroom soup, water, and wine. Add rice; blend together. Pour mixture into buttered casserole; top with chops. Sprinkle top with dry soup mix followed by slivered almonds. Bake covered for 1½ hours at 350°. Yield: 6 servings.

FLORIDA ORANGE PORK CHOPS

6 loin pork chops
¾ cup orange juice
1 teaspoon salt
¼ teaspoon pepper
½ teaspoon dry mustard
¼ cup brown sugar

Place chops in roasting pan. Mix remaining ingredients and pour over chops. Bake at 350° for 1 hour. Baste occasionally. Yield: 6 servings.

GRILLED PORK CHOPS

1 tablespoon brown sugar
1 tablespoon cornstarch
¼ teaspoon salt
¾ cup apple juice, fruit cocktail juice, or peach juice
¼ cup ketchup
1 tablespoon vinegar
1 tablespoon Worcestershire sauce
6 rib or loin chops, 1 to 1½-inches thick

Combine brown sugar, cornstarch, and salt in small saucepan. Stir in juice, ketchup, vinegar and Worcestershire sauce. Bring to boil, stirring constantly until thickened. Reduce heat and cook slowly 1 to 2 minutes. Place chops on grill 4 to 5 inches above coals. Cook at low to moderate temperatures for 10 minutes on each side. Continue cooking, turning, and basting with sauce for 10 to 20 minutes longer. Yield: 6 servings.

STUFFED PORK CHOPS

4 (1-inch thick) pork chops, split-pocketed
1 cup croutons
1 tablespoon onion
½ cup ground peanuts
1 tablespoon parsley
butter, melted
½ to ¾ cup apple jelly, melted
1 teaspoon lemon juice

Mix croutons, onion, peanuts, and parsley with enough melted butter to hold together. Stuff chops and close with toothpicks. Brown chops on both sides in butter. Bake uncovered at 350° for 1 hour. Baste with a mixture of melted apple jelly and lemon juice. Yield: 4 servings.

TROPICAL PORK CHOPS

1 cup long grain rice
6 to 8 pork chops
salt and pepper to taste
1 (1-pound 4-ounce) can pineapple chunks
1 envelope of brown gravy mix
1 cup water
¼ cup chopped green pepper

Cook rice according to package directions. Brown pork chops; season with salt and pepper. Drain pineapple, reserving ½ cup liquid. Combine pineapple liquid, gravy mix, water, green pepper, cooked rice, and pineapple. Spoon into baking pan and top with pork chops. Bake at 350° for 45 minutes. Yield: 6 to 8 servings.

HAM AND SWISS BUNS

1 (8-ounce) package refrigerated crescent dinner rolls
1 (4-ounce) package sliced cooked ham
4 ounces packaged sliced Swiss cheese
1 teaspoon prepared mustard
1 teaspoon mayonnaise
1 egg, slightly beaten

Preheat oven to 375°. On a floured surface, separate dough into 4 rectangles. Gently pinch diagonal perforations together on each rectangle. With lightly floured rolling pin, roll each rectangle into a 7x5-inch rectangle. Arrange ham and cheese slices on dough rectangles, cutting ham and cheese to fit and leaving ½ inch rim of dough around the edges. Mix mustard and mayonnaise and spread on ham and cheese filling. Brush rim of dough with beaten egg. Fold dough over filling so the 5-inch sides meet. With a fork, firmly press edges together to seal. Place on a cookie sheet; brush with egg. Bake for 12 to 15 minutes or until browned. Serve with apple wedges and carrot sticks. Yield: 4 servings.

GRILLED HAM

1 (2-pound) center cut ham slice, 1½-inches thick
1 cup apricot preserves
½ cup light brown sugar
⅓ cup margarine
⅛ teaspoon dried cloves

Slice ham fat diagonally to prevent curling. Heat preserves, sugar, margarine, and cloves until mixture boils. Grill ham over coals 5 minutes on each side. Spread preserve mixture over ham on each side and cook 5 more minutes on each side. Yield: 4 servings.

LAMB BASTILLE

1 (1-pound) rack of lamb, cut into 4-ounce chops

Chutney Topping:
2 medium onions
3 teaspoons herb oil
3 ounces chutney

Hollandaise Sauce:
½ cup butter, melted
3 egg yolks
1 tablespoon Dijon mustard
2 tablespoons lemon juice

Breadcrumb Topping:
½ cup fresh sour dough breadcrumbs
3 teaspoons olive oil
1 clove garlic, crushed

CHUTNEY TOPPING: Peel and slice onions thin. Heat herb oil in sauté pan and lightly brown onions quickly. Add chutney and mix well. Remove from heat. Set aside.

HOLLANDAISE SAUCE: Melt butter and set aside. In a metal mixing bowl, add 3 egg yolks. Whisking constantly, slowly add butter until thick. While whisking, add mustard and lemon juice. Set aside.

BREADCRUMB TOPPING: Mix breadcrumbs, olive oil and garlic until moist. Set aside.

TO ASSEMBLE: Grill rack of lamb to desired doneness, preferably medium. Place chops on oven broiler pan and top with chutney mixture, hollandaise sauce and seasoned breadcrumb topping. Glaze under broiler for 30 seconds or until golden brown.

Goldsmith's Casual Cuisine
Augusta, Georgia

LAMB STEAKS WITH BEARNAISE SAUCE

2 tablespoons soy sauce
1 tablespoon ketchup
1 tablespoon vegetable oil
½ teaspoon coarsely ground pepper
1 clove garlic, minced
4 (1-inch thick) lamb sirloins
Bearnaise Sauce (See Index)
carved tomato shell
fresh watercress

Combine first 5 ingredients, mixing well. Brush garlic mixture over both sides of each lamb steak. Place steaks in a large shallow dish. Cover and refrigerate overnight. Grill steaks over medium coals 5 to 8 minutes on each side or to desired degree of doneness. Arrange steaks around the tomato shell that is filled with the Bearnaise Sauce; garnish platter with watercress. Yield: 4 servings. *Beef may be substituted for lamb.*

VEGETABLES AND SIDE DISHES

BAKED APPLES

6 large baking apples, peeled and cored
6 tablespoons sugar, divided
1½ teaspoons cinnamon, divided
1½ teaspoons ground nutmeg, divided

2 tablespoons butter or margarine, divided
½ to ¾ cup apple juice
red food coloring (optional)

Place apples in a shallow 2-quart casserole; pour 1 tablespoon sugar into cavity of each apple. Sprinkle each with ¼ teaspoon cinnamon and ¼ teaspoon nutmeg; top with 1 teaspoon butter. Heat apple juice to boiling; add red food coloring, if desired. Pour juice into casserole dish. Bake apples uncovered at 400° for 50 to 60 minutes or until tender, basting occasionally with juice. Yield: 6 servings.

APPLE-CRANBERRY CASSEROLE

2 cups raw cranberries, washed
3 cups unpeeled, chopped red apples

1 cup sugar

Topping:
1 cup oatmeal, uncooked
½ cup butter or margarine, melted

½ cup brown sugar
½ cup chopped pecans

Mix cranberries, apples and sugar; pour into greased casserole. Mix topping ingredients and spoon over cranberry mixture. Bake at 350° for 45 minutes. Yield: 6 servings. *Pretty and easily prepared holiday dish.*

FRIED APPLES

6 large tart apples
4 tablespoons butter
¾ cup sugar

⅛ teaspoon salt
¼ cup water

Wash apples, quarter and core. Cut quarters into thick slices lengthwise. Melt butter in heavy skillet; add apples, sugar, salt and water. Cover; steam apples on high for 6 minutes. Remove cover, lower heat and continue cooking until apples are tender and transparent. The syrup should be very thick. Yield: 4 to 6 servings. *Excellent with pork roasts or ham.*

SPICED PEACHES

1 (29-ounce) can peach halves
1 teaspoon ground cinnamon
½ teaspoon ground cloves

1 teaspoon ground allspice
¾ cup brown sugar
½ cup white vinegar

Topping:
1 (3-ounce) package cream cheese, softened

1 tablespoon cream

Drain peaches; reserve ¾ cup juice. To juice add cinnamon, cloves, allspice, brown sugar and vinegar. Bring to a boil; simmer for 5 minutes. Pour sauce over peaches. Chill several hours. Just before serving, combine cream cheese and cream and top peaches. Yield: 6 to 8 servings.

CURRIED PEARS

3 fresh pears
lemon juice
1 (8-ounce) package cream cheese, softened
2 tablespoons powdered sugar

½ teaspoon curry powder
⅓ cup chopped pecans, divided
⅓ cup coconut
maraschino cherries

Quarter and core each pear. Brush with lemon juice and refrigerate in covered container. Combine cream cheese, sugar, curry powder, coconut and half of the nuts in food processor and mix for 15 seconds. Refrigerate until firm. When ready to serve spread curry mixture on top of each wedge. Sprinkle with remaining nuts. Top with half of a cherry. Yield: 12 servings. *Delicious side dish or appetizer.*

PINEAPPLE-CHEESE CASSEROLE

1 (20-ounce) can chunk pineapple, drained, reserving 3 tablespoons juice
3 tablespoons all-purpose flour
½ cup sugar

1 cup shredded Cheddar cheese
¼ cup butter
½ cup butter-flavored crackers, crushed

Mix all ingredients, except crackers. Place in a 1-quart casserole. Top with cracker crumbs. Bake at 350° for 20 to 30 minutes. Yield: 4 servings. *Good with ham dishes.*

PINEAPPLE SOUFFLÉ

½ cup margarine, softened
1½ cups sugar
3 eggs, beaten
1 (16-ounce) can crushed pineapple, including juice
1 cup evaporated milk
5 slices bread with crust trimmed off
dash of vanilla extract

Cream margarine and sugar. Add other ingredients; pour into buttered casserole. Bake at 350° for 50 to 60 minutes. Yield: 6 servings. *Especially good with ham.*

HOT SHERRIED FRUIT

1 (1-pound) can pineapple chunks
1 (1-pound) can pear halves, cubed
1 (1-pound) can peach slices
1 (1-pound) can apricots
½ cup margarine
2 tablespoons all-purpose flour or cornstarch
½ cup sugar
1 teaspoon cinnamon
1 cup sherry

Drain all fruit; layer in a 1½ quart glass casserole dish. Melt margarine in saucepan; add flour or cornstarch, sugar, cinnamon and sherry. Blend and cook until thickened. Pour over fruit. Bake 30 minutes at 350°. Yield: 8 servings.

ALMOND RICE

2 cups uncooked instant rice
1 teaspoon butter or margarine
½ teaspoon salt
1⅔ cups hot water
¾ cup slivered almonds
¾ cup golden raisins

Combine rice, butter and salt in a deep 2-quart casserole; stir in hot water. Cover with heavy-duty plastic wrap, and *microwave* at high for 8 minutes. Let stand 3 minutes. Spread almonds in a pie plate; microwave at high 4 to 5 minutes. Stir almonds and raisins into rice; fluff rice with a fork. Yield: 6 servings.

FRIED RICE

1 cup long grain rice
1 medium potato, chopped
1 medium onion, chopped
1 carrot, grated
½ cup margarine
dash soy sauce

Prepare rice according to directions and refrigerate. Sauté potato, onion and carrot in margarine. Add rice and soy sauce. Stir, heat and serve. Yield: 4 servings.

BARBECUED RICE

1⅓ cups water
2 tablespoons dried minced onion
½ teaspoon salt
½ teaspoon pepper
¼ teaspoon oregano
1 teaspoon Worcestershire sauce
2 tablespoons ketchup
1⅓ cups precooked rice
butter

Make a sealed packet by pressing aluminum foil firmly against the inside of a mixing bowl until it takes the shape of the bowl. Mix ingredients and dot with butter. After placing ingredients in the foil, roll the edges together to form a tight seal. Remove packet from bowl. Bake over hot fire for 15 minutes or until done. Yield: 4 servings.

RICE CASSEROLE

1 (10¾-ounce) can beef bouillon
½ (10¾-ounce) can cream of mushroom soup
½ (10¾-ounce) can onion soup
1 (10¾-ounce) can water
1 cup uncooked rice
¼ cup butter or margarine

Combine all ingredients in 2½ to 3-quart casserole. Cover and bake 45 minutes at 475°. Uncover last 10 minutes of baking. Yield: 6 to 8 servings.

ASPARAGUS MORNAY

2 pounds fresh asparagus spears
2 tablespoons butter
1 tablespoon all-purpose flour
dash salt
dash white pepper
1 cup milk
½ cup shredded Cheddar cheese
¼ cup slivered almonds, toasted

Steam asparagus just until tender. Place on serving dish; keep warm. Melt butter in small saucepan over low heat. Add flour, salt and pepper; blend into butter. Add milk, stirring constantly, until mixture thickens. Reduce heat; cook 2 minutes. Add cheese; stir until melted. Pour cheese sauce over hot asparagus. Top with almonds. Serve immediately. Yield: 6 servings.

ASPARAGUS, CHEESE AND MUSHROOM CASSEROLE

2 (15-ounce) cans asparagus
2 tablespoons butter, melted
2 tablespoons all-purpose flour
2 tablespoons reserved asparagus juice
1 cup cream
¾ pound sharp cheese
1 (6-ounce) can mushrooms, drained
1 (14-ounce) can artichokes, drained
2 hard boiled eggs, diced
paprika, salt, and pepper to taste

Drain asparagus, reserving 2 tablespoons juice. Make cream sauce by mixing butter, flour, asparagus juice and cream. Add cheese. Layer half of the asparagus, mushrooms, artichokes and eggs in a 1½-quart casserole. Pour half the sauce over the vegetables. Repeat vegetable layer and top with remaining sauce. Season to taste. Bake at 325° until hot and bubbly. Yield: 8 servings.

ASPARAGUS WITH ORANGE BUTTER SAUCE

⅓ cup butter
2 tablespoons grated orange rind
¼ cup orange juice
1½ pounds fresh asparagus
peeled orange slices

Combine butter, orange rind and juice in a saucepan. Bring to a boil. Reduce heat and simmer until mixture is reduced by half and slightly thickened; stir occasionally. Set aside and keep warm. Snap off tough ends of asparagus and remove scales from stalks with a vegetable peeler. Cook asparagus, covered, in a small amount of boiling water 6 to 8 minutes or until tender; drain. Arrange asparagus in a serving dish. Pour orange sauce over asparagus. Garnish with orange slices. Yield: 6 servings.

GREEN BEAN AMANDINE

5 tablespoons butter or margarine, divided
¾ cup slivered almonds
½ teaspoon lemon-pepper seasoning
2 medium onions
3 (16-ounce) cans green beans, drained
1 teaspoon salt

Heat 2 tablespoons butter or margarine. Sauté almonds until browned. Add lemon-pepper seasoning. Remove from heat and set aside. In a saucepan, melt remaining butter; add onions; cook until tender. Add drained beans and salt; heat through. Add almond mixture just before serving. Yield: 8 to 10 servings.

SNIBBLED BEANS

2 (10-ounce) packages frozen French-style green beans
1 small onion, sliced paper-thin
6 slices bacon

Sauce:
1 egg, slightly beaten
¼ cup white vinegar
½ cup sugar
reserved bacon grease
salt and pepper to taste

BEANS: Cook beans, drain and place in 2-quart casserole. Place slices of onion on top of beans. Fry bacon until crisp; crumble and sprinkle over beans and onions.

SAUCE: Discard half of grease and heat remaining grease. Beat sauce ingredients thoroughly. Pour sauce mixture slowly into hot drippings, stirring rapidly to prevent egg from lumping. Allow dressing to come to a boil. Then pour over beans and toss well. Salt and pepper to taste. Yield: 6 servings.

PICKLED BEANS

2 (16-ounce) cans whole green beans
2 medium onions, sliced
⅓ cup bean liquid
1 cup sugar
1 cup white vinegar
2 tablespoons oil

Drain beans and reserve ⅓ cup liquid. Layer beans and onions in flat 2-quart casserole. Mix bean liquid, sugar, vinegar and oil in saucepan and bring to a boil. Remove from heat and slowly pour over beans and onion. Refrigerate overnight. Yield: 6 to 8 servings.

SPICY BAKED BEANS

1 (31-ounce) can pork and beans
1 teaspoon dry mustard
1 teaspoon salt
¼ cup brown sugar
1 green pepper, chopped
1 large onion, chopped

1 tablespoon cider vinegar
⅛ teaspoon ground cloves
¼ cup ketchup
1 teaspoon lemon juice
4 slices bacon

Combine all ingredients except bacon. Pour mixture into 2-quart baking dish. Top with bacon slices. Bake uncovered at 325° for 1½ hours. Yield: 6 servings. *Just plain good!*

RED BEANS AND RICE

1 pound dried red beans
1 meaty ham bone
2 quarts water
3 cups chopped onion
1 bunch green onions, chopped
2 cloves garlic, minced
1 tablespoon salt
dash red pepper
1 teaspoon black pepper

½ teaspoon sugar
dash liquid pepper sauce
¼ teaspoon dried oregano
¼ teaspoon dried thyme
1 tablespoon Worcestershire sauce
4 ounces tomato sauce
cooked rice
chopped green onions, garnish

Combine beans, ham bone and water. Bring to a boil and boil 3 minutes. Remove from heat and let stand one hour. Return to boil; lower heat and simmer for 3 hours. Remove ham bone from pot; tear meat from bone and return to pot. Add remaining ingredients, except rice and green onion garnish. Simmer for 1 hour. Remove ½ cup beans from pot. Mash beans and return to pot (this thickens the broth). Serve over hot cooked rice and garnish with chopped green onions. Yield: 8 servings. *Better if cooked the day before serving.*

SOUTHERN FRIED GREEN BEANS

3 pounds fresh green beans
3 tablespoons bacon or ham drippings

1 cup water
salt and pepper to taste

Wash and snap beans. Place bacon or ham drippings in a large skillet. Add beans and cook on medium high for about 10 minutes, stirring constantly. When dark brown spots appear on beans add water, salt and pepper to taste. Cover and cook for about 20 minutes. Yield: 6 servings. *Nice blend of stir-frying and southern flavor.*

BROCCOLI PUFF

2 (10-ounce) packages chopped broccoli
3 eggs, separated
1 tablespoon all-purpose flour
pinch of nutmeg
1 cup mayonnaise

1 tablespoon butter, melted
¼ teaspoon salt
¼ teaspoon pepper
¼ cup plus 1 tablespoon Parmesan cheese

Cook broccoli and drain. Beat egg yolks; add flour. Mix well. Stir in nutmeg, mayonnaise, butter, salt, pepper and cheese. Add broccoli and mix. Beat egg whites until stiff. Gently fold into mixture. Pour into lightly buttered 9-inch square baking dish. Bake at 350° for 30 minutes. Cut into squares to serve. Yield: 8 servings.

ORIENTAL BROCCOLI RICE CASSEROLE

2 cups cooked white rice
3 (10-ounce) packages frozen chopped broccoli, cooked and drained
1 (10¾-ounce) cans cream of mushroom soup
1 (8-ounce) can sliced water chestnuts, drained

1 (8-ounce) can bamboo shoots, drained
1 (8-ounce) jar processed cheese spread
½ cup butter, melted
1 cup shredded Cheddar cheese
1 (2-ounce) jar pimentos, drained

Combine all ingredients except Cheddar cheese and pimentos. Pour into greased 3-quart casserole. Sprinkle Cheddar cheese and pimentos over the top. Bake at 325° for 30 to 40 minutes. May be prepared ahead and frozen. Yield: 8 to 10 servings.

MARINATED BRUSSELS SPROUTS

2 (8-ounce) boxes frozen Brussels sprouts
½ cup tarragon vinegar
½ cup vegetable oil
1 clove garlic, minced

1 tablespoon sugar
1 teaspoon salt
dash of hot pepper sauce
1 small onion, minced

Cook Brussels sprouts just until tender and drain. Combine remaining ingredients and pour over hot Brussels sprouts. Marinate 3 to 4 days before serving. Drain and serve. Yield: 4 servings.

HONEY ORANGE BEETS

1 tablespoon minced onion
2 tablespoons margarine
2 tablespoons cornstarch
1 teaspoon grated orange rind
1 cup orange juice

¼ cup honey
2 tablespoons lemon juice
4 cups sliced beets, cooked and drained (may use canned beets)

In a large saucepan, sauté onion in butter. Stir in cornstarch. Add remaining ingredients, except beets. Bring to a boil, stirring constantly. Boil one minute. Reduce heat; add beets and cook until heated through. Yield: 8 servings.

CARROT CASSEROLE

6 large carrots
½ cup butter, softened
1 cup sugar

3 tablespoons all-purpose flour
3 eggs, beaten
½ teaspoon cinnamon

Cook carrots until tender. Grate carrots into large bowl. Add butter, sugar, flour, eggs and cinnamon. Mix well. Pour into greased casserole dish. Bake at 350° for 30 to 40 minutes. Yield: 4 servings. *Recipe may be doubled.*

QUICK ORANGE CARROTS

5 medium carrots, cut in thin strips

2 tablespoons butter
2 tablespoons orange marmalade

Cook carrots in salted water 15 minutes or until tender. Drain and add butter. Cover and let stand until butter melts. Stir in marmalade to glaze carrots. Serve immediately. Yield: 4 servings. *Note: Remove tops of carrots before refrigerating. Tops drain moisture from carrots, making them limp and dry.*

CAULIFLOWER WITH MUSTARD SAUCE

1 medium cauliflower
½ cup mayonnaise
½ teaspoon grated onion
1 teaspoon prepared mustard
¼ cup grated Parmesan cheese

Wash cauliflower and cut into bite-size pieces. Boil in salted water until tender (7 to 10 minutes) and drain. Mix remaining ingredients and pour over cauliflower. Serve immediately. Yield: 6 servings.

CREAMED CORN

3 tablespoons butter
3 tablespoons bacon grease
10 ears fresh corn, grated
water
salt and pepper to taste

Melt butter and bacon grease in heavy skillet. Grate corn and measure. Add corn and water (equal to ½ amount of corn) to skillet; season with salt and pepper. Cook over low heat until thickened, 30 to 45 minutes, stirring frequently. Yield: 6 to 8 servings.

CORN PUDDING

3 eggs
1 (16-ounce) can creamed corn
1 (16-ounce) can whole kernel corn
½ cup whole milk
½ cup sugar
½ teaspoon salt
⅛ teaspoon pepper
2 tablespoons cornstarch
2 tablespoons butter or margarine, melted
½ teaspoon vanilla extract

In a large mixing bowl, beat eggs just until blended. Add remaining ingredients and stir. Pour mixture into a greased 2-quart casserole dish. Bake at 350° for 1 hour. Yield: 6 servings.

SWEET AND SOUR CUCUMBERS

½ cup white vinegar
⅓ cup salad oil
2 tablespoons sugar
1 teaspoon salt
¼ teaspoon white pepper
¼ teaspoon oregano leaves
3 medium cucumbers, sliced very thin

In a large bowl, combine all ingredients. Cover and refrigerate at least 45 minutes, stirring occasionally. Yield: 4 cups. *Good with grilled meats and fish.*

CREOLE EGGPLANT

1 onion, chopped
1 green pepper, chopped
½ cup margarine
½ cup raw rice
1 large eggplant, peeled and chopped
1 (14-ounce) can tomatoes
¼ teaspoon dried basil
¼ teaspoon dried oregano
1 cup beef bouillon
½ teaspoon salt
½ teaspoon white pepper
2 dashes hot pepper sauce
1 cup grated Parmesan cheese

Sauté onion and green pepper in margarine. Add rice and sauté until rice is brown. Add remaining ingredients, except cheese. Pour into greased 2-quart casserole; cover and bake at 350° for 30 minutes. Remove cover and top with cheese. Bake for 20 minutes uncovered. Yield: 6 to 8 servings.

EGGPLANT CASSEROLE

1 eggplant, peeled, cooked and drained
1 egg, beaten
⅔ cup evaporated milk
2 tablespoons butter, melted
1 small onion, chopped
¾ cup dry breadcrumbs
1 cup shredded sharp Cheddar cheese, divided

Combine eggplant, egg, milk, butter, onion, crumbs and ½ cup cheese. Pour into 1½ to 2-quart baking dish. Sprinkle top with rest of cheese. Bake at 350° for 30 minutes. Yield: 6 servings.

FRIED EGGPLANT

2 eggs
¾ cup milk
2 medium eggplants, peeled
1 cup all-purpose flour
¾ cup cracker meal

½ teaspoon salt
½ teaspoon white pepper
oil for deep frying
Parmesan cheese

Beat eggs and milk together. Cut eggplant into julienne strips. Dredge in flour; dip in egg mixture. Roll strips in meal seasoned with salt and pepper. Fry strips in deep fat for 5 minutes. Drain and sprinkle with Parmesan cheese. Yield: 6 servings.

MUSHROOM CASSEROLE

1 pound fresh mushrooms
2 tablespoons butter
12 slices day-old white bread
5 eggs
2½ cups milk
1 teaspoon salt
¼ teaspoon pepper
¾ teaspoon dry mustard
½ pound sharp Cheddar cheese, shredded, divided

½ cup butter, melted, divided
⅛ teaspoon Worcestershire sauce
1 teaspoon prepared mustard
1 teaspoon lemon juice
1 (10-ounce) can cream of mushroom soup

Remove stems from mushrooms; sauté caps and stems separately in butter and set aside. Remove crusts from 6 slices of bread and crumble into 2-quart buttered baking dish. Mix eggs, milk, salt, pepper and dry mustard. Pour *half* of egg mixture over crumbled bread. Top with ¼ pound shredded cheese and ¼ cup melted butter. Combine sautéed stems with Worcestershire sauce, prepared mustard and lemon juice. Spread stems in baking dish. Crumble remaining 6 slices of bread into casserole. Top with remaining milk and egg mixture. Add remaining ¼ pound shredded cheese and ¼ cup melted butter. Spread caps of sautéed mushrooms on top. Refrigerate at least 8 hours (no longer than 48 hours). Top with soup. Bake at 350° for 45 minutes. Serve warm. Yield: 10 servings. *Delicious brunch casserole.*

VIDALIA ONION CASSEROLE

3 cups thinly sliced Vidalia onions
¼ cup butter or margarine
1 cup herb stuffing mix
2 tablespoons butter or margarine
2 eggs
¾ cup milk
salt and pepper to taste
½ to ¾ cup shredded Cheddar cheese

Cut onions in quarters and slice very thin. Set aside. Melt ¼ cup margarine or butter in saucepan and pour over stuffing. Mix thoroughly and line 8-inch pie pan or 1-quart casserole dish with stuffing mixture. Melt 2 tablespoons butter in frying pan. Sauté onions until tender; pour over stuffing in casserole dish. Mix eggs, milk, salt and pepper. Pour mixture over onions. Sprinkle cheese over onions. Bake at 350° for 45 minutes or until slightly brown. Yield: 8 to 10 servings.

FRENCH ONION PIE

1 9-inch pie shell
4 cups onions, sliced
3 tablespoons butter
2 eggs plus 2 egg yolks
1 teaspoon salt
dash of Worcestershire sauce
½ teaspoon prepared mustard
1½ cups half-and-half
¼ pound Swiss cheese, shredded
½ cup grated Parmesan cheese
½ pound Gruyére cheese, shredded

Sauté onions in 3 tablespoons butter until tender. Set aside. Bake pie shell 5 minutes. Remove from oven. Beat eggs and yolks. Add salt, Worcestershire sauce and mustard. Scald cream and add cheeses. Stir a small amount of hot cheese sauce into egg mixture; stir well. Gradually add egg mixture to sauce. Put onions in pie shell and top with egg mixture. Bake at 300° for 45 minutes. Yield: 6 servings. *Good with salad as main dish or serve as a side dish.*

FRIED OKRA

½ cup all-purpose cornmeal
¼ cup all-purpose flour
1 teaspoon salt
¼ teaspoon pepper

4 cups tender okra, cut into
 ½-inch slices
hot vegetable oil

Combine dry ingredients in a paper bag; mix well. Rinse okra; drain on paper towel. While damp, shake okra in paper bag to coat with dry ingredients. Fry okra in hot vegetable oil until golden brown. Yield: 6 servings.

OKRA AND TOMATOES

5 fresh ripe tomatoes or 1
 (16-ounce) can tomatoes,
 undrained
1 pound okra

1 large onion, chopped
2 tablespoons margarine or
 bacon fat
salt and pepper

Peel and chop tomatoes. Wash and slice okra into rounds ½-inch thick. Sauté onion and okra in margarine about 5 minutes. Add tomatoes, salt and pepper. Cover and simmer 20 minutes. Stir occasionally to prevent scorching. Yield: 4 to 6 servings.

GREEN PEA CASSEROLE

1 (10-ounce) can cream of
 mushroom soup
2 cups shredded Cheddar cheese
1 (2-ounce) jar diced pimento
2 (10-ounce) packages frozen
 green peas, cooked and
 drained

½ cup chopped green pepper
½ medium onion, chopped
½ cup margarine

Heat soup in a medium saucepan; add cheese, pimento and peas. Sauté pepper and onion in margarine. Combine with pea mixture; pour into 2-quart casserole. Bake at 350° for 30 minutes or until bubbly. Yield: 8 to 10 servings.

CLAFOUTI OF PEAS

3 eggs
1½ cups milk
⅔ cup all-purpose flour
2 tablespoons butter, melted
1 tablespoon sugar

½ teaspoon each pepper and thyme
1½ cup cooked English peas
2 tablespoons butter, melted

In a blender, combine eggs, milk, flour, 2 tablespoons melted butter, sugar, pepper and thyme; blend at high speed for 5 seconds. Scrape down any flour from sides of container and blend for 5 seconds longer. Pour batter into a bowl; cover and allow to stand at room temperature for 1 hour. Pour 1 cup of batter into 1½ quart soufflé dish. Toss peas with 2 tablespoons melted butter. Spread peas over batter; pour remaining batter over peas. Bake at 350° for 45 to 50 minutes or until puffed and browned. Yield: 4 servings.

STUFFED POTATOES

4 large baking potatoes
4 tablespoons margarine, softened
1½ cups buttermilk

⅓ cup sour cream
salt to taste
½ cup green onion, chopped
sharp Cheddar cheese, shredded

Wash potatoes thoroughly. Bake in conventional or microwave oven until done. Remove from oven. While potatoes are still warm, use sharp knife to cut in half lengthwise. Use spoon to scoop out potato pulp, being sure to keep shell intact. Place pulp in large mixing bowl; add margarine, buttermilk, sour cream and salt. Beat with electric mixer until creamy. Stir in onions. Spoon potato mixture back into shells and place on foil-lined cookie sheet. Just before serving, sprinkle cheese on top of each potato and place under broiler until cheese is melted and potatoes are hot. Serve immediately. Yield: 8 servings.

EASY POTATO BAKE

8 large potatoes
½ cup oil
4 tablespoons Parmesan, divided
salt, pepper and garlic salt to taste
paprika

Wash potatoes and cut into wedges. Do not peel. Arrange potatoes in shallow baking dish and coat with oil; add 2 tablespoons cheese and seasonings. Sprinkle paprika and 2 tablespoons Parmesan cheese on top. Bake at 350° uncovered for 1 hour or until golden brown. Yield: 6 to 8 servings.

POTATO CASSEROLE

1 (8-ounce) jar cheese spread
1 cup sour cream
½ cup butter
1 large onion
1 (32-ounce) package frozen shredded potatoes

Mix cheese and sour cream; set aside. Sauté onions in butter until tender. Place potatoes in a deep, medium baking dish; add cheese mixture. Pour butter and onion mixture over top and stir. Bake at 400° for 30 minutes, stirring mixture twice during baking. Yield: 6 to 8 servings.

COUNTRY POTATOES

12 red or new potatoes
salt and pepper to taste
3 cups grated sharp Cheddar cheese
8 strips cooked bacon, crumbled
½ cup butter, melted

Boil potatoes with skins on until done. Drain and let cool. Slice unpeeled potatoes thin. Butter bottom of 9x12-inch baking dish. Layer half of potatoes, salt, pepper, half of cheese and half of bacon in casserole. Dribble half of the butter over the layer. Repeat layers. Bake uncovered at 350° until bubbling hot, about 15 minutes. Yield: 8 servings. *This recipe is guaranteed to please! Freezes well.*

SESAME POTATO STICKS

8 medium baking potatoes
½ cup sesame seeds
½ cup butter or margarine, melted
salt
paprika

Peel potatoes; cut into 1-inch thick strips. Sprinkle sesame seeds on waxed paper. Dip potato sticks in butter; dip one side of potato sticks in sesame seeds. Place sticks, seed side up, on a well-greased baking sheet. Sprinkle with salt and paprika. Bake at 400° about 40 minutes or until done. Yield: 8 servings.

GRATED SWEET POTATO CASSEROLE

1½ cups sugar
½ cup milk
3 cups raw sweet potatoes, grated
2 eggs
½ cup butter or margarine
⅛ teaspoon soda
½ teaspoon cinnamon
¾ cup buttermilk
½ cup ground pecans
½ cup raisins

Mix sugar and milk; add potatoes, eggs and butter. Add soda, cinnamon, buttermilk, pecans and raisins. Bake at 400° for 1 hour in greased casserole. Stir occasionally. Yield: 6 to 8 servings.

YAM BAKE

2 apples, cored, sliced
⅓ cup chopped pecans
½ cup packed brown sugar
½ teaspoon cinnamon
2 (17-ounce) cans yams, drained
¼ cup margarine
2 cups miniature marshmallows

Toss apples and nuts with brown sugar and cinnamon. Beginning with yams, alternate layers of yams and apples in 1½-quart casserole. Dot with margarine. Cover and bake at 350° for 35 to 40 minutes. Remove cover; sprinkle marshmallows on top. Broil until lightly browned. Yield: 6 to 8 servings.

EASY SWEET POTATO SOUFFLÉ

3 cups cooked mashed sweet potatoes
2 eggs

½ cup milk
salt
1 cup brown sugar

Topping:
¼ cup butter
½ cup all-purpose flour

1 cup sugar
1 cup nuts

Beat first 5 ingredients together and pour into a 9-inch square baking dish. Mix butter, flour, sugar and nuts. Spread on top of potatoes. Bake at 350° for 30 minutes. Yield: 6 servings.

SPINACH-CHEESE CASSEROLE

⅓ cup butter
2 tablespoons chopped onion
½ teaspoon salt
¼ teaspoon garlic salt
¼ teaspoon pepper
2 eggs

¼ cup milk
2 cups cooked rice
2½ cups shredded sharp Cheddar cheese, divided
1 package frozen spinach, thawed

Melt butter and sauté onion. Add salt, garlic salt and pepper; mix well. Remove from heat. Beat eggs and milk. Combine the two mixtures. Combine rice, 2 cups cheese and spinach; mix well. Stir in egg mixture. Sprinkle top with remaining cheese. Bake at 350° for 25 to 30 minutes. Yield: 6 to 8 servings.

SPINACH-RICOTTA STUFFED TOMATOES

1 (10-ounce) box frozen spinach
8 ripe red tomatoes, the riper the better
salt
3 tablespoons olive oil
1 cup finely chopped onions
salt and freshly ground pepper
1 cup ricotta cheese
2 egg yolks
¼ cup grated Parmesan cheese
¼ cup chopped parsley
Parmesan for sprinkling on top
parsley for sprinkling on top

Defrost spinach and squeeze dry. Wash tomatoes and cut off tops. Remove pulp, being careful not to pierce sides of tomatoes. Salt cavities; turn tomatoes upside down on a paper towel and drain for 30 minutes. Heat oil in heavy skillet; add onions and cook until tender (about 15 minutes). Chop spinach and add to onions. Season with salt and pepper. Cook over low heat, stirring occasionally, for 10 minutes. In a mixing bowl beat the cheese and egg yolks thoroughly. Add spinach mixture, Parmesan and parsley. Pat tomato cavities dry. Spoon ½ cup spinach mixture into each tomato. Top with additional Parmesan and parsley. Arrange tomatoes in a shallow baking dish and bake at 350° for 20 minutes or until filling is hot and bubbly. Yield: 8 servings.

TOMATOES WITH ARTICHOKE HEARTS

4 fresh tomatoes
2 (6-ounce) jars marinated artichokes, quartered
3 green onions, chopped
4 tablespoons butter
½ teaspoon leaf basil
2 tablespoons sugar
salt and pepper to taste

Grease shallow baking dish. Slice tomatoes and place in bottom of casserole. Place quartered artichokes on top of tomatoes. Sauté onions in butter until tender. Add basil, sugar, salt and pepper; pour over tomatoes. Bake at 325° for 10 to 15 minutes. Yield: 4 to 6 servings. *Good side dish with fish.*

BAKED CHEDDAR TOMATOES

5 medium tomatoes, cut in half crosswise
olive oil
¾ teaspoon salt
1 cup soft breadcrumbs
1 cup shredded Cheddar cheese
¼ cup butter, melted
1 teaspoon dried whole basil
½ teaspoon red pepper

Brush the cut surface of tomato halves with olive oil; sprinkle with salt. Place tomato halves in a 13x9x2-inch baking dish. Combine the remaining ingredients, mixing well. Spoon over cut surface of tomatoes. Bake at 350° for 12 to 15 minutes or until tomatoes are thoroughly heated and cheese melts. Yield: 10 servings.

FRIED GREEN TOMATOES

4 large green tomatoes
½ cup all-purpose flour or all-purpose cornmeal
1 teaspoon salt
¼ teaspoon pepper
bacon fat

Cut firm tomatoes in ¼-inch slices. Mix flour or cornmeal with salt and pepper. Dip tomato slices in seasoned mixture. Place in heavy skillet containing melted bacon fat. Fry slowly until brown, turning once. Drain tomatoes on paper towels. Yield: 6 servings.

SAUTÉED CHERRY TOMATOES

6 tablespoons sweet butter
1 clove garlic, minced
3 pints cherry tomatoes, stemmed, rinsed and patted dry
salt and freshly ground pepper
2 tablespoons freshly chopped basil
Parmesan cheese

Melt butter in a heavy skillet. Sauté garlic for 1 minute; add tomatoes. Shake and roll tomatoes in butter until they are coated with butter and heated through (about 15 minutes). Do not overcook! Sprinkle with salt, pepper, basil and Parmesan cheese. Serve immediately. Yield: 6 to 8 servings. *Heating the tomatoes adds to their natural sweetness. Do not overcook or tomatoes will become mushy.*

BAKED STUFFED TOMATOES

8 ripe tomatoes
salt
1 bunch green onions, chopped
2 cloves garlic, minced
¼ cup butter
¼ cup olive or vegetable oil
1 tablespoon dried oregano leaves

½ teaspoon dried thyme
½ teaspoon dried basil
2 bay leaves
2 dashes liquid pepper sauce
2 (3-ounce) cans chopped mushrooms, undrained
1 cup Italian seasoned breadcrumbs
½ cup grated Parmesan cheese

Cut away stem end of tomatoes. Scoop out pulp; chop and set aside. Lightly salt inside of tomatoes; turn upside down on paper towel to drain. Sauté onions and garlic in butter and oil until soft; add oregano, thyme, basil, bay leaves, pepper sauce and mushrooms with liquid. Cook 5 minutes. Add tomato pulp. Simmer 20 minutes. Remove bay leaves. Add breadcrumbs and cheese; mix well. Stuff shells with mixture and sprinkle with additional cheese. Bake at 350° for 10 minutes. Yield: 8 servings.

SQUASH MEDLEY

1 pound zucchini squash, sliced
1 pound yellow crookneck squash, sliced
1 pound green scalloped-edge summer squash, cut up
¼ cup cracker crumbs
2 eggs, well beaten
½ green pepper, diced

2 stalks celery, chopped
6 green onions (scallions), chopped or ½ cup chopped yellow onions
¼ cup butter
½ cup Parmesan cheese
salt, pepper or cayenne to taste
paprika

Cook squash until tender. Pour off all but a small amount of liquid. Mash squash. Mix in cracker crumbs and eggs. Sauté green pepper, celery and onion in butter until soft. Add to squash mixture; add cheese and seasonings. Place in a greased casserole and refrigerate until ready to bake. Bake uncovered at 350° for 45 minutes. While hot, sprinkle with Parmesan cheese and paprika. Yield: 8 servings.

VEGETABLES AND SIDE DISHES

STUFFED SQUASH

3 medium yellow squash
½ cup thick White Sauce (See Index)
1 tablespoon grated onion
2 tablespoons chopped green pepper
3 hard boiled eggs, chopped, optional
1 cup grated Parmesan cheese
crumbled bacon or bacon bits to taste
½ cup buttered breadcrumbs
paprika

Boil whole squash about 10 minutes or until tender. Drain; cut squash in half and scoop out center leaving shell about ½ to ¾-inch thick. Mash pulp; add white sauce, onion, green pepper, eggs, half of cheese and bacon. Fill shells with mixture; sprinkle with crumbs, remaining cheese and dash of paprika. Place in shallow pan with a small amount of water. Bake at 375° for 25 to 30 minutes or until brown. Yield: 3 to 4 servings.

MOZZARELLA ZUCCHINI SPEARS

3 small zucchini
1 tablespoon salad oil
½ teaspoon salt
¼ teaspoon basil
½ cup mozzarella cheese, shredded

Cut each zucchini lengthwise into quarters. Over medium-low heat, in hot oil, cook zucchini until browned and tender, about 10 to 15 minutes. Turn occasionally. Sprinkle mozzarella over zucchini spears and season with salt and basil. Cover and cook until cheese melts. Yield: 4 to 6 servings.

ZUCCHINI PROVENÇAL

1½ pounds zucchini, cubed
3 tablespoons vegetable oil
1 clove garlic, minced
juice of ½ lemon
2 green onions, chopped
ground black pepper
¼ teaspoon dried oregano
¼ teaspoon parsley
¼ teaspoon dried thyme
¼ teaspoon dried basil
1 (14½-ounce) can tomato wedges

Sauté zucchini in oil with garlic, lemon, onion, pepper, oregano, parsley, thyme and basil for 5 minutes. Add tomatoes; simmer 15 minutes. Yield: 4 servings. *Excellent side dish with fish.*

VEGETABLES AND PASTA

4 tablespoons vegetable oil
1 large sweet onion, sliced
2 stalks celery, sliced
1 small green pepper, sliced in strips
1 small zucchini, sliced
2 small yellow squash, sliced
1 (16-ounce) can tomatoes
¼ cup black olives, sliced
1 cup flat, thin noodles cooked according to directions (2 cups cooked)
Parmesan cheese

Heat oil; sauté onion, celery, green pepper, zucchini and squash until tender. Add tomatoes and heat 2 to 3 minutes. Remove from heat and add olives. Serve over hot buttered noodles. Sprinkle cheese over vegetables before serving. Yield: 4 servings.

RATATOUILLE PROVENÇAL

6 tablespoons olive oil
3 onions, coarsely chopped
2 green peppers, cored, seeded, coarsely chopped
4 cloves garlic, minced
1 medium unpared eggplant, cut in 1-inch cubes
3 medium zucchini, quartered and cut in 1-inch lengths
1 bay leaf
2 pounds fresh tomatoes, peeled, seeded and cut in 1-inch cubes or may substitute 2 cups canned, drained, pear-shaped tomatoes
½ cup chopped fresh parsley
2 teaspoons fresh thyme or ½ teaspoon dried thyme
1 tablespoon fresh chopped basil or ¼ teaspoon dried basil
salt and pepper to taste

Heat oil in large skillet; add onions, green peppers and garlic. Cook until onions are transparent. Add eggplant, zucchini, bay leaf, tomatoes, herbs, salt and pepper. Simmer, uncovered, 20 minutes or until vegetables are tender. Serve hot or cold. If served cold, serve on cracker rounds with lemon wedge garnish. Yield: 6 servings.

VEGETABLE SPAGHETTI

¼ cup chopped celery
¼ cup chopped bell pepper
1 medium onion, chopped
bacon drippings
1 (16-ounce) can tomatoes, mashed
1 tablespoon sugar
salt and pepper
1½ cups shredded sharp Cheddar cheese
¼ pound spaghetti, cooked

Sauté celery, bell pepper and onion in small amount of bacon drippings. Add tomatoes, sugar, salt and pepper. Simmer about ½ hour. Add cheese and spaghetti. Let stand 5 minutes. Yield: 4 servings.

PASTA PRIMAVERA

3 tablespoons olive oil
1 clove garlic
1½ cups broccoli, chopped
1½ cups zucchini, chopped
½ cup fresh or frozen green peas
1 cup green beans, cut in 1-inch pieces
4 cups chopped ripe tomatoes
1 teaspoon parsley
1 teaspoon dried basil
½ teaspoon pepper
½ teaspoon dried thyme
1 teaspoon dried oregano
dash red pepper
1 quart water
1 pound spaghetti
½ cup grated Parmesan cheese

SAUCE: Heat oil in a large skillet and sauté minced garlic. Add broccoli, zucchini, peas and beans; stir until tender, yet crisp (3 to 4 minutes). Add tomatoes, parsley, basil, pepper, thyme, oregano and red pepper. Simmer 1 to 2 minutes or until tomatoes are tender but firm.

SPAGHETTI: Bring one quart of water to a rolling boil. Add pasta and cook 8 to 10 minutes. Drain pasta and put in a large bowl. Add the primavera sauce to the spaghetti and top with grated cheese. Toss and serve immediately. Yield: 6 servings.

SWEET TOOTH

186 DESSERTS

AMBROSIA

4 oranges, peeled and sectioned
2 grapefruit, peeled and sectioned
1 (20-ounce) can pineappple chunks, undrained
2 tablespoons California brandy
2 tablespoons powdered sugar
1 cup shredded coconut, toasted

In medium bowl, combine orange and grapefruit sections with pineapple chunks. Mix together brandy and powdered sugar. Pour over fruit. Cover and chill. At serving time, sprinkle with coconut. Yield: 6 servings.

BRANDIED FRUIT

1 (15¼-ounce) can pineapple chunks
1 (16-ounce) can sliced peaches
1 (10-ounce) jar maraschino cherries
1 (17-ounce) can apricot halves
1¼ cups sugar
1¼ cups brandy

Drain fruits. Combine all ingredients and place in nonmetalic container. Stir and cover. Let stand at room temperature 3 weeks. Stir 2 times a week. Serve over ice cream or pound cake. To replenish fruit, reserve 1 cup starter and add 1 cup sugar and 1 of the fruits every 1 to 3 weeks. Yield: 6 cups.

CARAMEL VANILLA FRUIT

1 (8-ounce) carton vanilla yogurt
3 tablespoons caramel vanilla liqueur
brown sugar
sliced bananas
seedless grapes

Combine yogurt and liqueur. Place bananas and grapes in individual serving dishes. Spoon sauce over fruit. Sprinkle with brown sugar. Yield: 1¼ cups sauce.

AMARETTO BLUEBERRIES

1 pint fresh blueberries
1 pint vanilla ice cream, softened

⅓ cup amaretto

Place blueberries in four dessert dishes. Combine softened ice cream and liqueur. Spoon over blueberries and serve immediately. Yield: 4 servings.

BLUEBERRY DUMPLINGS

2½ cups fresh blueberries
⅓ cup sugar
dash salt

1 cup water
1 tablespoon lemon juice

Dumplings:
1 cup all-purpose flour
2 tablespoons sugar
2 teaspoons baking powder
¼ teaspoon salt

1 tablespoon butter or margarine, softened
½ cup milk

Bring first four ingredients to a boil. Cover and simmer 5 minutes. Add lemon juice. Sift dry ingredients. Cut in butter or margarine. Add milk all at once. Stir only until flour is moistened. Drop batter from tablespoons into bubbling sauce. Cover tightly. Cook over low heat for 10 minutes and do not peek. Yield: 6 servings.

LEMON COOLER

3 cups water
1 cup sugar
juice of 3 lemons

3 bananas, mashed
1 (20-ounce) can crushed pineapple, drained

Boil water and sugar for 5 minutes. Cool and add fruit juice and fruit. Freeze, stirring occasionally. Process in blender before serving. Yield: 4 to 6 servings. *Good summer dessert!*

STRAWBERRY DELIGHT

1 envelope unflavored gelatin
¼ cup orange juice
1 (10¾-ounce) loaf frozen pound cake, thawed
¼ cup orange-flavored liqueur, divided
1 (14-ounce) can sweetened condensed milk
3 tablespoons lemon juice
3 egg whites, stiffly beaten
1 cup whipping cream, whipped
3 cups sliced fresh strawberries or frozen strawberries, drained
¾ cup slivered almonds

Sprinkle gelatin over orange juice in a cup; place cup in a bowl of hot water and stir until gelatin is dissolved. Set aside. Cut pound cake into ½-inch slices; cut each slice diagonally into 2 triangles. Dip triangles in liqueur. Place triangles in a 2½-quart round-bottomed bowl, placing narrowest end of triangles in center of bowl. Leave some space at the top of the bowl. Combine milk, lemon juice, gelatin mixture and remaining liqueur in a large bowl; fold in egg whites, whipped cream, strawberries and almonds. Spoon over cake. Cover; refrigerate overnight. Garnish with strawberries. Yield: 8 to 10 servings. *Glass bowl makes attractive serving dish.*

STRAWBERRIES ROMANOFF

2 pints ripe strawberries
⅓ cup sugar
⅓ cup orange liqueur
1 orange
¾ cup whipping cream
2 tablespoons sugar

Remove stems from strawberries. Rinse and drain well; pat dry. Place strawberries in a bowl and add ⅓ cup sugar and orange liqueur. Using a sharp knife, cut thin strips of peel from the orange (do not cut white pulp). Cut peel into thin strips. Fold into strawberries. Cover and refrigerate at least 1 hour. When ready to serve, whip cream with 2 tablespoons sugar. Top strawberries with whipped cream. Yield: 8 servings.

DIPPED STRAWBERRIES

1 pound white chocolate
2 quarts whole strawberries, chilled

1 (7-ounce) package flaked coconut

Wash berries but do not remove stems. Refrigerate berries. Bring water to boil in bottom of double boiler. Remove from heat; place chocolate in top boiler and melt slowly. Dry berries thoroughly. Holding berries by stem, dip into melted chocolate to coat half of berry. Dip coated strawberry in coconut. Place on waxed paper until set. May be made 24 hours ahead.

MACÉDOINE DE FRUITS

3 cups fresh fruits, peeled and sliced (peaches, nectarines, cantelope, pears, apricots, bananas; or, whole strawberries, raspberries or blueberries)

½ cup sugar
½ cup water
3 tablespoons fruit liqueur
sprinkling of toasted sliced almonds

Choose 2 to 4 fruits for macédoine (medley). Make a sugar syrup by boiling sugar and water for 5 minutes. Add liqueur to syrup. Pour over fruits. Cover and chill. Serve within 3 to 4 hours or fruit flavors will lose their individuality. Garnish with almonds. Yield: 4 to 6 servings.

CHERRIES JUBILEE

1 (16½-ounce) can pitted black cherries
¾ cup currant jelly

½ cup brandy
1½ quarts vanilla ice cream

Drain cherries. In chafing dish over low heat, melt currant jelly, stirring gently. Add cherries to jelly, stirring constantly until mixture simmers. Pour brandy into center of fruit and do not stir. Allow brandy to heat undisturbed in chafing dish. When warm, carefully light with match. Immediately spoon flaming fruit over ice cream. Serve immediately. Yield: 8 servings.

PEACH CLAFOUTI

5 tablespoons sugar divided
3 cups fresh peaches, peeled and sliced
1 cup milk
1 cup half-and-half

3 eggs
¼ cup all-purpose flour
pinch salt
1 teaspoon vanilla extract
vanilla ice cream

Butter a 1½-quart baking dish or deep dish pie pan. Sprinkle bottom with 2 tablespoons sugar. Arrange peaches in bottom of baking dish. Blend milk, half-and-half, eggs, flour and salt for 2 minutes. Add vanilla and remaining sugar. Blend for 30 seconds. Pour over fruit. Bake at 375° for 45 minutes or until puffed and golden brown. Serve hot, topped with vanilla ice cream. Yield: 6 servings.

CHERRY TORTE

1¼ cups graham cracker crumbs
4 tablespoons margarine, melted
¼ cup sugar
1 (8-ounce) package cream cheese, softened
1 cup powdered sugar
2 tablespoons milk

1 package powdered instant whipped topping
1 cup nuts, chopped
1 teaspoon almond extract
1 teaspoon vanilla extract
1 can cherry pie filling

FIRST LAYER: Line bottom of 8-inch square dish with crust made by mixing graham cracker crumbs, margarine and sugar.

SECOND LAYER: Blend cream cheese, powdered sugar and milk. Spread over crust.

THIRD LAYER: Mix whipped topping according to directions. Add nuts, almond and vanilla extracts. Spread over second layer. Spread pie filling over top. Chill several hours. Cut into squares and serve. Yield: 8 servings. *Very pretty when cut!*

BROWNIE BAKED ALASKA

1 quart coffee-almond ice cream
½ cup margarine, softened
2 cups sugar, divided
2 eggs
1 cup all-purpose flour
½ teaspoon baking powder
2 tablespoons cocoa
½ teaspoon salt
1 teaspoon vanilla extract
5 egg whites

Line a 1-quart mixing bowl (with 7-inch diameter) with waxed paper, leaving an overhang around the edges. Pack ice cream into bowl and freeze until very firm. Combine margarine and 1 cup sugar, creaming until light and fluffy. Add eggs, one at a time, beating well after each addition. Combine flour, baking powder, cocoa and salt; add to creamed mixture, mixing well. Stir in vanilla. Spoon batter into a greased and floured 8-inch round cake pan. Bake at 350° for 25 to 30 minutes. Let cool in pan 10 minutes; remove to wire rack and allow to cool completely. Place cake on a 9 or 10-inch pie pan. Invert bowl of ice cream onto brownie layer leaving waxed paper intact; remove bowl. Place ice cream-topped cake in freezer. Beat egg whites until frothy; gradually beat in 1 cup sugar. Continue beating until stiff peaks form. Remove cake from freezer and spread meringue over entire surface, making sure edges are sealed. Bake at 500° for 2 minutes or until meringue peaks are browned. Serve immediately. Yield: 10 to 12 servings. *Note: After meringue is sealed, dessert may be returned to freezer and kept frozen up to 1 week.*

LADY FINGER DESSERT

3 packages lady fingers
2 (3½-ounce) packages instant chocolate pudding
6 cups milk
2 (3½-ounce) packages instant vanilla pudding
1 (12-ounce) container frozen dairy topping

Line bottom and sides of 9-inch spring-form pan with split lady fingers. Mix chocolate puddings with 3 cups milk. Pour over lady fingers. Let set slightly. Top with layer of lady fingers. Mix vanilla puddings with 3 cups milk. Pour over 2nd layer of lady fingers. Let set slightly. Top with whipped dairy topping. Refrigerate. When ready to serve, remove pan sides. Place bottom of pan on serving plate. Yield: 12 servings.

LEMON ALMOND TART

Pastry:
1⅓ cups plus 1 tablespoon all-purpose flour
⅓ cup sugar
¼ teaspoon salt
⅓ cup sweet butter, chilled
3 egg yolks
½ teaspoon vanilla extract

Filling:
3 eggs
¾ cup sugar
7 tablespoons lemon juice
1 heaping tablespoon finely grated lemon peel
⅔ cup sweet butter, melted
1 cup ground blanched almonds
¼ cup slivered almonds

PASTRY: Combine flour, sugar and salt; blend well. Cut in butter until mixture resembles coarse meal. Beat yolks with vanilla. Add to flour mixture and blend until dough forms a ball. Flatten dough; wrap in plastic and refrigerate 1 hour or longer. Position rack in lower third of oven and preheat to 375°. Roll dough out onto lightly floured surface to ⅛-inch thickness. Fit into 10-inch pie plate. Set slightly smaller pie plate or pan inside crust and fill with dried beans. Bake 10 to 12 minutes. Let cool slightly before removing inside pan. Allow pastry to cool completely.

FILLING: Beat eggs and sugar together until light and lemon colored. Stir in lemon juice and peel. Add butter and almonds. Pour into pastry and bake until filling is golden brown and set, 25 to 30 minutes. During last 10 minutes of baking, arrange ¼ cup slivered almonds over top of pie. Serve at room temperature. Yield: 8 to 10 servings. *Pie is best baked and served on same day.*

CHOCOLATE-AIRE

1 (4-ounce) package sweet chocolate squares
3 tablespoons water
1 teaspoon orange flavoring or liqueur
1 (4-ounce) container frozen non-dairy topping
mandarin oranges, drained

Heat chocolate and water in saucepan over low heat, stirring until chocolate is melted and mixture is smooth. Cool and add flavoring. Fold into whipped topping (reserve 4 teaspoons of topping for garnish). Spoon into dessert glasses. Chill. Top with reserved whipped topping and drained mandarin orange slices. Recipe may be doubled. Yield: 4 servings.

CHOCOLATE ECLAIRS

Pastry:
¾ cup water
⅓ cup butter or margarine
⅛ teaspoon salt
¾ cup all-purpose flour (sift before measuring)
3 large eggs

Custard Filling:
1½ cups milk
¼ cup sugar
1½ tablespoons cornstarch
2 egg yolks, slightly beaten
1 teaspoon vanilla extract

Chocolate Glaze:
1 cup semisweet chocolate pieces
2 tablespoons butter or margarine
2 tablespoons light corn syrup
3 tablespoons milk

PASTRY: Preheat oven to 400°. In medium saucepan, bring water, ⅓ cup butter and salt to a boil. Remove from heat. Quickly add flour all at once. With a wooden spoon, beat constantly over low heat until mixture forms ball and leaves side of pan. Remove from heat. Using electric mixer or wooden spoon, beat in eggs, one at a time, beating well after each addition. Continue beating vigorously until dough is shiny and satiny and breaks away in strands. Dough will be stiff and hold its shape. Drop dough by rounded teaspoonsful 3 inches apart, on ungreased cookie sheet. With spatula, shape into 4x1½-inch strips, rounding ends and slightly indenting sides. Bake 35 to 40 minutes or until puffed and golden. Cool on rack.

FILLING: In small heavy saucepan, heat 1½ cups milk until bubbling around edge. Mix sugar and cornstarch; stir all at once into hot milk. Over medium heat, cook, stirring until bubbling. Reduce heat; simmer 1 minute. Beat a little of hot mixture into yolks. Add eggs to saucepan; cook, stirring over medium heat until thickened. Add vanilla. Pour into bowl; cover surface with waxed paper and refrigerate 1½ hours.

GLAZE: In top of double boiler over hot water, melt chocolate with butter. Blend in corn syrup and milk. Cool five minutes.

TO ASSEMBLE: With sharp knife, cut off tops of eclairs. Remove some of soft dough inside. Fill each eclair with ¼ cup custard. Replace tops. Place eclair on rack or tray. Spoon glaze over eclairs. Serve at once or refrigerate. Recipe may be doubled and tripled. Yield: 8 servings.

WHOOPIE PIES

Cookies:
- ½ cup shortening
- 1 cup sugar
- 1 egg
- 1 egg yolk
- 2 cups all-purpose flour
- ⅔ cup unsweetened cocoa
- ¼ teaspoon salt
- 1 teaspoon soda
- ½ cup hot water
- ⅔ cup buttermilk

Filling:
- 2 cups sifted powdered sugar
- 1 egg white
- 1 teaspoon vanilla extract
- ¼ cup butter, softened
- ½ cup shortening

In mixing bowl, beat together ½ cup shortening and 1 cup sugar on high speed until fluffy. Add egg and egg yolk. Stir together flour, cocoa and salt; set aside. Dissolve soda in hot water; cool slightly. Add flour mixture alternately with soda mixture and buttermilk to creamed mixture. Blend until well mixed. Drop batter by rounded tablespoonfuls 2 inches apart onto ungreased cookie sheets. Bake at 350° for 8 to 10 minutes. Cool cookies on wire racks.

FILLING: In medium mixing bowl, combine powdered sugar, egg whites and vanilla. Beating with mixer at low speed, gradually add butter and remaining shortening. Beat at high speed until light and fluffy. Spread filling on the bottom of one cookie, top with second cookie. Store in refrigerator. Yield: 24 filled cookies.

QUICK AND EASY POT DE CRÈME

- 1 (14-ounce) can sweetened condensed milk (remove label from can)
- 1 pint heavy cream
- ½ teaspoon vanilla extract
- pinch of sugar

Put unopened can in saucepan. Cover with water and simmer for 3 hours. Remove and cool. Whip cream, vanilla and sugar together until stiff peaks form. Open can; spoon out pot de crème into dessert dishes and top with whipped cream. Yield: 3 to 4 servings.

NOODLE KUGEL

1 (12-ounce) package medium noodles
1 cup cottage cheese
½ cup sour cream
3 eggs, separated
½ cup butter, melted
½ teaspoon salt
¼ cup sugar
1 (8-ounce) can crushed pineapple, drained
1 teaspoon vanilla extract
1 cup seedless raisins
cinnamon

Cook noodles according to package directions and drain. Combine cottage cheese, sour cream, egg yolks, butter, salt, sugar, pineapple and vanilla. Add raisins. Beat egg whites. Combine eggs, noodles and cheese mixture and pour into greased 13x9-inch pan. Sprinkle with cinnamon. Bake at 350° for 45 minutes to 1 hour. Yield: 8 to 10 servings.

INDIVIDUAL MERINGUE SHELLS

3 egg whites
1 teaspoon vanilla extract
¼ teaspoon cream of tartar
dash of salt
1 cup sugar

Allow egg whites to reach room temperature. Add vanilla, cream of tartar and dash of salt. Beat to soft peaks. Gradually add sugar, beating until stiff peaks form and sugar is dissolved (meringue will be glossy). Cover baking sheet with plain ungreased brown paper. Draw 8 circles, 3½ inches in diameter. Spoon meringue into circles and spread with back of spoon, shaping into shells. Bake at 275° for 1 hour. Turn off oven; leave shells in oven for 1 hour before removing. Fill shells with fresh fruit or ice cream. Yield: 8 shells.

TROPICAL ICE

1 (8½-ounce) can crushed pineapple
2 cups mashed bananas
1 cup sugar
2 tablespoons lemon juice
1 pinch salt
12 maraschino cherries, chopped

Combine all ingredients. Place in container and freeze until almost solid. Remove and beat with mixer until fluffy. Freeze several hours. Serve as ice cream or as a float with gingerale. Yield: 4 servings.

STRAWBERRY ICE CREAM

1 (5½-ounce) package vanilla instant pudding
2 cups sugar
4 cups milk
1 cup water
1 (13-ounce) can evaporated milk
2 cups fresh strawberries, mashed

Combine pudding and sugar in a large bowl. Add remaining ingredients, stirring well. Pour mixture into freezer can. Churn. Let ripen at least 1 hour. Yield: 1 gallon. *Any fresh fruit may be substituted for strawberries.*

UNCOOKED VANILLA ICE CREAM

2 cups sugar
1 (14-ounce) can sweetened condensed milk
2 tablespoons vanilla extract
pinch salt
6 eggs, beaten
1 pint whipping cream
milk

Mix sugar, condensed milk, vanilla, salt and eggs. Add cream and mix well. Pour into 1-gallon ice cream freezer. Add enough cold milk to fill ⅔ full or to fill line. Freeze. Yield: 1 gallon.

PRALINE ICE CREAM TOPPING

1 cup light corn syrup
½ cup sugar
⅓ cup butter or margarine
1 egg, beaten
1 tablespoon vanilla extract
1 cup coarsely chopped pecans

Combine first 4 ingredients in a heavy saucepan; mix well. Bring to a boil over medium heat, stirring constantly. Boil 2 minutes without stirring. Remove from heat and stir in vanilla and pecans. Serve warm or at room temperature over ice cream. Yield: 2½ cups.

BRANDY SYRUP

1½ cups granulated sugar
1 cup water
1 quart brandy

Combine sugar and water in a large saucepan. Heat over medium heat until sugar dissolves. Cool. Add brandy. Store in refrigerator. Yield: 5 pints. *Delicious over fresh fruit.*

CHOCOLATE SYRUP

½ cup cocoa
1 cup water
2 cups sugar
⅛ teaspoon salt
¼ teaspoon vanilla extract

Mix cocoa and water in a saucepan; stir to dissolve cocoa. Heat cocoa and water; add sugar, stirring to dissolve sugar. Boil 3 minutes. Add salt and vanilla. Pour into a sterilized pint jar. Store covered in refrigerator. Will keep several months. May be used for milk drinks or ice cream topping. Yield: 1 pint.

AMARETTO CAKE

Cake:
1 cup chopped pecans
1 (18-ounce) box yellow butter cake mix
1 (3¾-ounce) package instant vanilla pudding
4 eggs
½ cup amaretto
½ cup light rum
½ cup water
½ cup oil

Glaze:
½ cup butter
1 cup sugar
½ cup amaretto

Grease and flour bundt pan. Sprinkle nuts on bottom. Mix dry ingredients. Add eggs and liquid ingredients. Beat for 3 minutes. Pour into pan. Bake at 325° for 50 to 60 minutes. Mix glaze ingredients and boil for 3 minutes. Pour over hot cake and leave cake to cool at least 1 hour before removing from pan. Yield: 12 servings.

CAKES

BUTTERMILK CHOCOLATE CAKE

Cake:
1 cup margarine
4 tablespoons cocoa
1 cup water
2 cups sugar
2 cups all-purpose flour
2 eggs
½ cup buttermilk
1 teaspoon soda

Frosting:
1 cup margarine
4 rounded tablespoons cocoa
1 (16-ounce) box powdered sugar
1 teaspoon vanilla extract
3 tablespoons milk
1 cup chopped nuts

CAKE: Place margarine, cocoa and water in a saucepan and bring to a boil. Combine sugar and flour. Pour cocoa mixture over sugar and flour mixture. Mix well. Add eggs. Mix soda with buttermilk and then add to batter. Pour into greased 9½x13x2-inch pan. Bake at 300° for 1 hour or until done (may require 15 to 20 extra minutes to fully bake center of cake). Leave cake in pan to frost.

FROSTING: Melt margarine; add cocoa and bring to a boil. Remove from heat and add sugar and vanilla. Add milk. If frosting is too thick to spread, add more milk. Stir nuts into frosting. Pour frosting over cake. Yield: 12 to 15 servings.

GRANNY'S NEVER FAIL WHITE CAKE

2 cups sugar
½ cup shortening
¼ cup margarine
2½ cups sifted cake flour
2½ teaspoons baking powder
pinch of salt
1 cup milk
1 teaspoon vanilla extract
5 egg whites, stiffly beaten

Preheat oven to 350°. Cream sugar, shortening and margarine. Sift together flour, baking powder and salt. Add dry ingredients to creamed mixture. Add milk, vanilla and egg whites. Pour into 3 greased 9-inch round cake pans. Bake for 30 minutes or until cake pulls away from sides of pan. *As moist and delicious after a week as when first baked.*

CHEWY CAKE

1 (1-pound) box brown sugar
½ cup margarine, softened
3 large eggs
2½ cups self-rising flour
1 teaspoon vanilla extract
1 cup chopped nuts

Cream sugar and margarine until smooth; add eggs one at a time, beating well after each addition. Stir in flour, ⅓ cup at a time. Add vanilla and nuts and mix well. Spread in well greased 13x9-inch pan and bake in 325° oven 30 minutes. Yield: 12 servings.

HUMMINGBIRD CAKE

Cake:
3 cups all-purpose flour
2 cups sugar
1 teaspoon salt
1 teaspoon soda
1 teaspoon ground cinnamon
3 eggs, beaten
1½ cups salad oil
1½ teaspoons vanilla extract
1 (8-ounce) can crushed pineapple, undrained
2 cups chopped pecans or walnuts, divided
2 cups mashed bananas

Cream Cheese Frosting:
2 (8-ounce) packages cream cheese, softened
1 cup butter or margarine, softened
2 (16-ounce) packages powdered sugar
2 teaspoons vanilla extract

CAKE: Combine dry ingredients in a large mixing bowl; add eggs and salad oil, stirring until dry ingredients are moistened. Do not beat. Stir in vanilla, pineapple, 1 cup nuts and bananas. Spoon batter into 3 greased and floured 9-inch cake pans. Bake at 350° for 25 to 30 minutes or until done. Cool in pans 10 minutes. Remove from pans and cool completely.

FROSTING: Combine cream cheese and butter; cream until smooth. Add powdered sugar. Beat until light and fluffy. Stir in vanilla. Spread frosting between layers and on top and sides of cake. Sprinkle with remaining nuts. Yield: 12 servings.

ITALIAN CREAM CAKE

Cake:
½ cup margarine
½ cup vegetable shortening
2 cups sugar
5 egg yolks
2 cups all-purpose flour
1 teaspoon soda

1 cup buttermilk
1 teaspoon vanilla extract
1 small can flaked coconut
1 cup chopped nuts
5 egg whites, stiffly beaten

Frosting:
1 (8-ounce) package cream cheese, softened
¼ cup margarine

1 box powdered sugar
1 teaspoon vanilla extract
chopped pecans

CAKE: Cream margarine and shortening; add sugar and beat until mixture is smooth. Add egg yolks and beat well. Combine flour and soda and add to cream mixture alternately with buttermilk. Stir in vanilla. Add coconut and chopped nuts. Fold in stiffly beaten egg whites. Pour batter into 3 greased and floured 9-inch cake pans. Bake at 350° for 25 minutes or until cake tests done; cool.

FROSTING: Beat cream cheese and margarine until smooth; add sugar and mix well. Add vanilla and beat until smooth. Spread between layers and on top and sides of cake. Sprinkle top with pecans. Yield: 12 to 15 servings.

WINE CAKE

1 (18-ounce) package yellow cake mix
1 (3-ounce) package vanilla instant pudding
¾ cup salad oil

¾ cup sherry
4 eggs
1 teaspoon nutmeg
powdered sugar, optional

Combine all ingredients and beat at medium speed for 5 minutes. Bake in a greased bundt pan at 325° for 45 minutes or until inserted toothpick comes out clean. Allow to cool in pan for 5 minutes. Remove from pan; cool. Sprinkle with powdered sugar. Yield: 12 servings.

RED VELVET CAKE

Cake:
2 ounces red food coloring
2 tablespoons cocoa
½ cup shortening
1½ cups sugar
2 eggs, beaten
1 teaspoon salt
1 teaspoon vanilla extract
2½ cups sifted all-purpose flour
½ cup buttermilk
1 teaspoon soda
1 tablespoon vinegar

Frosting:
½ cup margarine, softened
1 (8-ounce) package cream cheese, softened
1 (1-pound) box powdered sugar
1 teaspoon vanilla extract
1 cup pecans, finely chopped

CAKE: Preheat oven to 350°. In small bowl, mix food color and cocoa; set aside. In a large bowl, cream shortening and sugar. Add eggs and beat well. Then add cocoa mixture, salt and vanilla. Add flour alternately with buttermilk and mix well. *Gently* fold in soda and vinegar. Pour into 2 well-greased 9-inch cake pans. Bake for 30 minutes. Cool in pan for 10 minutes; then remove. Cool thoroughly and frost.

FROSTING: Cream margarine and cream cheese together; gradually add sugar, beating thoroughly after each addition. Add vanilla; beat until smooth. Add pecans, reserving ¼ cup. Frost cake and sprinkle remaining nuts on top. Yield: 12 to 15 servings.

FRESH APPLE CAKE

2 cups sugar
1½ cups salad oil
3 eggs
3 cups cake flour
1 teaspoon soda
1 teaspoon baking powder
1 teaspoon salt
1 teaspoon cinnamon
1 teaspoon nutmeg
1 cup chopped dates, optional
2 teaspoons vanilla extract
3 cups chopped fresh apple
1 teaspoon chopped nuts

Mix sugar and oil with electric mixer. Beat at high speed for 1 minute. Add eggs, one at a time, beating 1 minute after each addition. Mix dry ingredients with chopped dates; add to oil and sugar. Fold in vanilla, apples and nuts. Mixture will be thick and stiff. Pour into greased and floured 10-inch tube pan. Bake at 325° for 1½ hours. Cool 15 minutes before removing from pan. Yield: 12 to 15 servings. *Better if allowed to age a couple of days.*

DEVIL'S FOOD SPICE CAKE

Cake:
½ cup cocoa
½ cup milk
2 cups sugar, divided
½ cup light corn syrup
1 cup buttermilk
1 teaspoon soda
2 cups all-purpose flour

1 teaspoon baking powder
½ cup butter, not margarine
3 eggs
1 teaspoon cinnamon
½ teaspoon ground cloves
1 teaspoon vanilla extract

Icing:
3 cups sugar
¾ cup butter
¼ cup margarine

¾ cup boiling water
1½ teaspoons vinegar
1 teaspoon vanilla

CAKE: In saucepan over medium heat, cook cocoa, milk, 1 cup sugar and corn syrup until sugar is dissolved; set aside. In a large bowl, combine buttermilk and soda. Set aside. Sift together flour and baking powder. Cream together butter and 1 cup sugar. Add eggs, one at a time, beating well after each addition. Add cinnamon, cloves and vanilla. Add ⅓ of buttermilk mixture and ⅓ of flour mixture; beat well. Repeat until buttermilk and flour are used. Slowly beat in cocoa mixture. Pour into 3 or 4 (9-inch) cake pans. Bake at 350° about 20 to 25 minutes or until an inserted toothpick comes out clean.

ICING: Place all ingredients in a saucepan. Bring to a rolling boil and cook for 5 minutes. Remove from heat and let cool 1 minute. As mixture cools, begin beating and beat until thick enough to spread. This icing sets rapidly. Quickly spread over cooled cake. Yield: 12 servings.

CRUNCH CAKE

1 cup shortening
2 cups sugar
6 eggs

2 cups all-purpose flour
⅛ teaspoon salt
¼ cup sherry

In a large mixing bowl, cream shortening and 2 cups sugar until light. Add eggs all at once and beat thoroughly. Stir in flour, salt, and sherry. Pour batter into a well greased 10-inch tube pan. Bake at 300° for 1 hour and 15 minutes. Let cool in pan 5 minutes. Remove from pan and cool completely. Yield: 12 servings.

FRESH RHUBARB CAKE

½ cup butter, softened
1½ cups brown sugar, packed
1 egg
1 teaspoon vanilla extract
2 cups all-purpose flour
¼ teaspoon salt
1 teaspoon soda
1 tablespoon fresh lemon juice
1 cup milk
2 cups fresh, coarsely chopped rhubarb
½ cup pecans or walnuts, chopped
½ cup granulated sugar
1 teaspoon ground cinnamon

Cream butter in large mixing bowl until light and fluffy. Gradually add brown sugar and continue to mix until fluffy. Add egg and vanilla and blend. In another bowl, sift together twice, flour, salt and soda. Combine lemon juice and milk and add to creamed mixture alternately with flour mixture. Fold in chopped rhubarb and pour into greased and floured 9x13x2-inch pan. In small bowl, blend nuts, granulated sugar and cinnamon and sprinkle evenly over top of batter. Bake at 350° for 45 to 50 minutes or until toothpick inserted in center comes out clean. Cool in pan at least ½ hour. Then cut into squares and serve. Yield: 12 servings. *Serve plain as coffee cake or as a dessert topped with slightly whipped cream and a dusting of cinnamon.*

LAURA'S LEMON CAKE

Cake:
½ cup butter
1 cup sugar
2 eggs
1½ cups all-purpose flour
1 teaspoon baking powder
½ teaspoon salt
½ cup milk
grated rind of 1 lemon

Glaze:
½ cup sugar
juice of 1 lemon
2 tablespoons butter, melted

CAKE: Cream butter and sugar. Add eggs, one at a time, beating after each addition. In a separate bowl mix together flour, baking powder and salt. Add dry ingredients alternately with milk to creamed mixture. Stir in grated lemon rind. Pour into greased 9x5x3-inch loaf pan and bake at 325° for 1 hour.

GLAZE: Bring lemon juice, sugar and butter to boil and pour over hot cake. Allow to cool in pan. Yield: 6 to 8 servings.

AUNT SARA'S CHOCOLATE POUND CAKE

Cake:
1½ cups shortening
3 cups sugar
1 teaspoon vanilla extract
5 eggs at room temperature
3 cups all-purpose flour
½ cup cocoa
¼ teaspoon salt
1 teaspoon baking powder
1½ cups milk

Frosting:
2 cups granulated sugar
¼ cup cocoa
⅔ cup milk
½ cup shortening, melted
2 teaspoons vanilla extract

CAKE: Preheat oven to 300°. Grease and flour large bundt or pound cake pan. In a large mixing bowl, cream shortening, sugar and vanilla; add eggs, one at a time, beating well after each addition. Sift dry ingredients together into separate bowl. Add to egg mixture alternately with milk, beginning and ending with flour. Bake 1½ hours. Let cool slightly in pan; remove from pan and cool completely.

FROSTING: Combine sugar and cocoa in large, heavy boiler. Add melted shortening and milk. Bring to boil over high heat and boil for 2 minutes, stirring constantly. Remove from heat and add vanilla. Beat until creamy. Add one teaspoon milk if frosting becomes too thick to spread easily. Frost cooled cake. Yield: 12 servings.

COCONUT POUND CAKE

1½ cups vegetable shortening
2½ cups sugar
5 large eggs
3 cups cake flour
1 cup milk
1 teaspoon salt
1 tablespoon coconut flavoring
½ can flake coconut

Cream shortening and sugar at high speed for 10 minutes. Add eggs, one at a time, and beat 1 minute after each egg. Add flour, milk and salt; stir in flavoring and coconut. Pour into tube pan and place in a cold oven. Bake 1 hour and 20 minutes at 325°. Check for doneness after 1 hour. Yield: 12 servings.

ORANGE POUND CAKE

1 cup vegetable oil
2 cups granulated sugar
4 eggs
1 tablespoon orange extract
½ teaspoon red food color
1 teaspoon yellow food color
1 teaspoon butter flavoring
½ teaspoon salt
3 cups all-purpose flour
¾ cup buttermilk
1 teaspoon soda
1 tablespoon white vinegar

Cream oil and granulated sugar. Add eggs, one at a time, beating well after each addition. Add extract, colors, butter flavoring and salt. Sift flour twice and add alternately with buttermilk. In a small bowl, mix soda and vinegar; add to batter. Blend well. Pour batter into a greased and floured 10-inch bundt pan. Bake at 325° for 65 minutes or until a toothpick inserted into the center of the cake comes out clean. Do not overbake. Yield: 12 servings.

DUMP POUND CAKE

1 cup butter
½ cup vegetable shortening
3½ cups all-purpose flour
2½ cups sugar
½ teaspoon salt
½ teaspoon soda dissolved in 1 teaspoon water
2 teaspoons vanilla extract
4 eggs
1 cup buttermilk

Mix all ingredients together and pour into bundt pan. Bake 1 hour and 20 minutes at 325°. Cool in pan 10 minutes before removing to rack to cool completely. Yield: 12 servings.

GRANDMA'S COLD OVEN POUND CAKE

1 cup margarine
¼ cup shortening
3 cups sugar
5 large eggs
1 cup milk
3 cups all-purpose flour
1 teaspoon vanilla extract
1 teaspoon lemon extract

Cream butter, shortening, and sugar. Add eggs one at a time, beating well after each one. Add milk and flour alternately to creamed mixture. Add remaining ingredients. Beat 5 minutes. Grease and flour 10-inch tube pan. Pour batter into pan and put into a COLD OVEN. Bake at 325° for 1½ hours. Yield: 12 servings.

CONFECTION FRUIT CAKE

3 cups lightly toasted pecan or walnut halves; or, whole almonds, filberts, brazil nuts; or, a combination of mixed nuts
3 cups candied fruits; or, a combination of candied fruits and chopped pitted dates
1 cup maraschino cherries, drained

3 eggs
1 teaspoon vanilla or 1 tablespoon brandy or rum
2 teaspoons grated orange rind
¾ cup sugar
¾ cup sifted all-purpose flour
½ teaspoon baking powder
½ teaspoon salt
honey or corn syrup for glazing

Combine nuts and fruits. Beat eggs and add vanilla and rind. Gradually beat sugar into egg mixture. Fold egg mixture into fruits and nuts. Add flour, baking powder and salt. Pour batter into greased and floured 9½x5½x3-inch pan. Bake at 300° for 1½ to 1¾ hours. Glaze cake with honey or syrup while hot. Cool cake in pan on cake rack. When cool, remove from pan. Wrap cooled cake in plastic wrap and store at room temperature at least 1 day before slicing. Cake may be sealed in freezer bag, aged at room temperature several days and then frozen. Recipe may be doubled or tripled. Yield: 1 loaf.

HOLIDAY GIFT CAKE

1 (8-ounce) package cream cheese, softened
1 cup butter or margarine
1½ cups sugar
1½ teaspoons vanilla extract
4 eggs
2¼ cups sifted cake flour, divided

1½ teaspoons baking powder
1 (8-ounce) jar maraschino cherries, chopped and drained
½ cup chopped pecans
½ cup finely chopped pecans
candied cherries and pecan halves

Glaze:
1½ cups sifted powdered sugar

2 tablespoons milk

Blend cream cheese, butter, sugar and vanilla until smooth. Add eggs, one at a time, mixing well after each addition. Gradually add 2 cups flour sifted with baking powder. Combine remaining flour with cherries and ½ cup chopped nuts. Fold into batter. Grease a 10-inch bundt or tube pan. Sprinkle with ½ cup finely chopped pecans. Pour batter into pan and bake at 350° for 1 hour and 20 minutes. Cool 10 minutes before removing from pan. Cool thoroughly and glaze. Decorate top of cake with candied cherries and pecans.

GLAZE: Combine sugar and milk. Drizzle over top and sides of cake. Yield: 12 to 15 servings.

PUMPKIN CREAM CAKE ROLL

Cake:
3 eggs
1 cup sugar
⅔ cup cooked pumpkin
1 teaspoon lemon juice
½ teaspoon salt
¾ cup flour

1 teaspoon baking powder
2 teaspoons cinnamon
1 teaspoon ginger
1 teaspoon nutmeg
1 cup finely chopped nuts

Cream Filling:
1 cup powdered sugar
7 ounces cream cheese, softened
4 tablespoons butter, softened
½ teaspoon vanilla

CAKE: Beat eggs at high speed for 5 minutes. Gradually beat in sugar. Combine pumpkin and lemon juice; stir into egg mixture. Combine dry ingredients (except nuts); fold into pumpkin mixture. Pour mixture into greased and floured 10x15-inch jellyroll pan; top with nuts. Bake at 375° for 15 minutes. Turn hot cake out onto towel which has been sprinkled with powdered sugar. Roll cake up in towel (long side to long side); cool.

CREAM FILLING: Combine all ingredients; beat until smooth.

TO ASSEMBLE: Unroll cake and fill with cream filling. Roll up cake. Chill and serve. Yield: 8 to 10 servings. *A wonderful holiday dessert.*

HAWAIIAN CAKE

Cake:
1 (18-ounce) package butter recipe yellow cake mix
½ cup butter, softened
¾ cup milk
3 eggs
1 (11-ounce) can mandarin oranges, drained
orange slices for garnish, optional

Hawaiian Icing:
1 pint whipping cream, whipped
1 (20-ounce) can crushed pineapple
1 (3¾-ounce) package instant vanilla pudding mix

CAKE: Preheat oven to 325°. Grease and flour three 9-inch round cake pans. Set aside. Put all ingredients into large mixing bowl. Blend until moistened. Scrape bowl and beaters. Beat at medium speed for 3 minutes. DO NOT OVERBEAT. Pour batter into prepared pans. Bake for 25 minutes. Cool cake in pans on rack at least 10 minutes. Remove from pans and cool, top side up, on rack. Frost with Hawaiian Icing when completely cool.

ICING: Place all ingredients in large mixing bowl. Mix at medium speed until well mixed. Spread between cooled layers and on top of cake. Decorate with orange slices. Refrigerate until time to serve. Yield: 12 to 15 servings.

EVERYDAY YELLOW CAKE

⅔ cup butter
1¾ cups sugar
2 eggs
1½ teaspoons vanilla
3 cups sifted cake flour
2½ teaspoons baking powder
1 teaspoon salt
1¼ cups milk

Preheat oven to 350°. Grease and lightly flour two 9x1½-inch round cake pans. Cream butter; gradually add sugar and cream until light. Add eggs and vanilla; beat until fluffy. Sift dry ingredients together; add to creamed mixture alternately with milk, beating after each addition. Beat 1 minute after last addition. Pour into cake pans and bake 30 to 35 minutes. Cool 10 minutes; remove from pans and cool on cake racks. Frost with Chocolate Butter Frosting (See Index). Yield: two 9-inch layers.

BUTTER FROSTING

6 tablespoons butter
1 (1-pound) box powdered sugar
¼ cup light cream
1½ teaspoons vanilla

Cream butter; gradually add half of sugar, blending well. Beat in 2 tablespoons cream and all of the vanilla. Gradually blend in remaining sugar. Add enough of remaining cream for spreading consistency.

CHOCOLATE BUTTER FROSTING: Add two 1-ounce squares unsweetened chocolate, melted, when vanilla is added. Yield: Enough frosting for two 8-inch layers.

CAKE NOTE: When testing a large cake for doneness, use a piece of uncooked spaghetti.

FUNNEL CAKES

2 beaten eggs
1½ cups milk
2 cups sifted all-purpose flour
1 teaspoon baking powder
½ teaspoon salt
2 cups cooking oil
powdered sugar

In mixing bowl, combine eggs and milk. Sift together flour, baking powder and salt. Add to egg mixture; beat with electric mixer until smooth. In 8-inch skillet, heat cooking oil to 360°. Cover bottom opening of funnel with finger. Pour a generous ½ cup batter into funnel. Holding funnel close to surface of oil, remove finger and release batter into hot oil in a spiral shape. Fry until golden, about 3 minutes. Using wide spatula and tongs, turn cake carefully. Cook 1 minute longer. Drain on paper toweling; sprinkle with sifted powdered sugar. Serve hot. Yield: 4 cakes.

AMARETTO CHEESECAKE

Cake:
- 2 cups graham cracker crumbs
- 2 tablespoons sugar
- 1 teaspoon ground cinnamon
- 6 tablespoons margarine or butter, melted
- 3 (8-ounce) packages cream cheese, softened
- 1 cup sugar
- 4 eggs
- ⅓ cup amaretto

Topping:
- 1 cup sour cream
- 1 tablespoon plus 1 teaspoon sugar
- 1 tablespoon amaretto
- 1 (1.2-ounce) chocolate candy bar, grated

Combine graham cracker crumbs, 2 tablespoons sugar, cinnamon, and butter; mix well. Press firmly into bottom and ½-inch up the sides of a 9-inch spring-form pan. Beat cream cheese with electric mixer until light and fluffy. Gradually add 1 cup sugar, mixing well. Add eggs, one at a time, beating well after each addition. Stir in ⅓ cup liqueur; pour into prepared pan. Bake at 375° for 45 to 50 minutes. Combine sour cream, 1 tablespoon plus 1 teaspoon sugar, and 1 tablespoon liqueur. Stir well, and spoon over cheesecake. Bake at 500° for 5 minutes. Let cool to room temperature and refrigerate 24 to 48 hours. Garnish with grated chocolate. Yield: 12 servings.

CREAMY CHEESE CAKE

- ¼ cup margarine or butter, melted
- 1 cup graham cracker crumbs
- ¼ cup sugar
- 2 (8-ounce) packages cream cheese, softened
- 1 (14-ounce) can sweetened condensed milk
- 3 eggs
- ¼ teaspoon salt
- ¼ cup reconstituted lemon juice
- 1 cup sour cream
- cherry pie filling, optional

Preheat oven to 300°. Combine margarine, crumbs, and sugar; pat firmly into bottom of buttered 9-inch spring-form pan. In large mixing bowl, beat cheese until fluffy. Beat in condensed milk, eggs and salt until smooth. Stir in lemon juice. Pour into prepared pan. Bake 50 to 55 minutes or until cake springs back when lightly touched. Cool to room temperature; chill. Spread sour cream on cheese cake. Garnish with cherry pie filling, if desired. Yield: 12 servings.

RICOTTA CHEESE CAKE

1 (29-ounce) can peach slices
¾ cup sugar, divided
2 envelopes unflavored gelatin
3 eggs, separated
¼ teaspoon salt
1½ cups low fat milk
3 cups ricotta cheese
3 tablespoons lemon juice
2 teapoons grated orange peel
½ teaspoon grated lemon peel
1 teaspoon vanilla extract
cinnamon

Drain peaches and set aside. In top of double boiler, combine ¼ cup of sugar and gelatin. Add egg yolks and beat until light and frothy. Add salt and milk. Cook over simmering water until mixture forms a custard (mixture will coat a metal spoon). In a food processor or blender, blend ricotta until smooth. Add ricotta, lemon juice, peels and vanilla to custard. In a large bowl, beat egg whites until soft peaks form. Gradually beat in remaining ½ cup sugar until stiff peaks form. Fold egg whites into cheese-custard mixture. Spread mixture in 9-inch spring-form pan. Arrange peach slices on top of mixture. Cover and refrigerate at least 4 hours. Sprinkle with cinnamon just before serving. Yield: 10 to 12 servings.

FRESH PEACH PIE

2 deep-dish pie shells
1⅓ cups sugar
1⅓ cups water
¼ cup cornstarch
⅓ cup apricot-flavored gelatin
½ teaspoon almond extract
4 cups sliced fresh peaches
frozen whipped topping or
   whipped cream
nutmeg

Bake pie shells; cool. Mix sugar, water and cornstarch in a saucepan and cook until thick. Remove from heat. Add gelatin, extract and let cool. Fold peaches into cooled apricot mixture. Divide into 2 shells. Chill. To serve, add topping and sprinkle with nutmeg. Yield: 12 servings. *Pies will keep in refrigerator for 2 to 3 days.*

BLUEBERRY CHEESE PIE

1 cup sugar
1 (8-ounce) package cream cheese
2 graham cracker pie crusts
3 bananas
1 (12-ounce) carton frozen non-dairy topping, thawed
1 (16-ounce) can blueberry pie filling

Cream sugar with cream cheese; spread on graham cracker crusts. Slice bananas and place on top of cheese mixture. Spoon non-dairy topping over bananas and top with blueberries. Cover and refrigerate until ready to serve. Yield: 12 servings or 2 pies.

FROZEN CRANBERRY PIE

1¼ cups vanilla wafer crumbs
6 tablespoons butter, melted
1 (8-ounce) package cream cheese, softened
1 cup whipping cream
¼ cup sugar
½ teaspoon vanilla extract
1 (1-pound) can whole cranberry sauce (not jellied)

Combine crumbs and butter. Press into 9-inch pie plate. Chill pie crust while preparing filling. Beat cream cheese until fluffy. Combine whipping cream, sugar and vanilla; whip until thick. Add to cheese. Fold into cranberry sauce and pour into crust. Freeze for 4 hours. Remove from freezer 15 to 30 minutes before serving. Yield: 6 servings.

FRUIT COBBLER

½ cup margarine
1 cup self-rising flour
1 cup sugar
1 cup milk
2 teaspoons baking powder
1 quart fresh fruit

Line bottom of 13x9-inch dish with margarine, cut into patties. Combine flour, sugar, milk and baking powder in bowl. Pour over margarine patties. Add fresh fruit; do not stir. Bake at 400° for 30 minutes or until crust is brown. Yield: 6 servings.

APRICOT PIE

1 (6-ounce) can crushed pineapple, undrained
1 (3-ounce) package apricot-flavored gelatin
1 cup sugar
1 (11-ounce) can evaporated milk
½ cup chopped pecans
¼ teaspoon almond flavoring
2 graham cracker pie crusts

Mix pineapple, gelatin, and sugar in a boiler. Bring to a boil and set aside to cool. Chill milk in freezer until ice crystals form. Whip chilled milk; add pineapple-gelatin mixture; fold in pecans. Stir in almond flavoring. Pour into crusts. Yield: 2 pies or 12 servings.

FRENCH APPLE COBBLER

Filling:
5 cups tart apples, peeled and sliced
¾ cup sugar
2 tablespoons all-purpose flour
½ teaspoon cinnamon
¼ teaspoon salt
1 teaspoon vanilla extract
¼ cup water
1 tablespoon margarine, softened

Batter:
½ cup sifted all-purpose flour
½ cup sugar
½ teaspoon baking powder
¼ teaspoon salt
2 tablespoons margarine, softened
1 egg, slightly beaten

FILLING: In medium bowl, combine apples, sugar, flour, cinnamon, salt, vanilla and water. Pour into 9-inch square pan. Dot apples with margarine.

BATTER: Combine batter ingredients. Beat with wooden spoon until smooth. Top apples with 9 portions of batter. Batter will spread during baking. Bake 35 to 40 minutes at 375° or until apples are fork tender and crust is golden brown. Serve warm with cream. Yield: 6 to 8 servings.

LEMON MERINGUE PIE

Filling:
1 cup sugar
1¼ cups hot water
1 tablespoon butter
4 tablespoons cornstarch
3 tablespoons cold water
6 tablespoons lemon juice
1 tablespoon grated lemon rind
3 egg yolks
2 tablespoons milk
pinch of salt

Meringue:
3 egg whites
1 teaspoon lemon juice
6 tablespoons sugar
1 (9-inch) baked pie shell

FILLING: Combine sugar, water and butter; heat until sugar dissolves. Add cornstarch blended with 3 tablespoons cold water. Cook slowly until clear (about 8 minutes). Add lemon juice and rind. Cook 2 minutes. Add egg yolks, salt, and milk and bring to a boil. Pour into baked pie shell.

MERINGUE: Beat egg whites until stiff but not dry. Add sugar, 2 tablespoons at a time. Beat well after each addition. Add lemon juice and beat. Spread over filling. Bake at 350° for 12 minutes. Yield: 6 servings. *Real old-time, lemon flavor!*

LEMONADE PIE

1 (6-ounce) can lemonade concentrate
1 (8-ounce) container frozen whipped topping
1 (14-ounce) can sweetened condensed milk
2 (8 or 9-inch) graham cracker crusts

Mix ingredients and pour into 2 graham cracker pie shells. Freeze. Yield: 2 pies or 12 servings. *May add yellow or green food coloring for more color.*

GRANDMA'S CHOCOLATE PIE

1 cup sugar
3 tablespoons cocoa
½ teaspoon salt
2½ tablespoons cornstarch
1 tablespoon all-purpose flour

3 cups milk
3 egg yolks
1 tablespoon butter
1½ teaspoons vanilla extract
1 deep (9-inch) baked pie shell

Meringue:
3 egg whites
¼ teaspoon cream of tartar

½ cup sugar

PIE: Mix sugar, cocoa, salt, cornstarch and flour in saucepan. Gradually stir in milk. Cook over moderate heat, stirring constantly, until mixture thickens and boils. Boil for one minute. Remove from heat. Slightly beat egg yolks in medium size bowl. Add a small amount of chocolate mixture to egg yolks and stir. Add yolk mixture to sauce and boil one minute more, stirring constantly. If mixture gets lumpy, beat with a wire whisk or hand mixer until smooth. Remove from heat. Add butter and vanilla, mixing well. Pour into baked pie shell.

MERINGUE: Beat egg whites until stiff peaks form. Add sugar and cream of tartar. Beat to blend. Top chocolate with meringue. Bake at 350° until delicately browned. Cool and serve. Yield: 6 servings.

CHOCOLATE PECAN PIE

⅔ cup evaporated milk
2 tablespoons butter
1 (12-ounce) package semisweet
  chocolate chips
2 eggs, slightly beaten
1 cup sugar

2 tablespoons all-purpose flour
¼ teaspoon salt
1 cup whole pecans
1 teaspoon vanilla extract
1 (9-inch) unbaked pie shell

Combine milk, butter and chocolate in saucepan. Stir over low heat until smooth. Mix eggs, sugar, flour and salt; add to chocolate mixture. Stir in pecans and vanilla. Pour into pie shell. Bake for 35 minutes at 375°. Yield: 8 servings. *Can be topped with whipped cream or vanilla ice cream.*

DAVID'S NOT-SO-SWEET PECAN PIE

1½ cups coarsely broken pecans
¼ cup butter
1 cup light brown sugar
3 eggs
½ cup light corn syrup
1 teaspoon vanilla
pinch salt
¼ cup pecan halves
9-inch unbaked pie shell, chilled

Preheat oven to 375°. Cream butter; add sugar and beat until soft and light. Beat in eggs, one at a time; stir in corn syrup, pecans, vanilla and salt. Pour filling into pie shell and place pecan halves on top. Bake for 40 minutes or until knife inserted in center comes out clean. Serve hot or cold. Yield: 6 servings.

FUDGE SUNDAE PIE

1 cup evaporated milk
1 (6-ounce) package semisweet chocolate morsels
1 cup miniature marshmallows
¼ teaspoon salt
1 quart vanilla ice cream
vanilla wafers
½ cup chopped pecans

Combine milk, chocolate morsels, marshmallows and salt in heavy saucepan. Stir constantly over medium heat until morsels and marshmallows melt and mixture thickens. Remove from heat. Cool to room temperature. Line sides and bottom of a 9-inch pie pan with vanilla wafers. Spoon half of ice cream over wafers. Cover with half the chocolate mixture. Repeat with ice cream and chocolate sauce layers. Top with pecans. Freeze until firm (3 to 5 hours). Keep frozen. Yield: 6 servings.

CHARLESTON CHESS PIE

1 tablespoon all-purpose flour
1½ cups sugar
3 eggs
½ cup butter, melted
2 teaspoons grated lemon rind
2 tablespoons lemon juice
½ cup buttermilk
1 teaspoon vanilla extract
1 unbaked (9-inch) pie shell

Combine flour and sugar in large bowl. Add eggs and butter; beat at low speed until well blended. Stir in lemon rind, juice, buttermilk and vanilla. Pour into pie shell. Bake at 325° for 45 minutes or until top is golden brown. Yield: 6 servings. *Add 1 cup coconut for a different taste.*

IMPOSSIBLE COCONUT PIE

4 eggs, beaten
1¾ cups sugar
½ cup self-rising flour
2 cups milk
¼ cup butter, melted
1 (7-ounce) can flaked coconut
1 teaspoon lemon flavoring

Preheat oven to 350°. Grease two (9-inch) pie plates slightly and sprinkle with flour. Beat eggs. Continue beating while adding remaining ingredients in order given. Pour into pie plates and bake 30 to 40 minutes. Yield: 12 servings.

PINEAPPLE COCONUT PIE

4 eggs, beaten
2 cups sugar
¼ cup margarine, melted
1 (1-pound) can crushed pineapple
1 cup coconut
2 (9-inch) pie shells, unbaked
whipped cream

Mix all ingredients. Pour into pie shells and bake at 325° for 45 minutes. Cool. Serve with whipped cream. Yield: 8 servings.

CUSTARD PIE

3 eggs, beaten
3 tablespoons all-purpose flour
1 cup sugar
2 tablespoons butter, melted
1 (13-ounce) can evaporated milk
1 teaspoon vanilla extract

Mix all ingredients together. Pour into greased and floured 9-inch pie plate. Bake at 350° for 40 minutes or until knife inserted in center comes out clean. Yield: 6 servings.

MINIATURE PECAN TARTS

Crust:
1 (3-ounce) package cream cheese, softened
½ cup butter or margarine, softened
1 cup sifted all-purpose flour

Topping:
1 egg
¾ cup brown sugar
1 tablespoon margarine or butter, melted
1 teaspoon vanilla extract
dash salt
1 cup chopped pecans

CRUST: Blend together cheese and butter. Stir in flour and chill slightly. Shape in 1½-inch balls and place in miniature muffin tins. Press dough on bottom and up sides. Set aside.

FILLING: Combine all ingredients. Pour filling into each miniature tart. Fill ¾ full. Bake at 350° for 25 to 30 minutes. Let cool completely before removing from pan. Yield: 12 servings.

WALNUT MAPLE TARTS

½ cup butter
¾ cup firmly packed light brown sugar
½ cup maple syrup
3 eggs, lightly beaten
¼ cup heavy cream
1¼ cups chopped walnuts
½ teaspoon vanilla extract
8 unbaked tart shells
whipped cream
walnut halves

Heat butter, brown sugar and syrup in saucepan just to boiling point. Mix eggs, cream, walnuts and vanilla together; stir in hot syrup mixture gradually. Mix well. Pour into tart shells. Bake in preheated 375° oven for 20 minutes or until golden brown and custard is set. Let cool. Garnish with fluffs of whipped cream; top with walnut halves. Yield: 8 servings.

CREAM CHEESE TARTS

2 (8-ounce) packages cream cheese, softened
1 cup sugar
2 eggs
1 teaspoon vanilla extract
12 vanilla wafers
1 (15-ounce) can blueberry pie filling
whipped cream

Beat cream cheese in a medium mixing bowl until soft and creamy. Gradually add sugar and beat until light and fluffy. Add eggs and vanilla. Place 1 vanilla wafer in each paper-lined muffin cup; spoon cream cheese mixture over wafer. Fill cups. Bake at 350° for 20 minutes. Refrigerate and leave in muffin pans overnight. Top with blueberry pie filling and whipped cream before serving. Yield: 12 servings.

CHEESE CAKE TARTS

Muffins:
3 (8-ounce) packages cream cheese, softened
5 eggs
1 cup powdered sugar
1½ teaspoons vanilla extract

Topping:
1 cup sour cream
¼ cup sugar
½ teaspoon vanilla extract
strawberry preserves

Preheat oven to 300°. Mix first four ingredients and spoon into paper-lined muffin pans, filling each ¾ full. Bake at 300° for 40 minutes. Muffins will fall in center. Cool for 30 minutes. Mix together sour cream, sugar and vanilla. Fill depressions in muffins with sour cream mixture. Bake 10 minutes. Remove from oven and top with 1 teaspoon preserves. Yield: 24 regular muffins.

CREAM CHEESE BITES

butter
graham cracker crumbs
3 eggs, separated
¾ cup sugar

2 (8-ounce) packages cream
  cheese, softened
¼ teaspoon lemon extract

Filling:
1 cup sour cream
2 tablespoons sugar
1 teaspoon vanilla extract

cherry or blueberry pie filling,
  optional

Butter 4 dozen (1½-inch) muffin tins and coat generously with graham cracker crumbs; set aside. Cream egg yolks, sugar, cream cheese and lemon extract until fluffy. Beat egg whites until stiff and fold into creamed mixture. Fill muffin tins ¾ full. Bake at 350° for 20 minutes. Cool 10 to 15 minutes. Centers will fall, forming an indentation. Combine filling ingredients and spoon 1 teaspoon into each indentation. Bake 5 additional minutes. Top with pie filling, if desired. Store in refrigerator. *Freezes well.* Yield: 48 servings.

BASIC PIE CRUST

2 cups all-purpose flour
1 teaspoon salt

⅔ cup shortening
¼ cup ice water

Sift flour and salt into bowl. Cut shortening into flour until mixture is consistency of coarse meal. Add water, one teaspoon at a time, mixing to form a ball. Roll dough between 2 sheets of waxed paper or on lightly floured pastry cloth or board. For baked shell, prick crust with fork and cook 10 to 12 minutes at 450°. Yield: 2 (9-inch) crusts.

ANISE COOKIES

1 cup butter, softened
½ cup sifted powdered sugar
1 egg yolk
1½ teaspoons anise extract

2½ cups sifted all-purpose flour
powdered sugar for dusting
candied lilac floret, optional

Heat oven to 350°. Blend butter, sugar, yolk and extract; blend in flour slowly. Place mixture in pastry bag with star tip. Press mixture onto ungreased baking sheet in tiny but tall swirls 1 inch apart. Bake 8 minutes or until set but not brown. Cool. Dust with powdered sugar. Decorate with candied lilac floret, if desired. Yield: 3 dozen.

CHINESE TEA COOKIES

2¾ cups sifted all-purpose flour
1 cup sugar
½ teaspoon soda
½ teaspoon salt

1 cup butter or margarine
1 slightly beaten egg
1 teaspoon almond extract
⅓ cup whole almonds

Sift flour, sugar, soda and salt together. Cut in butter until mixture resembles cornmeal. Add egg and almond extract. Mix well. Shape dough into 1-inch balls and place 2 inches apart on ungreased cookie sheet. Place 1 almond on top of each cookie and press to flatten slightly. Bake at 325° for 15 to 18 minutes. Remove to rack to cool. Yield: 4 dozen.

COLLEEN'S WEDDING COOKIES

½ cup butter
2 tablespoons granulated sugar
1 cup pecans, ground (measure before grinding)

1 cup less 2 tablespoons all-purpose flour
powdered sugar

Mix together butter, granulated sugar, pecans and flour. Roll into balls. Bake at 300° for 25 to 30 minutes. Roll immediately in powdered sugar. Yield: 3 dozen.

SPICE BALLS

2¼ cups sifted all-purpose flour
1 teaspoon baking powder
2 teaspoons cinnamon
½ teaspoon ground cloves
½ teaspoon mace
¼ teaspoon pepper
2 eggs
1 cup sugar
1 teaspoon grated lemon peel
1 (14-ounce) jar candied citron, chopped
powdered sugar

Sift flour, baking powder and spices together. Beat eggs until light. Beat in sugar. Stir in dry ingredients. Mix in peel and citron. Break off small pieces of dough; roll into 1 inch balls. Place cookies 1 inch apart on greased cookie sheet. Cover with waxed paper; let stand overnight. Bake at 350° for 20 minutes. Cool. Roll in powdered sugar. Store in airtight container. Cookies are better if allowed to mellow for a week. Yield: 4 dozen.

CHOCOLATE-COCONUT BALLS

2 (12-ounce) packages coconut
1 (16-ounce) box powdered sugar
½ cup butter or margarine, melted
½ teaspoon vanilla extract
1 (14-ounce) can sweetened condensed milk
½ bar paraffin
1 (12-ounce) package semi-sweet chocolate chips

BALLS: Mix together first 5 ingredients. Press into 13x9-inch glass dish. Place in refrigerator overnight or in freezer for 15 minutes. Form into small balls or use cookie cutter to cut large bars.

COATING: Melt together over low heat in top of double boiler the paraffin and chocolate chips. Stir often. Using toothpicks inserted in balls, dip balls in chocolate mixture. Place on waxed paper until cool. Keep in refrigerator. Yield: 1 dozen large bars or 36 balls.

ORANGE BALLS

1 (12-ounce) box vanilla wafers
1 (1-pound) box powdered sugar
½ cup margarine, melted
1 (6-ounce) can frozen orange juice
¾ cup nuts, chopped
flaked coconut

Crush vanilla wafers in blender. Add sugar, margarine, orange juice and nuts. Mix well. Form into small balls. Roll in coconut. Store in cool, dry place. Yield: 6 dozen.

DATE CRISPIES

½ cup butter or margarine, melted
1 (1-pound) package pitted dates, finely chopped
1 egg
⅔ cup sugar
2 cups crisp rice cereal
½ cup chopped walnuts
1 cup coconut

Melt butter or margarine in saucepan. Add dates, egg and sugar. Cook slowly for 10 minutes or until sugar has dissolved, stirring occasionally. Allow to cool. Add cereal and walnuts; mix thoroughly. When cool enough to handle, shape into small balls and roll in coconut. Yield: 2 dozen.

ICEBOX COOKIES

1 cup butter
2 cups brown sugar
2 eggs
3½ cups all-purpose flour
½ teaspoon salt
1 teaspoon soda
½ teaspoon allspice
½ cup nuts

Cream butter, sugar and eggs together. Sift flour, salt, soda and allspice together. Add to creamed mixture. Add nuts. On waxed paper, roll into 4 long rolls. Wrap in waxed paper. Put in refrigerator for 1 hour. Slice and bake on cookie sheet at 375° to 400° 10 to 12 minutes or until lightly browned. Yield: 3 dozen.

VARIATION: Use chocolate chips, toffee bits or coconut in place of nuts. May keep in icebox for up to 2 weeks.

PEANUT BUTTER KISS COOKIES

1¾ cups all-purpose flour
1 teaspoon soda
½ teaspoon salt
½ cup sugar
½ cup firmly packed brown sugar
½ cup shortening
½ cup peanut butter
1 egg
2 tablespoons vanilla extract
granulated sugar, for topping
48 chocolate kisses

Sift flour, soda and salt into large mixing bowl. Add remaining ingredients except sugar for topping and kisses. Mix on lowest speed with electric mixer until dough is formed. Shape dough into balls using 1 teaspoon dough for each. Roll balls in sugar and place on ungreased cookie sheet. Bake at 375° for 10 to 12 minutes. Peel kisses while cookies are baking. Top each cookie immediately after removing from oven. Press kiss firmly into cookie (edges of cookie will crack). Yield: 4 dozen.

BROWN SUGAR ALMOND BARS

½ cup butter or margarine, softened
½ cup sifted powdered sugar
1 cup all-purpose flour
3 tablespoons butter or margarine
1 tablespoon water
½ cup packed brown sugar
¾ teaspoon lemon juice
¾ cup sliced almonds
¾ teaspoon vanilla

Cream together ½ cup butter or margarine and powdered sugar. Add flour; mix well. Pat into ungreased 9x9x2-inch baking pan. Bake at 350° for 12 to 15 minutes. Melt remaining butter. Add brown sugar, 1 tablespoon water and lemon juice; bring to a boil, stirring constantly. Remove from heat; stir in almonds and vanilla. Spread over crust. Bake 15 to 20 minutes. Cool and cut in bars while warm. Yield: 2 dozen.

JOHNNY APPLESEED BARS

2 cups whole wheat flour
¼ cup toasted wheat germ
2 teaspoons soda
1 teaspoon ground cinnamon
1 teaspoon salt
½ teaspoon ground nutmeg
4 cups diced tart cooking apples (pared or unpared)
1 cup granulated sugar
1 cup packed brown sugar
½ cup oil
1 cup chopped pecans
2 eggs, well beaten
1 teaspoon vanilla extract

Stir together flour, wheat germ, soda, cinnamon, salt and nutmeg; set aside. In a large bowl, combine apples, sugars, oil, nuts, eggs and vanilla. Add flour mixture to apple mixture. Stir gently to blend well. Pour into greased 13x9x2-inch baking pan. Bake at 350° for 50 minutes. Cool in pan. When cool, cut into bars. Yield: 24 bars.

CARROT BARS

2 cups all-purpose flour
2 cups sugar
1 teaspoon salt
2 teaspoons soda
2 teaspoons cinnamon
1½ cups cooking oil
4 eggs
3 (4½-ounce) jars of baby food strained carrots
½ cup raisins (optional)
½ cup chopped nuts (optional)

Frosting:
¼ cup butter
½ (8-ounce) package cream cheese
1¾ cups powdered sugar
1 teaspoon vanilla extract

BARS: Mix well first 6 ingredients in bowl. Add eggs, one at a time, beating after each egg is added. Add carrots; mix well. Add raisins and nuts, if desired. Pour into greased 13x15-inch pan. Bake at 350° for 30 to 40 minutes.

FROSTING: Cream butter and cheese with vanilla. Add sugar, beating well. Frost when cooled. Cut into bars. Yield: 42 (2-inch) bars.

2 sticks
3 C graham crackers
1 Cup p butter
1 box p. sug.
1½ pack ch. ch.

PEANUT BUTTER SQUARES

1½ sticks 1 cup margarine
2 Cups 1 (16-ounce) box powdered sugar
1pkg 1⅓ cups graham cracker crumbs
1 C. ½ cup peanut butter
1 (12-ounce) package chocolate chips, melted
½ cup peanut butter

Mix margarine, sugar, crumbs and ½ cup peanut butter and pat into a jellyroll pan. Chill thoroughly. Combine melted chips with remaining peanut butter and spread over cold graham cracker mixture. Yield: 1 to 1½ dozen squares.

RASPBERRY SQUARES

½ cup softened butter
1 cup packed brown sugar
1½ cups all-purpose flour
½ teaspoon salt
½ teaspoon soda
1½ cups quick cooking oats
¼ cup water
1 teaspoon lemon juice
⅔ cup raspberry jam

Cream butter and sugar until fluffy. Stir together flour, salt and soda. Stir into creamed mixture. Add oats and ¼ cup water. Mix until crumbly. Pat half of the crumb mixture into 13x9x2-inch pan. Stir lemon juice into jam and spread over base. Sprinkle remaining mixture on top. Bake at 350° for 25 minutes. Cool and cut into bars. Yield: 36 bars.

OATMEAL BROWNIES

½ cup self-rising flour
1 cup sugar
2 eggs, well beaten
½ cup melted butter or margarine
½ cup cocoa
½ cup quick-cooking oats, uncooked
½ cup chopped pecans

Combine flour, sugar and eggs in large mixing bowl and mix well. Combine butter and cocoa and stir in flour mixture. Add oats and pecans and mix until blended. Spread batter in well-greased 8-inch square pan. Bake at 350° for 30 minutes or until done. Cool and cut into bars. Yield: 16 bars.

OATMEAL HERMITS

2 cups all-purpose flour
1 teaspoon soda
½ teaspoon salt
1 teaspoon cinnamon
¼ teaspoon cloves
¼ teaspoon nutmeg
¾ cup butter or margarine
1 cup firmly packed dark brown sugar
½ cup granulated sugar
2 large eggs
⅓ cup milk
1 teaspoon vanilla
1½ cups quick-cooking oats
1 cup raisins
½ cup chopped walnuts

Combine flour, soda, salt, cinnamon, cloves and nutmeg and set aside. In a large bowl cream butter, brown sugar and granulated sugar. Beat in eggs, milk and vanilla. Add flour mixture and mix well. Stir in oats, raisins and walnuts. Drop by rounded tablespoons on ungreased cookie sheets. Bake at 375° for 10 to 12 minutes. Remove from pan and cool on wire racks. Yield: 3½ dozen.

SNICKERDOODLES

½ cup sweet butter
¾ cup sugar
1 whole egg plus 1 egg yolk
1⅔ cups flour
½ teaspoon soda
½ teaspoon nutmeg
½ cup walnut pieces
½ cup raisins

Cream butter and sugar. Beat in egg plus egg yolk. Sift flour and soda with nutmeg. Mix into batter. Fold in nuts and raisins. Drop by rounded teaspoons onto greased cookie sheet. Sprinkle with sugar and cinnamon. Bake at 375° for 10 to 12 minutes. Yield: 5 dozen.

AUNT HAUTIE'S FRUITCAKE COOKIES

½ cup butter, softened
1 cup dark brown sugar
4 eggs
2½ cups all-purpose flour, divided
2 teaspoons soda
1 teaspoon ground cinnamon
1 teaspoon ground nutmeg
1 teaspoon ground cloves
2¼ cups white raisins
½ pound red candied cherries, finely chopped
½ pound green candied pineapple, finely chopped
1½ pounds pecans, chopped
¼ cup cooking sherry

In a medium mixing bowl, cream butter and brown sugar. Add eggs, one at a time. Add 2 cups flour, soda, cinnamon, nutmeg and cloves. Combine fruit, raisins and ½ cup flour and mix to coat fruit. Pour butter mixture over fruit and mix well. Add pecans and sherry, stirring until well mixed. Line cookie sheets with waxed paper. Drop by teaspoons 1 to 1½ inches apart on cookie sheet. Bake at 250° for 35 minutes. Yield: 6 dozen.

LAST MINUTE CHOCOLATE DROP COOKIES

2 cups sugar
¼ cup cocoa
½ cup evaporated milk
½ cup margarine
½ cup peanut butter
2 cups crispy rice cereal
1 teaspoon vanilla extract

Mix sugar and cocoa together in saucepan. Add milk and margarine. Bring to a boil and boil 1 minute. Remove from heat. Add peanut butter, cereal and vanilla. Mix well and drop by teaspoons on waxed paper. Immediately after cooling, the cereal will be tough. When thoroughly cooled the cookies will be crisp and taste like crispy chocolate candy. Yield: 4 dozen.

GOOD FOR YOU COOKIES

1 cup light brown sugar, firmly packed
½ cup corn oil margarine, softened
2 eggs or ½ cup egg substitute
⅓ cup skimmed milk
1 cup chopped raw carrots or grated raw apple
2 cups unbleached flour
1 teaspoon baking powder
½ teaspoon soda
½ teaspoon salt
½ teaspoon ground cinnamon
½ teaspoon ground nutmeg
2 cups quick-cooking oatmeal
1 cup raisins
1 cup chopped pecans, optional

Cream sugar and margarine. Beat in eggs. Add milk and carrots (or apples). In a separate bowl, sift flour with baking powder, soda, salt and spices. Add oatmeal, raisins and nuts to dry ingredients. Add dry ingredients to creamed mixture. Mix thoroughly. Drop mixture by tablespoons onto greased cookie sheet. Bake at 375° for 12 to 15 minutes. Yield: 4 to 5 dozen.

QUICK CHOCOLATE COOKIES

2 tablespoons butter
1 (12-ounce) package chocolate chips
1 (14-ounce) can sweetened condensed milk
1 cup self-rising flour
1 cup chopped nuts

Melt butter and chocolate chips in double boiler. Stir to blend. Add milk. Continue stirring mixture until melted and blended. Add flour and mix well. Stir in nuts. Drop by teaspoonsful on foil-covered cookie sheets. Bake at 325° 8 to 10 mintues. *Do not overcook.* Let cool 1 to 2 minutes; remove from pans to cool. Yield: 5 dozen.

POTATO CHIP SHORTBREAD COOKIES

1 cup butter or margarine
½ cup butter-flavored
  shortening
1 cup sugar
¾ teaspoon vanilla extract

3 cups plus 2 tablespoons
  all-purpose flour
1½ cups crushed potato chips
½ cup pecans, chopped, optional
powdered sugar

Cream butter, shortening and sugar well. Add vanilla and flour; stir in potato chips and nuts. Drop by teaspoons onto greased cookie sheet and bake at 350° for 15 minutes or until browned around the edges. These cookies do not spread while cooking and are very rich; therefore, drop dough by small teaspoons and place close together on cookie sheet. When done, dust lightly with powdered sugar. Yield: 6 to 7 dozen.

MOLASSES PEANUT BUTTER COOKIES

½ cup shortening
½ cup sugar
½ cup light molasses
½ cup chunky peanut butter
1 egg

2 cups all-purpose flour
¼ teaspoon soda
¼ teaspoon baking powder
¼ teaspoon salt

In mixing bowl, cream together shortening and sugar; beat in molasses, peanut butter and egg. Combine flour, soda, baking powder and salt. Stir into peanut butter mixture. Mix well. Drop dough by rounded teaspoons 2 inches apart on ungreased cookie sheet. Flatten slightly with fork tines. Bake at 375° for 8 minutes or until done. Yield: 4 dozen cookies.

CHEWY CHOCOLATE MACAROONS

1 (14-ounce) package flaked
  coconut
1 (14-ounce) can sweetened
  condensed milk

2 teaspoons vanilla extract
4 squares unsweetened
  chocolate, melted

Combine all ingredients in a bowl and mix well. Drop teaspoons, 1 inch apart, on well greased baking sheet. Bake at 350° for 10 to 12 minutes. Remove from baking sheet immediately. Yield: 8 dozen.

MERINGUE COOKIES

3 egg whites
1 pinch salt
1 pinch cream of tartar
1 cup sugar
¾ teaspoon almond flavoring
1 cup chopped pecans

Preheat oven to 350°. Beat first 5 ingredients until stiff. Fold in nuts. Drop by teaspoons onto pan covered with aluminum foil. Turn off oven. Leave cookies in oven 3 hours or overnight. Yield: 1 dozen cookies.

NUT SMACKERS

1 egg white
¾ cup brown sugar
2 tablespoons sifted self-rising flour
½ teaspoon vanilla extract
2 cups pecan halves

Heat oven to 250°. Beat egg whites until soft peaks form. Mix in sugar, flour and vanilla. Fold in pecans. Place pecans, well-coated, on a cookie sheet 1 inch apart. Bake for 30 minutes. Remove from oven and cool on pan. Store in airtight container. Yield: 2 cups.

ALMOND BRICKLE

1¼ cups toasted almonds, coarsely chopped
1 cup butter
1½ cups firmly packed brown sugar
2 cups milk chocolate morsels

Sprinkle almonds over bottom of well greased 13x9-inch baking pan; set aside. In a heavy saucepan, melt butter. Stir in brown sugar until dissolved. Bring to a boil over medium heat. Boil, stirring constantly, for 7 minutes. Pour over nuts. Let stand for a few minutes. Sprinkle with chocolate morsels; let chocolate become shiny and spread over nut mixture. Chill in refrigerator 20 minutes. Cut into 1¼-inch squares. Yield: 4 dozen.

ANNE'S FUDGE

2 tablespoons butter, melted
3 cups sugar
5 tablespoons cocoa
½ cup light corn syrup
1 cup evaporated milk
½ teaspoon salt
½ cup chopped nuts
½ cup peanut butter, optional

Melt butter and set aside. Mix sugar, cocoa, syrup, milk and salt. Cook over medium heat, stirring constantly until soft ball stage. Remove from heat and stir in melted butter. Beat until thick and smooth. Add nuts and peanut butter. Mix well. Pour into buttered 8-inch square baking dish. Yield: 36 servings.

GRANNY'S PRALINES

2 cups sugar
½ cup milk
½ cup light corn syrup
2 tablespoons butter or margarine
¼ teaspoon baking soda
1 teaspoon vanilla extract
2 cups pecans

Combine first 5 ingredients in a heavy saucepan; mix well. Cook over medium heat, stirring until sugar dissolves; cook until mixture reaches soft ball stage (232°). Remove from heat; add vanilla and beat until creamy. Stir in pecans. Drop by tablespoonsful onto waxed paper; let stand until firm. Yield: 3 dozen.

ENGLISH TOFFEE

1 cup butter or margarine
1 cup sugar
2 (1.2-ounce) plain chocolate bars

1 cup chopped nuts

Melt butter or margarine over low heat. Add sugar and continue to cook over medium heat, stirring constantly, until mixture turns golden brown. Turn quickly onto cookie sheet and spread out as thin as possible. Break candy bars into small pieces and place on top of butter mixture. As chocolate melts, spread evenly. Top with chopped nuts. Candy will crack into irregular pieces easily. Store candy in a covered container in refrigerator. Candy may be frozen. Yield: 12 servings.

PEANUT BRITTLE

1 cup sugar
½ cup dark corn syrup
¼ cup water

1 cup raw peanuts
1 tablespoon butter
1 teaspoon soda

Grease cookie sheet and set aside. In a heavy iron skillet, combine sugar, syrup and water. Cook on high heat, stirring constantly, until all water vapor disappears. Add raw peanuts. Lower heat to medium and continue to cook and stir 3 to 4 minutes. Add butter and soda and stir quickly. Pour onto cookie sheet and spread with the back side of a spoon. When cool break into pieces and store in airtight container. Yield: 1 pound.

PEANUT BUTTER LOGS

1 (12-ounce) jar extra crunchy peanut butter
2 cups graham cracker crumbs
1 (1-pound) box powdered sugar
1 cup margarine

1 teaspoon vanilla extract
1 cup chopped peanuts
12 ounces semisweet chocolate morsels
½ bar parrafin

Mix first six ingredients with hands; shape into small logs. Melt chocolate and wax in the top of a double boiler. Dip peanut butter logs into chocolate. Place on waxed paper until dry. Yield: 1 to 1½ dozen.

MOCHA-BOURBON BALLS

12 (1-ounce) squares semisweet chocolate
½ cup butter
⅓ cup sugar
½ cup whipping cream
¼ cup bourbon
1 tablespoon instant coffee granules
2 cups ground pecans, divided
¾ cup chocolate wafer crumbs

Combine chocolate, butter and sugar in top of a double boiler; bring water to a boil. Reduce heat to low; cook until chocolate and butter melt. Remove from heat; stir in cream, bourbon, coffee granules and 1 cup pecans. Cover and refrigerate until firm. Combine remaining pecans and wafer crumbs; mix well. Shape chocolate mixture into 1 inch balls and roll in crumb mixture. Store in refrigerator. Yield: 5 dozen.

DOODADS

1 pound (approximately) white chocolate
2 cups thin pretzels, broken into small pieces
12 ounces salted Spanish peanuts

Melt white chocolate in top of double boiler. Stir in pretzel pieces and peanuts. Drop by teaspoonsful onto waxed paper. Cool. Candy will harden. Store in airtight container. Yield: approximately 2 dozen.

CHEWIES

2 (6-ounce) packages butterscotch bits
1 (6-ounce) package chocolate bits
1 can Chinese noodles (small size)
½ cup cashews

Melt bits over low heat. Stir in noodles and nuts. Drop by teaspoon onto waxed paper. Cool. Yield: 2 dozen.

SOMETHING SPECIAL

SOMETHING SPECIAL

Many of the recipes in this section may be prepared with minimal adult assistance. However, for safety's sake, adult supervision is encouraged.

ORNAMENT DOUGH

1 cup salt
1½ cups warm water

4 cups all-purpose flour

Mix salt and water; cool. Add flour; knead dough for 10 minutes. Shape dough or roll out and cut with cookie cutters. Use a drinking straw to punch hole for hanging. Bake at 300° for 45 to 60 minutes. Cool. Paint with tempra, acrylics or magic markers. When paint dries, ornaments may be sprayed or painted with varnish.

SOAP BUBBLES

When all the "bought" bubble solution has been used or spilled, replace with:

½ cup warm water
1½ teaspoons liquid detergent

¾ teaspoon sugar
¾ teaspoon glycerin (optional)

Combine ingredients (glycerin will make bubbles iridescent). Pour into plastic jar or container.

NONHARDENING CLAY

1 cup all purpose flour
1 cup water
½ cup salt

2 teaspoons cream of tartar
1 tablespoon cooking oil
Food color of choice

Combine all ingredients in medium sauce pan. Cook over medium heat, stirring until mixture forms a dough consistency. Store in air tight container.

FINGER PUDDING PAINT

1 (3-ounce) package instant pudding mix

butcher paper or plastic coated paper plates

Prepare pudding according to directions. Spoon pudding in small helpings and paint. *Children can "lick and paint" at the same time. Add food coloring to vanilla pudding for a variety of colors.*

HOT DOG PIZZA

2 English muffins
4 tablespoons ketchup
1 weiner, sliced in circles

4 tablespoons shredded Cheddar cheese

Split muffins. Spread 1 tablespoon ketchup on each muffin. Put weiner circles on muffin halves. Top with cheese. Bake at 350° for 5 to 7 minutes. Yield: 4 servings.

CORN DOGS

oil for frying
1 egg
½ cup milk
1 cup biscuit mix
2 tablespoons yellow corn meal
¼ teaspoon paprika

½ teaspoon dry mustard
⅛ teaspoon cayenne
1 (1-pound) package frankfurters
8 to 10 wooden sticks

Heat oil in deep fryer to 375°. Blend egg and milk. Stir in dry ingredients and seasonings. Push wooden stick in one end of each frankfurter. Dip franks in batter. Fry 2 to 3 minutes or until brown. Yield: 8 to 10 servings.

ORANGE-SICLES

1 (6-ounce) can orange juice concentrate, undiluted
3 cans cold water

1 egg white
2 tablespoons sugar or honey

Mix in blender. Pour into molds or small paper cups; insert wooden stick. Freeze.

FROZEN GRAPES

For a different treat, freeze green seedless grapes and serve in paper cups.

BANANA MILKSHAKE

1 banana
1 cup milk

1 large scoop ice cream

Place all ingredients in a blender. Blend until smooth. Yield: 1 shake.

BANANA WHIP

1½ cups milk
1 large banana

1 teaspoon sugar
½ teaspoon vanilla extract

Mix well in blender. Yield: 1 serving.

B.O.S. FRUIT DRINK

1 banana
2 cups orange juice
1 cup strawberries, fresh or frozen

½ cup powdered milk
1 tablespoon honey

Blend and freeze until "slushy". Yield: 4 servings.

ORANGE WHIP

1 (6-ounce) can orange juice concentrate

3 cups water
1 cup powdered milk

Thaw frozen concentrate. Put all ingredients in a blender. Whip and serve. Yield: 4 servings.

JUICE-SICLES

1 (6-ounce) can juice concentrate (apple, grape, mixed fruit), undiluted
1 (6-ounce) can water
2 cups ice cream, softened

Mix in blender. Pour into molds; insert sticks. Freeze.

PEACH-SICLE

1 cup cream
1 (16-ounce) can peaches in light syrup, drained
1 teaspoon sugar
¼ teaspoon cinnamon

Beat cream in blender for 1 minute. Add peaches, sugar and cinnamon. Blend until smooth. Pour into molds. Insert sticks and freeze.

SUNSHINE PUNCH

2 quarts orange juice, chilled
2 quarts lemonade, chilled
2 quarts ginger ale, chilled
4 cups crushed ice

Combine chilled ingredients just before serving. Stir gently. Add 4 cups crushed ice. Makes 1¾ gallons delicious, light punch. *Great for children's parties - no caffeine and no artificial coloring. Good with birthday cake!* Yield: 45 (5-ounce) servings.

HOT CHOCOLATE MIX

1 (1-pound) can powdered chocolate milk mix
1 (25.6-ounce) box non-fat dry milk
1 (7-ounce) jar non-dairy creamer
⅔ cup sifted powdered sugar

Mix all ingredients and store in airtight container. To serve, put 2 tablespoons mix in a cup and add hot water. Yield: 3-pounds 3-ounces. *Spoon into pint jars and give as gifts. Perfect Teacher's gift.*

APPLESAUCE

8 medium apples   ½ cup sugar
water

Wash, peel, quarter and core apples. Put apples in a large saucepan and add water to ½ inch depth. Cover tightly; bring to a boil. Lower heat and simmer until apples are very soft. Add sugar. Stir and cook 15 minutes longer. For a spicy flavor and pink color add 2 tablespoons of cinnamon red hot candies at the simmer stage, stirring to dissolve. Yield: 4 servings.

APPLE-WICHES

1 medium apple   peanut butter

Wash and core apple. Slice apple horizontally into thin slices. Spread one slice of apple with peanut butter. Top with a second apple slice like a sandwich. Yield: 2 servings.

CANDLESTICK SALAD

1 pineapple slice   ½ cherry
1 lettuce leaf
1 small banana, cut in half
   crosswise

Place pineapple slice on lettuce leaf. Stand banana half in center and top with cherry. Yield: 1 serving.

PETER RABBIT SALAD

1 pear half   1 cherry slice
lettuce leaf   2 raisins
1 large marshmallow

Place pear half, cut side down, on lettuce leaf. Cut marshmallow in half; use ½ for tail and ¼ for each ear. Use cherry slice for mouth and raisins for eyes. Small end of the pear is the head. Yield: 1 serving.

FRAME THOSE EGGS

4 large eggs
4 slices bread
margarine
salt and pepper to taste

Heat skillet or griddle. With a round biscuit cutter, cut the center from each slice of bread and store for future use. Butter both sides of bread and brown each in skillet on one side only. Turn and carefully drop egg in center hole. Cook until egg is set. Salt and pepper to taste and serve. Yield: 4 servings.

GRILLED CHEESE PLUS

2 slices bacon
1 English muffin
butter
2 slices tomato
2 slices American cheese

Cook bacon and set aside. Split and butter muffins; toast until lightly browned. Break bacon in half and put 2 halves on each muffin. Put tomato on top of bacon. Top tomato with cheese. Broil 5 inches from heat until cheese melts. Yield: 2 servings.

CHEESE 'N MARSHMALLOW CRACKERS

saltine crackers
American cheese slices
marshmallows

Top one saltine cracker with ¼ slice American cheese. Place marshmallow on top of cheese. Broil in oven until marshmallow is soft and golden brown. Let cool. *Store marshmallows in the freezer to keep them from drying. Cut marshmallows while frozen to prevent shears or knife from getting sticky.*

POPCORN BALLS

1 (3-ounce) package flavored
   gelatin, flavor of choice
1 cup sugar
1 cup light corn syrup
3 quarts popped popcorn

Mix first 3 ingredients. Bring to a boil, stirring constantly. Pour over popcorn and toss. When the mixture has cooled enough to be handled, form into firm balls with buttered hands. Cool on waxed paper. Yield: 2 to 4 dozen, depending on size.

GRAPE SHAKIES

3 envelopes unflavored gelatin
1 (12-ounce) can frozen grape juice concentrate, thawed

1½ cups water

Soften gelatin in grape juice. Bring water to a boil; add juice mixture and stir until gelatin dissolves. Remove from heat and pour into a lightly greased (may use aerosol spray) 9x13-inch pan; chill. When firm, cut into squares. Refrigerate in covered container. Shakies may go unrefrigerated for 4 hours under normal conditions. May substitute apple or cranberry juice for grape. Yield: 24 servings.

QUICKIE DOUGHNUTS

2 (10 to 11-ounce) cans biscuits
hot shortening for deep fat frying

granulated or powdered sugar
cinnamon, optional

Punch a hole in the center of each biscuit. Fry dough in hot shortening (350°). Brown 1 minute on each side. Drain; shake doughnuts in a bag containing granulated or powdered sugar. Cinnamon may be mixed with sugar, if desired. Yield: 20 doughnuts.

CUPCAKE CONES

1 (18-ounce) box cake mix, any flavor

waffle ice cream cones

Prepare cake batter according to directions. Instead of using paper cupcake liners, use ice cream cones. Pour ¼ cup cake batter in each cone (cones should be ½ full). Do not overfill. Stand cones in muffin pans. Bake according to directions on box. Ice with favorite icing. Yield: 24 cupcakes. *To steady cones in muffin pans, wrap base of cone with aluminum foil.*

QUICK CUPCAKE ICING: *Remove cupcakes from oven and, while hot, top with chocolate chips. Spread chips as they melt. Or, top cupcakes with one large marshmallow. Return to oven to melt marshmallow.*

MICROWAVE FUDGE

2½ cups semisweet chocolate chips
1 (14-ounce) can sweetened condensed milk
¼ cup butter
1 cup chopped pecans

Place chips, milk and butter in microwave or glass dish. Microwave on 70% power until chocolate melts, stirring several times (4 minutes). Add nuts and pour into a well buttered 8-inch square baking dish. Refrigerate. Yield: 36 pieces.

CHOCOLATE CHIP CANDY

¼ cup powdered sugar
1 cup chocolate chips
½ cup sweetened condensed milk
1 cup peanut butter

Combine powdered sugar, chocolate chips, milk and peanut butter. Stir until well mixed. Drop by rounded teaspoons onto waxed paper. Chill. Yield: 24 servings.

LOLLIPOPS

2 cups sugar
1 cup light corn syrup
½ cup water
few drops oil flavoring and color of choice
lollipop sticks

Put first 3 ingredients in a heavy saucepan; cook over high heat until mixture reaches hard crack stage (290°). Remove immediately. Stir in coloring and flavoring and pour into molds. Place sticks in lollipops as they cool. Remove from molds as soon as candy pops out easily. Use only oil flavorings. Mini-muffin pans (well buttered) may be substituted for molds. Yield: approximately 24 lollipops.

PEANUT BUTTER BALLS

½ cup peanut butter, plain or crunchy
1 cup powdered milk
½ cup honey
toasted wheat germ (straight from jar)

Mix peanut butter, dry milk and honey. Shape into walnut size balls. Roll balls in wheat germ.

HONEY MILK BALLS

½ cup honey or dark corn syrup
½ cup peanut butter
1 cup powdered milk

1 cup uncooked rolled oats or
1½ cups graham cracker crumbs

Combine ingredients and mix well. Knead until blended. Shape into small balls.

VARIATION: Wrap dough around a pecan or roll in coconut. Yield: 24 balls.

WONDERFUL SUGAR COOKIES

⅔ cup shortening
¾ cup sugar
½ teaspoon grated orange peel
½ teaspoon vanilla extract
1 egg

4 teaspoons milk
2 cups sifted all-purpose flour
1½ teaspoons baking powder
⅛ teaspoon salt

Thoroughly cream shortening, sugar, orange peel and vanilla. Add egg; beat until fluffy. Stir in milk. Sift together dry ingredients; add to creamed mixture and blend. Divide dough in half; wrap in waxed paper and chill at least one hour (may be refrigerated as long as 24 hours). On floured surface, roll half of dough to ⅛-inch thickness. Keep remaining dough refrigerated until ready to use. Cut into shapes with cookie cutters. Bake on greased cookie sheet at 375° for 6 to 7 minutes or until lightly brown on edges. Cool and decorate. Store in airtight container. Yield: 2 dozen. *Perfect for Cookie Painting Party (See Index).*

OLD MCDONALD'S FARM PARTY

Invite children to come dressed as farmers.

GAMES:
1. Haystack: Have children dig through a pile of hay filled with wrapped penny candies, stickers and small toys.
2. Fishing pond: Use a small plastic swimming pool without water. Attach a paper clip to light-weight, wrapped candies. Scatter in the pool. Make fishing poles out of dowel pins, string and a magnet tied to the end.
3. Shell the Peas: Give each child a paper plate filled with unshelled blackeyed peas. After 3 to 5 minutes call time. The child with the most shelled peas wins.
4. Sing and play "The Farmer in the Dell."

CLOWN PARTY

Invite children to come dressed as clowns with makeup. As part of the games supply makeup and mirror for older children or paint faces for younger children.

GAMES:
1. Pin the Nose on the Clown: Draw a large clown without a nose. Make round circles for noses.
2. Balloon Relay: Divide children into teams. Give the first child on each team a balloon. Have them place the balloon between their knees and run to a designated spot and back to the team. The first team to finish wins.
3. Clown Parade: Give each child a toy whistle, kazoo or horn. Have them march around the yard playing their instruments.
4. Big Shoe Race: Divide children into teams. Give the first child a pair of men's shoes. Have them run to a designated spot and back to the team.

OLYMPIC PARTY

Invite children to come dressed in red, white and blue. Decorate the yard with flags, streamers and balloons. Have "athletes" salute the flag and march around yard before games commence.

GAMES:
    Relay races (Batons can be made from paper towel rolls decorated with streamers.)
    Weight lifting (Barbells can be made from broom stick handles with balloons attached to ends.)
    Jumps - Extend a streamer between poles - raise and lower.
    Basketball - Shoot for baskets
    Soccer - Kick for goals
    Frisbee throw (Be sure to throw the same direction!)

ACCESSORIES:
    Miniature flags for children to wave
    Party goods (Take advantage of July 4th decorations)
    Sports equipment

SUGGESTIONS:
    Decorate cake to resemble a flag. Mold ice cream in a star shape. Serve Strawberry Punch (See Index). Stash party gifts in a sled or small pool. Present children with ribbons at the end of the games.

COOKIE PAINTING PARTY

Make Wonderful Sugar Cookies (See Index) and cut in shapes appropriate for the season. These should be baked and cooled prior to party time.

Buy several packages small paint brushes (watercolor type); wash and dry them.

The "paint" is a mixture of sifted powdered sugar and small amounts of hot water colored with food coloring in colors appropriate for the party. (Valentines would have red, pink and white, for example.)

Mix one cup sifted powdered sugar with hot water until of relatively thin painting consistency. Color with drops of food coloring. The amount you need depends on the number of children who will paint cookies. Allow 6 to 8 cookies per child. Put 2 brushes in each cup of colored cookie paint. About 3 cups of "paint" are needed for 5 to 6 children.

Spread the table with waxed paper. Give the children aprons to cover their clothes and each a plate full of cookies to paint. Stand back and watch the fun and creativity.

TEA PARTY

Invite girls to come dressed in hats, gloves and "Mom's old dress". Set a small table with lace tablecloth and napkins. Serve punch instead of tea in teacups.

GAMES:
1. Pocketbook Game: Fill a large pocketbook with small toy make-up objects. (Such as: lipsticks, mirrors, combs, nailpolish). Each child reaches in and feels an object. If they can name it, it is theirs.
2. Jewelry: Supply each child with colored cereal with holes and some yarn. Children make their own necklaces and bracelets.
3. Paint cookies: See Index.

SUBSTITUTIONS AND EQUIVALENTS

SUBSTITUTIONS

For this:	Use this:
1 teaspoon baking powder	½ teaspoon cream of tartar plus ¼ teaspoon baking soda
1 cup fine breadcrumbs	3 to 4 slices oven dried bread
¾ cup soft breadcrumbs	1 slice bread
1 cup butter	1 cup margarine or 1 cup hydrogenated fat plus ½ teaspoon salt
1 cup ketchup or chili sauce *(for cooking only)*	1 cup tomato sauce plus ½ cup sugar and 2 tablespoons vinegar
1 square (1-ounce) chocolate, unsweetened	3 tablespoons cocoa, plus 1 tablespoon butter
1 square (1-ounce) chocolate, semi-sweet	3 tablespoons cocoa plus 4 teaspoons sugar plus 1 tablespoon butter, or 1 ounce unsweetened chocolate plus 4 teaspoons sugar
1½ teaspoons cornstarch	1 tablespoon flour
¾ cup cracker crumbs	1 cup breadcrumbs
1 cup light cream, half-and-half *(for baking only)*	3 tablespoons butter plus ⅞ cup milk
1 cup heavy cream *(for cooking only, not whipping)*	⅓ cup butter plus ¾ cup milk
1 cup cream, sour	⅓ cup butter plus ¾ cup milk or 1 cup cottage cheese and ¼ cup buttermilk blended with ½ teaspoon lemon juice
1 whole egg	2 egg yolks plus 1 tablespoon water (for thickening or baking) or 2 egg yolks (for custards)
2 large eggs	3 small eggs
1 tablespoon flour, all-purpose *(for thickening)*	½ tablespoon cornstarch or 2 teaspoons quick-cooking tapioca
1 cup all-purpose flour	1 cup plus 2 tablespoons cake flour
1 cup cake flour	1 cup minus 2 tablespoons all-purpose flour
1 clove garlic	⅛ teaspoon dehydrated minced garlic or ⅛ teaspoon garlic powder
1 tablespoon fresh snipped herbs	1 teaspoon dried
1 cup honey	1¼ cups sugar plus ¼ cup water
1 tablespoon grated lemon rind	1 medium lemon
1 cup milk, whole	½ cup evaporated milk plus ½ cup water or 4 tablespoons dry whole milk plus 1 cup water

3 tablespoons grated orange rind — 1 medium orange
1 cup sour milk or buttermilk — 1 tablespoon vinegar or lemon juice plus enough sweet milk to make 1 cup (let stand 5 minutes)
1 pound fresh mushrooms — 6 ounces canned mushrooms
1 tablespoon prepared mustard — 1 teaspoon dry mustard
1 tablespoon instant onion — 1 small fresh onion
1 cup sugar — 1 cup molasses plus ¼ teaspoon baking soda (omit baking powder)
1 cup tomatoes, canned — 1⅓ cups cut-up fresh tomatoes, simmered 10 minutes
1 cup tomato juice — ½ cup tomato sauce plus ½ cup water
1 cake compressed yeast — 1 package or 2 teaspoons active dry yeast
1 cup yogurt — 1 cup buttermilk

EQUIVALENTS

3 teaspoons = 1 tablespoon

4 tablespoons = ¼ cup

5⅓ tablespoons = ⅓ cup

8 tablespoons = ½ cup

10⅔ tablespoons = ⅔ cup

12 tablespoons = ¾ cup

16 tablespoons = 1 cup

2 cups = 1 pint

4 cups = 1 quart

4 quarts = 1 gallon

8 quarts = 1 peck

4 pecks = 1 bushel

16 ounces = 1 pound

32 ounces = 1 quart

8 ounces, liquid = 1 cup

1 ounce, liquid = 2 tablespoons

INDEX

INDEX

A

Almond Brickle	232
Almond Rice	162
Almost Yeast Rolls	80
Amaretto Blueberries	187
Amaretto Cake	197
Amaretto Cheese Cake	210
Amaretto Chicken Salad	113
Ambrosia	186
Anise Cookies	221
Anne's Fudge	232

APPETIZERS
  CHEESE AND SOUR CREAM
Cheese and Date Dip	8
Cheese Crackers	23
Cheese in a Bread Bowl	8
Cheese-Olive Balls	11
Cheese Spread	8
Chili Cheese Cubes	12
Easy Cheese Straws	10
Ham Cheese Spread	10
Hot Broccoli and Cheese Dip	22
Party Sandwich Bites	11
Pecan Curry Spread	9
Pimento Cheese Spread	12
Pineapple Cheese Ball	11
Pizza Bread	16
Sour Cream Dip	12

  MEATS
Bacon Rye Balls	13
Bacon Tater Bites With Mustard Sauce	13
Bacon Wrapped Olives	14
Chicken Nachos	15
Cocktail Meatballs	14
Curried Chicken Bites	15
Curried Ham Roll	15
Ham Cheese Spread	10
Hot Rye Rounds	14
Red Devil Balls	16
Saucy Franks	16

  NUTS
Dry Roasted Pecans	24
Italian Wheat Snack	24
Sugared Peanuts	23
Toasted Pecans	24

  SEAFOOD
Caviar Pie	17
Crab Meat Dip	17
Creamy Tuna Dip	19
Hot Crab Appetizer	17
Lobster Dip	18
Salmon Party Ball	18
Seafood Spread	18
Shrimp Beignets	19
Shrimp Celery	19

  VEGETABLE
Artichoke Squares	20
Asparagus Dip	20
Broccoli Dip	21
Con Queso Dip	21
Fresh Vegetable Dip	21
Hot Broccoli and Cheese Dip	22
Mushroom Appetizer	22
Party Sandwich Bites	11
Spinach Feta Triangles	9
Vegetable Marinade	22
Zucchini Bites	23

APPLE
Apple Brandy Pork Chops	154
Apple Cranberry Casserole	160
Apple Salad	65
Applesauce	240
Apple-wiches	240
Baked Apples	160
French Apple Cobbler	213
Fresh Apple Cake	201
Fried Apples	160
Johnny Appleseed Bars	225
Apricot Brandy Chicken	103
Apricot Pie	213
Artichoke Squares	20
Artichoke, Tomatoes With Artichoke Hearts	178
Arved's Orange Biscuits	78
Asheville Salad	56

ASPARAGUS
Asparagus, Cheese And Mushroom Casserole	164
Asparagus Dip	20
Asparagus Mornay	164
Asparagus With Orange Butter Sauce	164

INDEX

Augusta's Favorite Salad 56
Aunt Hautie's Fruitcake Cookies 228
Aunt Sarah's Chocolate Pound Cake 204
Autumn Punch 31

B

BACON
Bacon And Egg Cake 91
Bacon Muffins 79
Bacon-Rye Balls 13
Bacon Tater Bites With Mustard
  Sauce 13
Bacon Wrapped Olives 14
Baked Apples 160
Baked Cheddar Tomatoes 179
Baked Crab Casserole 129
Baked Dove 116
Baked Pork Chops 154
Baked Red Snapper 124
Baked Salmon Steaks 123
Baked Scrambled Eggs 92
Baked Spaghetti 146
Baked Stuffed Flounder Fillets 120
Baked Stuffed Tomatoes 180
Baked Ziti 147
Banana, Frozen Banana Salad 65
Banana Milkshake 238
Banana Whip 238
Barbecue Beef Sandwiches 144
Barbecued Rice 163
Barbecue Sauce 46
Barbecue Sauce (Fondue) 50
Basic Omelet 96
Basic Pie Crust 220
Basic White Sauce 44
Batter For Fried Shrimp 131

BEANS
Black Bean Gazpacho 34
Green Beans Amandine 165
Hearty Bean Soup 34
Pickled Beans 165
Red Beans and Rice 166
Snibbled Beans 165
Southern Fried Green Beans 166
Spicy Baked Beans 166
Three Bean Salad 57
Bearnaise Sauce 45
Beautiful Bread 74

BEEF
Barbecue Beef Sandwiches 144
Beef Burgundy 139
Beef Carbonnade 137
Beef Pasty 144
Beef Quiche 93
Beef Stroganoff 143
Broiled Sirloin Steak with
  Garlic Sauce 140
Curried Beef and Peppers 141
Grilled Round Steak 140
Individual Beef Wellingtons 136
New Orleans Steak Diane 138
Oriental Beef 142
Pepper Steak 141
Reuben Casserole 151
Skirt Steak Oriental 139
Steak and Vegetable Kabobs 138
Sweet 'N' Sour Flank Steak 140
Swiss Steak 143
Teriyaki Fondue 142

BEEF, GROUND
Baked Spaghetti 146
Baked Ziti 147
Chili 149
Chili Casserole 149
Hamburger Casserole 148
Marinated Grill Burgers 151
Marvelous Meatloaf 147
Moussaka 145
Perfect Pizza 150
Stuffed Peppers 146
Taco Dinner 150
Vegetable-Burger Soup 40
Zucchini-Beef Casserole 148
Beer Biscuits 77

BEETS
Borscht Salad 56
Honey Orange Beets 168
Better-For-You Sour Cream 48

BEVERAGES
Autumn Punch 31
Banana Milkshake 238
Banana Whip 238
B.O.S. Fruit Drink 238
Brandy Ice 26
Champagne Punch 26
Easy Coffee Liqueur 30
Eggnog Bowl 32
Frozen Fruit Daiquiri 26
Fruit Milk Shake 28
Hot Buttered Rum 31
Hot Chocolate Mix 239
Hot Eggnog 32
Hot Mulled Cider 31
Irish Cream 30
Mimosa Hawaiian 29
Montgomery Christmas Punch 32
Orange Jewel 29
Orange Whip 238
Party Style Mint Julep 26

252 INDEX

Peach Sour 28
Pina Colada 27
Russian Coffee 30
Strawberry Punch 29
Strawberry Spritzers 27
Summer Punch 29
Sunshine Punch 239
Syllabub 27
Tomato Wow 28
Tropical Milk 28
Watermelon Screwdrivers 27
Whiskey Punch 30

BISCUITS *(see* **BREADS)**

Black Bean Gazpacho 34
Blueberries, Amaretto 187
Blueberry Cheese Pie 212
Blueberry Dumplings 187
Blueberry Salad 66
Blue Cheese Dressing 71
Blue Cheese Quiche 93
Borscht Salad 56
B.O.S. Fruit Drink 238
Boston Brown Bread 85
Brandied Fruit 186
Brandy Ice 26
Brandy Syrup 196

BREADS
  BISCUITS
    Arved's Orange Biscuits 78
    Beer Biscuits 77
    Cheese Biscuits 77
    Mile-High Biscuits 78
  BREADS
    Beautiful Bread 74
    Boston Brown Bread 85
    Cheese and Onion Bread 76
    Christmas Stollen 83
    Corn Spoon Bread 76
    Date Nut Loaf 87
    Dill Cottage Cheese Bread 75
    English Muffin Loaves 74
    Hobo Bread 85
    Lemon Loaf 84
    Orange French Toast 83
    Pizza Bread 16
    Poppy Seed Bread 85
    Prune Bread 86
    Pumpkin Loaf 87
    Soft Bread Sticks 77
    Strawberry Bread 86
    Stuffed French Toast 84
    White Batter Bread 75
    Zucchini Bread 76

COFFEE CAKES
  Caramel Orange Coffee Ring 81
  Overnight Coffee Cake 82
  Streusel Coffee Cake 82
CORNBREAD, HUSHPUPPIES
  Sausage Cornbread Stuffing 88
  Hush Puppies 88
MUFFINS
  Bacon Muffins 79
  Broccoli Muffins 79
  Buttermilk Blueberry Muffins 79
  Carrot Bran Muffins 80
ROLLS
  Almost Yeast Rolls 80
  Icebox Parkerhouse Rolls 80
Breakfast Casserole 97
BROCCOLI
  Broccoli Dip 21
  Broccoli Muffins 79
  Broccoli Puff 167
  Buttermilk Broccoli Soup 35
  Hot Broccoli and Cheese Dip 22
  Oriental Broccoli Rice Casserole 167
Broiled Sirloin Steak with Garlic Sauce ... 140
Broiled Trout Fillets 125
Broken Glass Salad 64
Brownie Baked Alaska 191
Brown Sugar Almond Bars 224
Brunswick Stew 39
Brussels Sprouts, Marinated 167
Butter Frosting 209
Butter, Strawberry 88
Buttermilk Blueberry Muffins 79
Buttermilk Broccoli Soup 35
Buttermilk Chocolate Cake 198

C

Cabbage, Marinated Cole Slaw 57
CAKES
  Amaretto Cake 197
  Aunt Sarah's Chocolate Pound Cake 204
  Buttermilk Chocolate Cake 198
  Chewy Cake 199
  Coconut Pound Cake 204
  Confection Fruit Cake 206
  Crunch Cake 202
  Cupcake Cones 242
  Devil's Food Spice Cake 202
  Dump Pound Cake 205
  Everyday Yellow Cake 208
  Fresh Apple Cake 201
  Fresh Rhubarb Cake 203
  Funnel Cakes 209
  Grandma's Cold Oven Pound Cake . 205
  Granny's Never Fail White Cake . 198

INDEX

Hawaiian Cake	208
Holiday Gift Cake	206
Hummingbird Cake	199
Italian Cream Cake	200
Laura's Lemon Cake	203
Orange Pound Cake	205
Pumpkin Cream Cake Roll	207
Red Velvet Cake	201
Wine Cake	200
California Quiche	93
Candlestick Salad	240

CANDY

Almond Brickle	232
Anne's Fudge	232
Chewies	234
Chocolate Chip Candy	243
Doodads	234
English Toffee	233
Granny's Pralines	232
Lollipops	243
Microwave Fudge	243
Mocha-Bourbon Balls	234
Peanut Brittle	233
Peanut Butter Logs	233
Cantaloupe Soup, Fresh	36
Caramel Orange Coffee Ring	81
Caramel Vanilla Fruit	186

CARROT

Carrot Bars	225
Carrot Bran Muffins	80
Carrot Casserole	168
French Carrot Soup	35
Quick Orange Carrots	168
Sweet and Sour Carrot Salad	58

CASSEROLES

Apple-Cranberry Casserole	160
Asparagus, Cheese and Mushroom Casserole	164
Baked Crab Casserole	129
Baked Spaghetti	146
Baked Ziti	147
Breakfast Casserole	97
Carrot Casserole	168
Chicken Tetrazzini	111
Chili Casserole	149
Crab and Shrimp Casserole	129
Eggplant Casserole	170
Grated Sweet Potato Casserole	176
Green Pea Casserole	173
Hamburger Casserole	148
Mushroom Casserole	171
Oriental Broccoli Rice Casserole	167
Pineapple-Cheese Casserole	161
Potato Breakfast Casserole	98
Potato Casserole	175
Reuben Casserole	151
Rice Casserole	163
Shrimp Casserole	131
Six Layer Venison Dish	118
Spinach-Cheese Casserole	177
Vidalia Onion Casserole	172
Zucchini-Beef Casserole	148
Catfish Stew	124
Cauliflower Salad	58
Cauliflower with Mustard Sauce	169
Caviar Pie	17
Celery Seed Dressing	71
Celery, Shrimp	19
Champagne Punch	26
Charleston Chess Pie	216

CHEESE

Asparagus, Cheese and Mushroom Casserole	164
Baked Cheddar Tomatoes	179
Baked Scrambled Eggs	92
Basic Omelet	96
Beef Quiche	93
Blue Cheese Quiche	93
Breakfast Casserole	97
California Quiche	93
Cheese and Date Dip	8
Cheese and Onion Bread	76
Cheese and Sausage Crepes	90
Cheese Biscuits	77
Cheese Crackers	23
Cheese in a Bread Bowl	8
Cheese 'N Marshmallow Crackers	241
Cheese-Olive Balls	11
Cheese Spread	8
Cheesy Chicken	111
Chili Cheese Cubes	12
Christmas Quiche	94
Easy Cheese Straws	10
Egg and Cheese Strata	90
Golden Onion Quiche	94
Greek Egg and Spinach Pie	91
Grilled Cheese Plus	241
Ham Cheese Spread	10
Hot Broccoli and Cheese Dip	22
Macaroni and Cheese	98
Microwave Cheese Sauce	45
Molded Cheese Salad	59
Mozzarella Zucchini Spears	181
Mushroom Quiche	95
Nightmare Sandwiches	98
Onion Frittata	92
Perfect Cheese Souffle	97

254 INDEX

Pimento Cheese Spread 12
Pineapple Cheddar Salad 68
Pineapple Cheese Ball 11
Pineapple-Cheese Casserole 161
Potato Breakfast Casserole 98
Potato Quiche 95
Salmon Potato Cheese Soup 43
Salsa Alla Carbonara 96
Spinach-Cheese Casserole 177
Spinach Feta Triangles 9
Spinach-Ricotta Stuffed Tomatoes 178
Tuna Cheese Burger 128
CHEESE CAKES
   Amaretto Cheese Cake 210
   Cheese Cake Tarts 219
   Cream Cheese Bites 220
   Cream Cheese Tarts 219
   Creamy Cheese Cake 210
   Ricotta Cheese Cake 211
Cheesy Chicken 111
Cherries Jubilee 189
Cherry, Frozen Cherry Salad 66
Cherry Torte 190
Chewies 234
Chewy Cake 199
Chewy Chocolate Macaroons 230
CHICKEN (see also **POULTRY**)
   Chicken and Sausage Jambalaya 112
   Chicken Breasts in Wine 104
   Chicken Breasts with Cream 104
   Chicken Cordon Bleu 100
   Chicken Curry Salad 114
   Chicken Gumbo 112
   Chicken Nachos 15
   Chicken Noodle Soup 40
   Chicken Normandy 102
   Chicken Tetrazzini 111
   Chicken with Mushrooms 110
CHILDREN
   Applesauce 240
   Apple-wiches 240
   Banana Milkshake 238
   Banana Whip 238
   B.O.S. Fruit Drink 238
   Candlestick Salad 240
   Cheese 'N Marshmallow Crackers 241
   Chocolate Chip Candy 243
   Clown Party 245
   Cookie Painting Party 246
   Corn Dogs 237
   Cupcake Cones 242
   Finger Pudding Paint 237
   Frame Those Eggs 241
   Frozen Grapes 238

Grape Shakies 242
Grilled Cheese Plus 241
Honey Milk Balls 244
Hot Chocolate Mix 239
Hot Dog Pizza 237
Juice-sicles 239
Lollipops 243
Microwave Fudge 243
Nonhardening Clay 236
Old McDonald's Farm Party 244
Olympic Party 245
Orange-sicles 237
Orange Whip 238
Ornament Dough 236
Peach-sicle 239
Peanut Butter Balls 243
Peter Rabbit Salad 240
Popcorn Balls 241
Quickie Doughnuts 242
Soap Bubbles 236
Sunshine Punch 239
Tea Party 246
Wonderful Sugar Cookies 244
Chili 149
Chili Casserole 149
Chili Cheese Cubes 12
Chili Sauce (Fondue) 49
Chinese Tea Cookies 221
CHOCOLATE
   Aunt Sarah's Chocolate Pound Cake 204
   Buttermilk Chocolate Cake 198
   Chewy Chocolate Macaroons 230
   Chocolate-aire 192
   Chocolate Chip Candy 243
   Chocolate-Coconut Balls 222
   Chocolate Eclairs 193
   Chocolate Pecan Pie 215
   Chocolate Syrup 197
   Grandma's Chocolate Pie 215
   Hot Chocolate Mix 239
   Last Minute Chocolate Drop Cookies ... 228
   Quick Chocolate Cookies 229
Christmas Quiche 94
Christmas Stollen 83
Clafouti of Peas 174
Clams Casino 129
Clown Party 245
Cocktail Meatballs 14
Coconut, Chocolate-Coconut Balls ... 222
Coconut Chicken Salad 52
Coconut, Impossible Coconut Pie 217
Coconut Pound Cake 204
COFFEE CAKES (see **BREADS**)
Cole Slaw, Marinated 57

INDEX

Colleen's Wedding Cookies 221
Colorful Pasta Salad 55
Condensed Milk, Sweetened 48
Confection Fruit Cake 206
Con Queso Dip 21
Cookie Painting Party 246
COOKIES
  BARS
    Brown Sugar Almond Bars 224
    Carrot Bars 225
    Johnny Appleseed Bars 225
    Oatmeal Brownies 226
    Peanut Butter Squares 226
    Raspberry Squares 226
  DROP
    Aunt Hautie's Fruitcake Cookies 228
    Chewy Chocolate Macaroons 230
    Good For You Cookies 229
    Last Minute Chocolate Drop
      Cookies 228
    Meringue Cookies 231
    Molasses Peanut Butter Cookies 230
    Nut Smackers 231
    Oatmeal Hermits 227
    Potato Chip Shortbread Cookies 230
    Quick Chocolate Cookies 229
    Snickerdoodles 227
    Whoopie Pies 194
  SHAPED
    Anise Cookies 221
    Chinese Tea Cookies 221
    Chocolate-Coconut Balls 222
    Colleen's Wedding Cookies 221
    Date Crispies 223
    Honey Milk Balls 244
    Icebox Cookies 223
    Orange Balls 223
    Peanut Butter Balls 243
    Peanut Butter Kiss Cookies 224
    Spice Balls 222
    Wonderful Sugar Cookies 244
Coq au Vin 101
Coquilles St. Jacques 133
CORN
    Corn Chowder 36
    Corn Dogs 237
    Corn Pudding 169
    Corn Salad 59
    Corn Spoon Bread 76
    Creamed Corn 169
Cornbread, Sausage Cornbread
  Stuffing 88
Cornish Hens 115
Country Potatoes 175

Country Soup 40
CRAB *(see also* **SEAFOOD)**
  Crab and Shrimp Casserole 129
  Crab Meat Dip 17
  Crab Stuffed Eggplant 132
  Hot Crab Appetizer 17
Crackers, Cheese 23
CRANBERRY
  Apple Cranberry Casserole 160
  Cranberry Cream Salad 66
  Cranberry Sauce 47
  Frozen Cranberry Pie 212
Cream Cheese Bites 220
Cream Cheese Tarts 219
Creamed Corn 169
Creamy Baked Chicken Breasts 102
Creamy Cheese Cake 210
Creamy Orange-Lime Mold 68
Creamy Squash Soup 39
Creamy Tuna Dip 19
Creme Crecy 36
Creole Eggplant 170
Creole Fish 126
Creole, Shrimp 130
Crepes, Cheese and Sausage 90
Crescent Chicken Squares 110
Crunch Cake 202
Crunchy Rice Salad 62
Crust, Basic Pie Crust 220
Cucumber Salad 59
Cucumbers, Sweet and Sour 170
Cupcake Cones 242
Curried Beef and Peppers 141
Curried Chicken Bites 15
Curried Fish Fillets 126
Curried Ham Roll 15
Curried Pears 161
Curried Rice Salad 62
Curried Tuna-Mushroom Soup 41
Curry, Pecan Curry Spread 9
Curry Sauce (Fondue) 50
Custard Pie 217
D
Date, Cheese and Date Dip 8
Date Crispies 223
Date-Nut Loaf 87
David's Not-So-Sweet Pecan Pie 216
DESSERTS *(see also* **CAKES, COOKIES,**
PIES and **CANDY)**
  CHEESE CAKES
    Amaretto Cheese Cake 210
    Cheese Cake Tarts 219
    Cream Cheese Bites 220
    Cream Cheese Tarts 219

256 INDEX

Creamy Cheese Cake 210
Ricotta Cheese Cake 211
CUSTARDS
  Chocolate Eclairs 193
  Noodle Kugle 195
  Quick and Easy Pot de Creme 194
FROZEN
  Brownie Baked Alaska.............191
  Lemon Cooler 187
  Strawberry Ice Cream 196
  Tropical Ice 195
  Uncooked Vanilla Ice Cream 196
FRUIT
  Amaretto Blueberries 187
  Ambrosia 186
  Blueberry Dumplings 187
  Brandied Fruit 186
  Caramel Vanilla Fruit 186
  Cherries Jubilee 189
  Cherry Torte 190
  Dipped Strawberries 189
  French Apple Cobbler 213
  Fruit Cobbler 212
  Macedoine de Fruits 189
  Peach Clafouti 190
  Strawberries Romanoff 188
MERINGUES
  Individual Meringue Shells 195
REFRIGERATOR
  Chocolate-aire 192
  Lady Finger Dessert 191
  Strawberry Delight 188
SAUCES
  Brandy Syrup 196
  Chocolate Syrup 197
  Praline Ice Cream Topping.........196
  Sweetened Condensed Milk 48
TARTS
  Cream Cheese Tarts 219
  Lemon Almond Tart..............192
  Miniature Pecan Tarts 218
  Walnut Maple Tarts 218
Devil's Food Spice Cake 202
Dill Cottage Cheese Bread 75
Dill, Lemon Dill Horseradish Sauce 47
Dipped Strawberries..................189
DIPS
  Asparagus Dip 20
  Broccoli Dip 21
  Cheese and Date Dip   8
  Con Queso Dip 21
  Crab Meat Dip 17
  Creamy Tuna Dip 19
  Fresh Vegetable Dip 21

  Hot Broccoli and Cheese Dip 22
  Lobster Dip 18
  Sour Cream Dip 12
Doodads 234
Dove, Baked 116
Dove, Drunken 115
DRESSINGS, SALAD (see **SALAD DRESSING**)
Dry Roasted Pecans 24
Dump Pound Cake 205

E

Easy Cheese Straws 10
Easy Chicken Chop Suey 103
Easy Coffee Liqueur 30
Easy Hollandaise Sauce 45
Easy Potato Bake 175
Easy Sweet and Sour Chicken 108
Easy Sweet Potato Souffle 177
Eggnog Bowl...................... 32
EGGPLANT
  Creole Eggplant..................170
  Crab Stuffed Eggplant 132
  Eggplant Casserole 170
  Fried Eggplant 171
  Ratatouille Provencal 183
EGGS
  Bacon and Egg Cake 91
  Baked Scrambled Eggs 92
  Basic Omelet.................... 96
  Beef Quiche 93
  Blue Cheese Quiche 93
  Breakfast Casserole 97
  California Quiche................ 93
  Christmas Quiche 94
  Egg and Cheese Strata 90
  Frame Those Eggs 241
  Golden Onion Quiche 94
  Greek Egg and Spinach Pie 91
  Mushroom Quiche 95
  Nightmare Sandwiches 98
  Onion Frittata 92
  Perfect Cheese Souffle 97
  Potato Breakfast Casserole 98
  Potato Quiche 95
  Salsa Alla Carbonara 96
English Muffin Loaves................ 74
English Toffee 233
Equivalents 248
Everyday Yellow Cake 208
Excellent Vinaigrette................ 72

F

Faucon Salad 58
Finger Pudding Paint 237

FISH *(see also* **SEAFOOD)**
  Baked Red Snapper 124
  Baked Salmon Steaks 123
  Baked Stuffed Flounder Fillets 120
  Broiled Trout Fillets 125
  Catfish Stew 124
  Creole Fish 126
  Curried Fish Fillets 126
  Fish and Chips..................127
  Flounder a la Moutarde 120
  French Fried Fish 128
  Grilled Salmon..................124
  Grilled Swordfish with
    Horseradish Sauce..............127
  Grouper Soup 43
  Quick and Easy Fish 126
  Salmon Cutlets with Browned Butter ...122
  Salmon Potato Cheese Soup 43
  Salmon Timbales.................123
  Sauteed Scrod 121
  Savory Baked Fish................128
  Striped Bass in Butter Sauce 122
  Stuffed Dover Sole 121
  Trout Baked with Shrimp 125
  Tuna Cheese Burger 128
Five Cup Salad 65
Florida Orange Pork Chops 154
Flounder a la Moutarde 120
Fondue Sauces 49-50
Fondue, Teriyaki 142
Frame Those Eggs 241
Franks, Saucy 16
French Apple Cobbler.................213
French Carrot Soup 35
French Fried Fish 128
French Onion Pie 172
French Onion Soup 37
Fresh Apple Cake 201
Fresh Cantaloupe Soup................ 36
Fresh Peach Pie 211
Fresh Rhubarb Cake 203
Fresh Tomato Dressing 71
Fresh Vegetable Dip 21
Fried Apples 160
Fried Chicken 106
Fried Eggplant 171
Fried Green Tomatoes 179
Fried Okra 173
Fried Quail 116
Fried Rice 163
Frosting, Butter 209
Frozen Banana Salad.................. 65
Frozen Cherry Salad.................. 66
Frozen Cranberry Pie 212

Frozen Fruit Daiquiri 26
Frozen Grapes 238
Fruitcake, Aunt Hautie's Fruitcake
  Cookies 228
Fruit Milk Shake 28
FRUITS *(see individual listings also)*
  Ambrosia......................186
  Fruit Cobbler...................212
  Hot Sherried Fruits 162
Fudge, Anne's.....................232
Fudge Sundae Pie 216
Funnel Cakes 209

G

GAME
  Cornish Hens 115
  Dove, Baked 116
  Doves, Drunken 115
  Pheasant 116
  Quail, Fried 116
  Six Layer Venison Dish 118
  Venison Roast 117
  Venison Stew...................117
Game Sauce 48
Gazpacho 37
German Potato Salad 61
Golden Onion Quiche 94
Good For You Cookies 229
Grandma's Chocolate Pie 215
Grandma's Cold Oven Pound Cake 205
Granny's Giblet Gravy................ 48
Granny's Never Fail White Cake 198
Granny's Pralines 232
Grape Shakies 242
Grated Sweet Potato Casserole 176
Greek Egg and Spinach Pie............. 91
Greek Salad 60
Green Beans Amandine 165
Green Pea Casserole 173
Green Pea Salad 60
Grilled Cheese Plus 241
Grilled Chicken with Marinade 105
Grilled Ginger Chicken 105
Grilled Ham 156
Grilled Pork Chops 155
Grilled Round Steak 140
Grilled Salmon 124
Grilled Swordfish with
  Horseradish Sauce 127
Grouper Soup 43
Gumbo, Chicken 112
Gumbo, Seafood 42

H

HAM
  Curried Ham Roll 15

258 INDEX

Grilled Ham	156
Ham and Swiss Buns	156
Ham Cheese Spread	10
Ham Glaze	46
Nightmare Sandwiches	98
Red Devil Balls	16
Hamburger Casserole	148
Hawaiian Cake	208
Hawaiian Shrimp Curry	132
Hearty Bean Soup	34
Herbed Chicken	107
Hickory Barbecue Sauce	46
Hobo Bread	85
Holiday Gift Cake	206
Honey Milk Balls	244
Honey Orange Beets	168
Hot and Sour Soup	38
Hot Broccoli and Cheese Dip	22
Hot Buttered Rum	31
Hot Chicken Salad	113
Hot Chocolate Mix	239
Hot Crab Appetizer	17
Hot Dog Pizza	237
Hot Eggnog	32
Hot Mulled Cider	31
Hot Mustard Sauce (Fondue)	49
Hot Rye Rounds	14
Hot Sherried Fruit	162
Hot Spinach Salad	63
Hummingbird Cake	199
Hush Puppies	88

I

Icebox Cookies	223
Icebox Parkerhouse Rolls	80

ICE CREAM *(see* **DESSERTS***)*

Impossible Coconut Pie	217
Individual Beef Wellingtons	136
Individual Meringue Shells	195
Irish Cream	30
Italian Cream Cake	200
Italian Wheat Snack	24

J

Jambalaya, Chicken and Sausage	112
Johnny Appleseed Bars	225
Juice-sicles	239

L

Lady Finger Dessert	191
Lamb Bastille	157
Lamb Steaks with Bearnaise Sauce	158
Last Minute Chocolate Drop Cookies	228
Laura's Lemon Cake	203
Lemonade Pie	214
Lemon Almond Tart	192
Lemon Cooler	187

Lemon Dill Horseradish Sauce	47
Lemon Loaf	84
Lemon Meringue Pie	214
Linguini Salad	55
Lobster Dip	18
Lollipops	243

M

Macaroni and Cheese	98
Macedoine de Fruits	189
Mandarin Salad Molds	68
Marinade, Vegetable	22
Marinated Brussels Sprouts	167
Marinated Cole Slaw	57
Marinated Grill Burgers	151
Marinated Zucchini Salad	64
Marvelous Meatloaf	147
Meatballs, Cocktail	14

MEATS *(see individual listings)*

Meringue Cookies	231
Microwave Cheese Sauce	45
Microwave Fudge	243
Mile-High Biscuits	78
Milk, Sweetened Condensed	48
Mimosa Hawaiian	29
Miniature Pecan Tarts	218
Mocha-Bourbon Balls	234
Molasses Peanut Butter Cookies	230
Molded Cheese Salad	59
Molded Gazpacho Salad	60
Montgomery Christmas Punch	32
Moussaka	145
Mozzarella Chicken	106
Mozzarella Zucchini Spears	181

MUFFINS *(see* **BREADS***)*
MUSHROOM

Mushroom Appetizer	22
Mushroom Casserole	171
Mushroom Quiche	95
Mustard Chicken	105
Mustard Sauce	47

N

Nachos, Chicken	15
New Orleans Steak Diane	138
New Potato Salad	61
Nightmare Sandwiches	98
Nonhardening Clay	236
Noodle Kugle	195
Nut Smackers	231

O

Oatmeal Brownies	226
Oatmeal Hermits	227

OKRA

Fried Okra	173
Okra and Tomatoes	173

INDEX

Old Fashioned Vegetable Soup 41
Old McDonald's Farm Party 244
Olives, Bacon Wrapped................ 14
Olives, Cheese-Olive Balls 11
Olympic Party 245
Omelet, Basic 96
ONION
   French Onion Pie 172
   French Onion Soup 37
   Golden Onion Quiche 94
   Onion Frittata 92
   Vidalia Onion Casserole 172
Orange Balls 223
Orange Chicken 108
Orange French Toast 83
Orange Jewel 29
Orange Pound Cake 205
Orange Salad Cups 67
Orange-sicles 237
Orange Whip 238
Oriental Beef 142
Oriental Broccoli Rice Casserole 167
Ornament Dough 236
OUTDOOR COOKING
   Broiled Sirloin Steak with
      Garlic Sauce.................... 140
   Grilled Chicken with Marinade 105
   Grilled Ginger Chicken 105
   Grilled Ham....................... 157
   Grilled Pork Chops 155
   Grilled Round Steak 140
   Grilled Salmon.................... 124
   Grilled Swordfish with
      Horseradish Sauce................ 127
   Lamb Steaks with Bearnaise Sauce 157
   Marinated Grill Burgers 151
   Skirt Steak Oriental................. 139
   Steak and Vegetable Kabob 138
   Sweet 'N' Sour Flank Steak 140
   Venison Roast 117
Overnight Coffee Cake 82
Oyster Stew 44

P
Paella Salad 52
PARTIES
   Clown Party....................... 245
   Cookie Painting Party 246
   Old McDonald's Farm Party 244
   Olympic Party 245
   Tea Party 246
Party Sandwich Bites 11
Party Style Mint Julep................. 26
PASTA
   Baked Spaghetti 146

Baked Ziti 147
Colorful Pasta Salad.................. 55
Linguini Salad 55
Macaroni and Cheese 98
Pasta Primavera.................... 184
Summer Pasta Salad 54
Vegetables and Pasta 182
Vegetable Spaghetti 183
Peach Clafouti 190
Peaches, Spiced 161
Peach-sicle 239
Peach Sour 28
Peanut Brittle 233
Peanut Butter Balls.................. 243
Peanut Butter Kiss Cookies 224
Peanut Butter Logs.................. 233
Peanut Butter Squares 226
Peanuts, Sugared 23
Pear Gelatin Salad 69
Pears, Curried 161
PEAS
   Clafouti of Peas 174
   Green Pea Casserole................ 173
   Green Pea Salad 60
Pecan Curry Spread 9
Pecan Pie, Chocolate Pecan Pie 215
Pecan Pie, David's Not-So-Sweet
   Pecan Pie........................ 216
Pecans, Dry Roasted 24
Pecans, Toasted 24
Pecan Tarts, Miniature 218
Penthouse Chicken 109
Pepper Steak 141
Perfect Cheese Souffle 97
Perfect Pizza...................... 150
Peter Rabbit Salad 240
Pheasant 116
Pickled Beans 165
PIES
   Apricot Pie 213
   Basic Pie Crust 220
   Blueberry Cheese Pie............... 212
   Caviar Pie 17
   Charleston Chess Pie 216
   Chocolate Pecan Pie 215
   Custard Pie 217
   David's Not-So-Sweet Pecan
      Pie 216
   French Apple Cobbler............... 213
   French Onion Pie 172
   Fresh Peach Pie 211
   Frozen Cranberry Pie 212
   Fruit Cobbler..................... 212
   Fudge Sundae Pie 216

INDEX

Grandma's Chocolate Pie 215
Greek Egg and Spinach Pie 91
Impossible Coconut Pies.............217
Lemonade Pie 214
Lemon Meringue Pie.................214
Pineapple Coconut Pie 217
PIES (TARTS)
  Cheese Cake Tarts 219
  Cream Cheese Bites.................220
  Cream Cheese Tarts 219
  Lemon Almond Tart 192
  Miniature Pecan Tarts 218
  Walnut Maple Tarts 218
Pimento Cheese Spread 12
Pina Colada 27
PINEAPPLE
  Pineapple Cheddar Salad.............68
  Pineapple Cheese Ball................11
  Pineapple-Cheese Casserole 161
  Pineapple Coconut Pie 217
  Pineapple Souffle..................162
Pizza Bread.........................16
Pizza, Hot Dog.....................237
Pizza, Perfect 150
Popcorn Balls 241
Poppy Seed Bread 85
PORK
  Apple Brandy Pork Chops...........154
  Baked Pork Chops 154
  Florida Orange Pork Chops.........154
  Grilled Ham.......................157
  Grilled Pork Chops 155
  Ham and Swiss Buns 158
  Stuffed Pork Chops 155
  Tropical Pork Chops 155
Potato Breakfast Casserole............98
Potato Chip Shortbread Cookies......230
POTATOES
  Country Potatoes 175
  Easy Potato Bake 175
  German Potato Salad................61
  New Potato Salad 61
  Potato Breakfast Casserole 98
  Potato Casserole 175
  Potato Quiche 95
  Potato Soup 38
  Salmon Potato Cheese Soup 43
  Sesame Potato Sticks 176
  Stuffed Potatoes 174
  Yugoslavian Potato Salad............61
POULTRY
  Amaretto Chicken Salad 113
  Apricot Brandy Chicken 103
  Cheesy Chicken 111

Chicken and Sausage Jambalaya 112
Chicken Breasts in Wine 104
Chicken Breasts with Cream..........104
Chicken Cordon Bleu 100
Chicken Curry Salad 114
Chicken Gumbo 112
Chicken Nachos 15
Chicken Noodle Soup 40
Chicken Normandy 102
Chicken Tetrazzini..................111
Chicken with Mushrooms 110
Coconut Chicken Salad 52
Coq au Vin........................101
Cornish Hens 115
Creamy Baked Chicken Breasts 102
Crescent Chicken Squares 110
Curried Chicken Bites................15
Easy Chicken Chop Suey 103
Easy Sweet and Sour Chicken........108
Fried Chicken 106
Grilled Chicken with Marinade 105
Grilled Ginger Chicken 105
Herbed Chicken 107
Hot Chicken Salad 113
Mozzarella Chicken 106
Mustard Chicken 105
Orange Chicken....................108
Penthouse Chicken 109
Petti di Pollo alla Bolognese 101
Spicy Baked Chicken...............109
Stuffed Chicken Breasts with Brandy
  Sauce 100
Sweet and Sour Chicken 107
Tarragon Chicken Salad.............52
Turkey Breast In A Bag 114
Practically No-Calorie Soup 37
Praline Ice Cream Topping 196
Prune Bread 86
Pumpkin Cream Cake Roll 207
Pumpkin Loaf 87

Q

QUAIL
  Fried Quail 116
QUICHE
  Beef 93
  Blue Cheese 93
  California..........................93
  Christmas 94
  Golden Onion 94
  Mushroom.........................95
  Potato 95
Quick and Easy Fish 126
Quick and Easy Pot de Creme 194
Quick Chocolate Cookies 229

INDEX 261

Quickie Doughnuts 242
Quick Orange Carrots 168

R
Raspberry Orange Mold 69
Raspberry Squares 226
Ratatouille Provencal 183
Red Beans and Rice 166
Red Devil Balls 16
Red Devil Sauce (Fondue) 49
Red Velvet Cake 201
Reuben Casserole. 151
RICE
  Almond Rice 162
  Barbecued Rice 163
  Crunchy Rice Salad 62
  Curried Rice Salad 62
  Fried Rice 163
  Oriental Broccoli Rice Casserole 167
  Red Beans and Rice 166
  Rice Casserole 163
Ricotta Cheesecake 211
ROLLS *(see* BREADS*)*
Russian Coffee 30

S
SALAD DRESSINGS
  Blue Cheese Dressing 71
  Celery Seed Dressing 71
  Excellent Vinaigrette 72
  Fresh Tomato Dressing 71
  Thousand Island Dressing. 71
SALADS
  CONGEALED
    Asheville Salad. 56
    Borscht Salad. 56
    Broken Glass Salad 64
    Cranberry Cream Salad 66
    Creamy Orange-Lime Mold 68
    Mandarin Salad Molds 68
    Molded Cheese Salad 59
    Molded Gazpacho Salad. 60
    Pear Gelatin Salad 69
    Pineapple Cheddar Salad 68
    Raspberry Orange Mold 69
    Screwdriver Salad 70
    Strawberry Nut Salad 70
  FRUIT
    Apple Salad 65
    Blueberry Salad 66
    Candlestick Salad. 240
    Five Cup Salad. 65
    Frozen Banana Salad 65
    Frozen Cherry Salad 66
    Orange Salad Cups 67
    Pear Gelatin Salad 69

    Peter Rabbit Salad 240
    Pineapple Cheddar Salad 68
    Strawberry Nut Salad 70
    Summer Fruit Salad. 67
  MEAT
    Amaretto Chicken Salad 113
    Chicken Curry Salad 114
    Coconut Chicken Salad 52
    Hot Chicken Salad 113
    Taco Salad 63
    Tarragon Chicken Salad 52
  PASTA
    Colorful Pasta Salad 55
    Linguini Salad. 55
    Summer Pasta Salad 54
    Tuna Salad 54
  SEAFOOD
    Asheville Salad 56
    Paella Salad 52
    Salade Nicoise 53
    Shrimp Remoulade 131
    Shrimp Salad 53
    Tuna Salad 54
    Tuna Salad with Chinese Noodles 54
  VEGETABLE
    Augusta's Favorite Salad. 56
    Borscht Salad. 56
    Cauliflower Salad 58
    Corn Salad 59
    Crunchy Rice Salad 62
    Cucumber Salad 59
    Curried Rice Salad. 62
    Faucon Salad 58
    German Potato Salad 61
    Greek Salad 60
    Green Pea Salad 60
    Hot Spinach Salad 63
    Marinated Cole Salw 57
    Marinated Zucchini Salad 64
    New Potato Salad 61
    Salade Nicoise 53
    Sauerkraut Salad 62
    Sweet and Sour Carrot Salad 58
    Three Bean Salad 57
    Yugoslavian Potato Salad 61
SALMON
  Baked Salmon Steaks 123
  Grilled Salmon. 124
  Salmon Cutlets with Browned Butter . . . 122
  Salmon Party Ball 18
  Salmon Potato Cheese Soup 43
  Salmon Timbales 123
Salsa Alla Carbonara 96

INDEX

SANDWICHES
- Barbecue Beef Sandwiches 144
- Beef Pasty 144
- Grilled Cheese Plus 241
- Ham and Swiss Buns 156
- Nightmare Sandwiches 98
- Party Sandwich Bites 11
- Tuna Cheese Burger 128

SAUCES
- Barbecue Sauce 46
- Barbecue Sauce (Fondue) 50
- Basic White Sauce 44
- Bearnaise Sauce 45
- Better-For-You Sour Cream 48
- Chili Sauce (Fondue) 49
- Cranberry Sauce 47
- Curry Sauce (Fondue) 50
- Easy Hollandaise Sauce 45
- Game Sauce 48
- Granny's Giblet Gravy 48
- Ham Glaze 46
- Hickory Barbecue Sauce 46
- Hot Mustard Sauce (Fondue) 49
- Lemon Dill Horseradish Sauce 47
- Microwave Cheese Sauce 45
- Mustard Sauce 47
- Red Devil Sauce (Fondue) 49
- Sweetened Condensed Milk 48
- Saucy Franks 16
- Sauerkraut Salad 62

SAUSAGE
- Cheese and Sausage Crepes 90
- Chicken and Sausage Jambalaya 112
- Sausage Cornbread Stuffing 88
- Sauteed Cherry Tomatoes 179
- Sauteed Scrod 121
- Savory Baked Fish 128
- Screwdriver Salad 70

SEAFOOD
- Caviar Pie 17
- Clams Casino 129
- CRAB
  - Baked Crab Casserole 129
  - Crab and Shrimp Casserole 129
  - Crab Stuffed Eggplant 132
- SCALLOPS
  - Coquilles St. Jacques 133
  - Scallops Florentine 134
  - Scallops in Wine Sauce 134
- SHRIMP
  - Batter for Fried Shrimp 131
  - Crab and Shrimp Casserole 129
  - Hawaiian Shrimp Curry 132
  - Shrimp Beignets 19

- Shrimp Bisque 42
- Shrimp Casserole 131
- Shrimp Celery 19
- Shrimp Creole 130
- Shrimp in Patty Shells 130
- Shrimp Remoulade 131
- Shrimp Salad 53
- Shrimp Sea Island 133
- Trout Baked with Shrimp 125
- Seafood Bisque 43
- Seafood Gumbo 42
- Seafood Spread 18
- Sesame Potato Sticks 176

SHRIMP *(see* **SEAFOOD)**
- Six Layer Venison Dish 118
- Skirt Steak Oriental 139
- Snibbled Beans 165
- Snickerdoodles 227
- Soap Bubbles 236
- Soft Bread Sticks 77

SOMETHING SPECIAL
- Applesauce 240
- Apple-wiches 240
- Banana Milkshake 238
- Banana Whip 238
- B.O.S. Fruit Drink 238
- Candlestick Salad 240
- Cheese 'N Marshmallow Crackers 241
- Chocolate Chip Candy 243
- Clown Party 245
- Cookie Painting Party 246
- Corn Dogs 237
- Cupcake Cones 242
- Equivalents 248
- Finger Pudding Paint 237
- Frame Those Eggs 241
- Frozen Grapes 238
- Grape Shakies 242
- Grilled Cheese Plus 241
- Honey Milk Balls 244
- Hot Chocolate Mix 239
- Hot Dog Pizza 237
- Juice-sicles 239
- Lollipops 243
- Microwave Fudge 243
- Nonhardening Clay 236
- Old McDonald's Farm Party 244
- Olympic Party 245
- Orange-sicles 237
- Orange Whip 238
- Ornament Dough 236
- Peach-sicle 239
- Peanut Butter Balls 243
- Peter Rabbit Salad 240

INDEX

Popcorn Balls 241
Quickie Doughnuts 242
Soap Bubbles 236
Substitutions 247-248
Sunshine Punch 239
Tea Party 246
Wonderful Sugar Cookies 244

SOUFFLES
  Easy Sweet Potato Souffle 177
  Perfect Cheese Souffle 97
  Pineapple Souffle 162

SOUP
  Black Bean Gazpacho 34
  Brunswick Stew 39
  Buttermilk Broccoli Soup 35
  Catfish Stew 124
  Chicken Noodle Soup 40
  Corn Chowder 36
  Country Soup 40
  Creamy Squash Soup 39
  Creme Crecy 36
  Curried Tuna-Mushroom Soup 41
  French Carrot Soup 35
  French Onion Soup 37
  Fresh Cantaloupe Soup 36
  Gazpacho 37
  Grouper Soup 43
  Hearty Bean Soup 34
  Hot and Sour Soup 38
  Old Fashioned Vegetable Soup 41
  Oyster Stew 44
  Potato Soup 38
  Practically No-Calorie Soup 37
  Salmon Potato Cheese Soup 43
  Seafood Bisque 43
  Seafood Gumbo 42
  Shrimp Bisque 42
  Vegetable-Burger Soup 40
Sour Cream Dip 12
Southern Fried Green Beans 166
Spice Balls 222
Spiced Peaches 161
Spicy Baked Beans 166
Spicy Baked Chicken 109

SPINACH
  Greek Egg and Spinach Pie 91
  Hot Spinach Salad 63
  Spinach-Cheese Casserole 177
  Spinach Feta Triangles 9
  Spinach-Ricotta Stuffed Tomatoes .. 178

SPREADS
  Cheese Spread 8
  Ham Cheese Spread 10
  Pecan Curry Spread 9

Pimento Cheese Spread 12
Seafood Spread 18

SQUASH
  Creamy Squash Soup 39
  Ratatouille Provencal 183
  Squash Medley 180
  Stuffed Squash 181

STEAK
  Broiled Sirloin Steak with Garlic
    Sauce 140
  Grilled Round Steak 140
  New Orleans Steak Diane 138
  Pepper Steak 141
  Skirt Steak Oriental 139
  Steak and Vegetable Kabob 138
  Sweet 'N Sour Flank Steak 140
  Swiss Steak 143

STRAWBERRY
  Dipped Strawberries 189
  Strawberries Romanoff 188
  Strawberry Bread 86
  Strawberry Butter 88
  Strawberry Delight 188
  Strawberry Ice Cream 196
  Strawberry Nut Salad 70
  Strawberry Punch 29
  Strawberry Spritzers 27
Streusel Coffee Cake 82
Striped Bass in Butter Sauce 122
Stuffed Chicken Breasts with
  Brandy Sauce 100
Stuffed Dover Sole 121
Stuffed French Toast 84
Stuffed Peppers 146
Stuffed Pork Chops 155
Stuffed Potatoes 174
Stuffed Squash 181
Stuffed Veal Chops Crabes 153
Substitutions 247-248
Sugared Peanuts 23
Summer Fruit Salad 67
Summer Pasta Salad 54
Summer Punch 29
Sunshine Punch 239
Sweet and Sour Carrot Salad 58
Sweet and Sour Chicken 107
Sweet and Sour Cucumbers 170
Sweetened Condensed Milk 48
Sweet 'N Sour Flank Steak 140

SWEET POTATOES
  Easy Sweet Potato Souffle 177
  Grated Sweet Potato Casserole 176
  Yam Bake 176
Sweet Veal Loaf 152

Swiss Steak 143
Swordfish, Grilled with Horseradish
  Sauce.............................. 127
Syllabub 27

T

Taco Dinner 150
Taco Salad........................... 63
Tarragon Chicken Salad 52
TARTS *(see* **PIES)**
Tea Party 246
Teriyaki Fondue 142
Thousand Island Dressing 71
Three Bean Salad 57
TOAST
  Orange French Toast................ 83
  Stuffed French Toast 84
Toasted Pecans 24
TOMATO
  Baked Cheddar Tomatoes 179
  Baked Stuffed Tomatoes 180
  Fresh Tomato Dressing 71
  Fried Green Tomatoes 179
  Okra and Tomatoes 173
  Ratatouille Provencal 183
  Sauteed Cherry Tomatoes 179
  Spinach-Ricotta Stuffed Tomatoes...178
  Tomatoes with Artichoke Hearts 178
  Tomato Wow 28
Tropical Ice 195
Tropical Milk....................... 28
Tropical Pork Chops 155
Trout Baked with Shrimp 125
TUNA
  Creamy Tuna Dip 19
  Salade Nicoise..................... 53
  Tuna Cheese Burger 128
  Tuna Salad......................... 54

Tuna Salad with Chinese Noodles 54
Turkey Breast in a Bag 114

U-V

Uncooked Vanilla Ice Cream 196
VEAL
  Stuffed Veal Chops Crabes 153
  Sweet Veal Loaf 152
  Veal Grillades 152
  Veal Marsala 151
  Veal Scallopini 153
VEGETABLES *(see individual listings also)*
  Fresh Vegetable Dip 21
  Vegetables and Pasta 182
  Vegetable-Burger Soup 40
  Vegetable Marinade................. 22
  Vegetable Soup, Old Fashioned 41
  Vegetable Spaghetti 183
Venison Roast 117
Venison Stew 117
Vidalia Onion Casserole 172

W-X-Y-Z

Walnut Maple Tarts 218
Watermelon Screwdrivers 27
Whiskey Punch 30
White Batter Bread 75
Whoopie Pies 194
Wine Cake 200
Wonderful Sugar Cookies 244
Yam Bake 176
Yugoslavian Potato Salad 61
ZUCCHINI
  Marinated Zucchini Salad 64
  Mozzarella Zucchini Spears 181
  Ratatouille Provencal 183
  Zucchini-Beef Casserole 148
  Zucchini Bites 23
  Zucchini Bread 76
  Zucchini Provencal 182

NOTES

NOTES

NOTES

NOTES

NOTES

NOTES

The Market Place
P. O. Box 3133
Augusta, Georgia 30904

Please send me _____ copies of *The Market Place* at $9.95 per copy, plus $1.50 for postage and handling. Georgia residents add 4% sales tax.

Name _____

Address _____

City _____ State _____ Zip _____

All proceeds will be used for community service projects sponsored by the Augusta Junior Woman's Club, Inc.

The Market Place
P. O. Box 3133
Augusta, Georgia 30904

Please send me _____ copies of *The Market Place* at $9.95 per copy, plus $1.50 for postage and handling. Georgia residents add 4% sales tax.

Name _____

Address _____

City _____ State _____ Zip _____

All proceeds will be used for community service projects sponsored by the Augusta Junior Woman's Club, Inc.

The Market Place
P. O. Box 3133
Augusta, Georgia 30904

Please send me _____ copies of *The Market Place* at $9.95 per copy, plus $1.50 for postage and handling. Georgia residents add 4% sales tax.

Name _____

Address _____

City _____ State _____ Zip _____

All proceeds will be used for community service projects sponsored by the Augusta Junior Woman's Club, Inc.

Reorder Additional Copies

p. 179 "FRIED GREEN TOMATOES"
Oct. 1992
Tawanda

p. 226 Peanut Butter Squares

58 Carrot Salad

Carol Crombie's Pound Cake

1 lb butter, softened
3 Cups sugar
6 large eggs
4 Cups flour - all purpose
3/4 C. milk
1 tsp almond extract
1 tsp vanilla extract

Directions
Beat butter at medium speed with an electric mixer until creamy. (Batter becomes paler yellow with the incorporation of air so the cake will rise. 1-7 minutes
Gradually add sugar at med. speed until light & fluffy.
Add eggs, 1 at a time, until yolk disappears
Add flour alternately with milk. Beginning & ending with flour, beating at low speed. Stir in extracts.
Pour into a greased + floured 10 inch tube pan.
Bake at 300° for 1 hour and 40 minutes.
Cool pan on a wire rack for 10-15 minutes. Remove from pan & cool on wire rack.